# GETTING THE LOWDOWN ON EMPLOYERS

# AND A LEG UP ON THE JOB MARKET

## Leila K. Kight

**TEN SPEED PRESS**
**BERKELEY, CALIFORNIA**

# ACKNOWLEDGMENTS

The author is indebted to Barbara Ferry for her creative research and stolid commitment to the success of this project, Michele Newman for her finishing touches, and Morton Leeds for his inspiration. For their generous gifts of time and expertise, the author acknowledges: Kathy Sims, Director of Career Services, George Washington University; Jennifer Reagan, Director of Career Services, American University; Bob Lynch, Director of Career Services, Georgetown University; James Woods, Coordinator, State Occupation Information, National Occupational Information Coordinating Committee (NOICC); Walton Webb, Coordinator, State and Interagency Network, National Occupational Information Coordinating Committee (NOICC); Robert Calvert, Publisher, Garrett Park Press; Edward Sturgeon, Research Manager, Lexington, Kentucky Chamber of Commerce; Rhea Nagle, Information Specialist, College Placement Council; Frederick MacDonald, Director of Professional Services, Right Associates; Martha Redstrom-Plourd, Managing Principal, Right Associates; Sara Pritchard, Communications Manager, American Association of Cost Engineers; Jane Shore, Conceptual Systems, Inc.; E. Neil Carey, Executive Director, National Career Development Association; Dick Ellis, Director of Manpower Studies, Engineering Manpower Commission; and Doug Braddock, Analyst, Science and Engineering Occupations, Bureau of Labor Statistics.

❊ ❊ ❊ ❊ ❊

1☯
TEN SPEED PRESS    P.O. Box 7123, Berkeley, CA 94707

Originally published by Washington Researchers; this is a revised and updated edition.

Cover design by Fifth Street Design
Text design by Sarah Levin

Library of Congress Card Number: 93-648749


FIRST PRINTING 1994
Printed in the United States
1  2  3  4  5 — 98  97  96  95  94

# CONTENTS

INTRODUCTION    vii

     Why Do Job Research?    viii

     Where To Begin    ix

**PART I: TOOLS & TECHNIQUES OF RESEARCH**    1

CHAPTER 1: USING THE LIBRARY & THE TELEPHONE    2

     Library Research    2

     Telephone Research    3

CHAPTER 2: INTERVIEWING THE EXPERTS    12

     Preparing Properly    13

     Getting Through to the Source    14

     Introducing Yourself    15

     Overcoming Barriers    17

     Maintaining Cooperation    19

     Closing Productively    20

**PART II: OCCUPATIONS**    21

CHAPTER 3: WHICH OCCUPATIONS ARE GROWING, WHICH DECLINING?    23

CHAPTER 4: RESEARCHING THE PROFESSIONS    51

     Government Publications    52

     Clearinghouses    56

     Other Useful Publications    58

     Job Listings    60

**PART III: INDUSTRIES**    61

CHAPTER 5: QUICK REFERENCE TO HIGH-GROWTH INDUSTRIES    62

CHAPTER 6: EVALUATING AN INDUSTRY    77

CHAPTER 7: TAPPING THE EXPERTS IN THE PRIVATE SECTOR    81

     Established Industries    81

     Experts in Industry    84

     Emerging Industries    86

     Specialized Information    88

CHAPTER 8: TAPPING THE EXPERTS IN GOVERNMENT    90
     Library Research    91
     Telephone Research    93

CHAPTER 9: READING UP ON INDUSTRIES    101
     Government Reports    101
     Industry Surveys    104
     Business Periodicals    105
     Industry Reports    107
     Directories    108

## PART IV: COMPANIES & EMPLOYERS    111

CHAPTER 10: SHORTCUTS TO SUCCESSFUL COMPANIES    113
     The Most Profitable Companies    114
     The Regional Stars    117

CHAPTER 12: WHO'S WHO    118
     Public or Private?    120
     Owned by Another Company?    120
     Foreign-Owned or American?    121
     For Profit or Not for Profit?    122

CHAPTER 12: FINANCIAL INFORMATION ABOUT PUBLIC COMPANIES    123
     Interstate Public Companies    123
     Intrastate Public Companies    130

CHAPTER 13: FINANCIAL INFORMATION ABOUT OTHER COMPANIES    136
     Private Companies    136
     Divisions and Subsidiaries    140
     Foreign Firms    140
     Not-for-Profit Organizations    143

CHAPTER 14: LOOKING BEYOND THE FINANCIAL STATEMENTS    144
     Reputation    144
     Sources of Information    149

CHAPTER 15: THE VALUE OF YOUR CONTRIBUTION    156
     Asking the Right Questions    157

CHAPTER 16: COMPATABILITY    162
     Shortcuts to Finding Congenial Companies    164

CHAPTER 17: EMPLOYEE BENEFITS AND THE COMPANY CULTURE     168

    Employee Benefits     168

    Employment Environment     172

    Company Culture     173

CHAPTER 18 : A SOCIAL CONSCIENCE     176

    Charitable Contributions     177

    Environmental Awareness     178

    Occupational Safety     180

    Equal Employment Opportunities     183

    Other Issues     184

**PART V: GEOGRAPHY AND THE QUALITY OF LIFE**     185

    The Best Places     187

CHAPTER 19: A GEOGRAPHIC FOCUS FOR OCCUPATIONS     188

    Professional Associations     189

    Special-Interest Associations     191

    Placement Organizations     192

CHAPTER 20: TARGETING A PARTICULAR PLACE     194

    State-level Job Research     195

    Local-level Job Research     206

CHAPTER 21: THE QUALITY OF LIFE     224

    The Arts and Cultural Events     225

    Climate     226

    Cost of Living     227

    Safety Rates     228

    Education     228

    Air Quality     232

    Health Care     232

    Recreation, Sports, and Leisure     233

    Transportation     233

    References for Research     235

APPENDIX I: INTERVIEWING EMPLOYERS     240

    The Cover Letter     240

    Your Appearance     241

    Asking Good Questions     242

    Giving Good Answers     243

APPENDIX II:  EMPLOYMENT ABROAD                                      247
              Publications                                           248
              Organizations                                         250

APPENDIX III: DATABASE VENDORS                                       252

APPENDIX IV:  STATE CHAMBERS OF COMMERCE                             253

APPENDIX V:   STATE ECONOMIC DEVELOPMENT OFFICES                     259

APPENDIX VI:  PUBLISHERS AND OTHER ORGANIZATIONS                     264

INDEX                                                                271

# TABLES

TABLE 1: Fastest Growing Occupations, 1990–2005                       25

TABLE 2: Occupations with the Largest Job Growth, 1990–2005           26

TABLE 3: Growth or Decline in Jobs, 1990–2005                         27

TABLE 4: Fastest Growing Manufacturing Industries in 1993             63

TABLE 5: Trends in Selected Service Industries, 1990–1993             63

TABLE 6: Declining Manufacturing Industries                           64

TABLE 7: Forecast Growth Rates for 156 Manufacturing Industries       65

TABLE 8: Employment, by Industry, 1975, 1990, and Projected to 2005   70

TABLE 9: Cost of Living Index for Selected Cities, 1992              227

TABLE 10: Estimated Education Expenditures, 1992–1993               230

# INTRODUCTION

)•(( )•(( )•((

W hen the research for this book began, the job market was strong and most job hunters could find job opportunities without making a great effort. Job seekers could be highly selective, and when this book was originally conceived it was to show them how to find the best positions with the best employers. Now, the overall job market is much weaker. Many employers are still cutting back their workforce. Especially hard hit are middle-management positions, a development that is stunting opportunities for professional growth for entry-level, white-collar workers and young managers.

In this economy, selective job hunting is more important than ever. When growth in many industries is at a standstill, when company profits have plummeted, and when educated and competent workers stand in unemployment lines around the country, savvy job seekers must focus their efforts on successful employers. They must look for the strong employment positions among the weak.

When there are fewer growth positions available, you must work harder to find them—and obtain them. There are many great jobs available. By doing the right kind of research, as described in this book, you can optimize your opportunities. The skills you master with the help of this book will serve you throughout your career. During your lifetime, you are likely to be in the job market several times. You may change jobs by choice, as you look for better opportunities, or involuntarily as your employer's needs change. For an array of reasons, from changing technologies to a sagging economy, few people can expect to remain with the same employer for their entire career.

Your job not only consumes at least forty hours of your week, but also determines how you can afford to spend the remaining hours. Despite the importance of job decisions, most people base them on little or no information. In fact, most job seekers do not know how to go about finding the information they need to evaluate a position or an employer adequately.

Recognizing that people come to the job-hunting process with different agendas, we address a number of needs:

- If you have a specific employer in mind, you will learn how to research that employer.

- If you want to find the best employer for your particular interests, you will learn how to scan the field efficiently for top companies. (Many job seekers overlook great opportunities because they focus their search too narrowly, concentrating on the few employers they are familiar with rather than doing a broader scan for prospective employers.)

- If you are committed to a particular occupation, you will learn how to discover which companies and geographical areas provide the best opportunities.

- If you are committed to a specific locale, you will learn which employers are your best bets in that region.

In short, this book shows how you can improve your opportunities, financially and otherwise, by systematically searching for the best employers within your chosen parameters of geography, industry, or profession.

## WHY DO JOB RESEARCH?

But why spend time doing research? Surely employers will give me all the facts I need. Where is the payoff in conducting my own investigation?

First, your own research will produce a more complete and realistic picture of a prospective employer. The employer provides information that is superficial, selective, and often biased. With a little research of your own, you can compile information about a company's financial health, its hiring and cutback activities, and its treatment of employees. With a little more research, you can discover where, within the company, the jobs are and more about the advancement track for people in your particular field.

Second, through research, you can not only expand your job possibilities beyond your current frame of knowledge and experience, but also focus your search on the best opportunities by determining where the best jobs are—in which careers, geographical regions, industries, and companies.

Third, your research can greatly increase your effectiveness in landing the job you want. You can not only identify specific areas of opportunity that others will miss, but also use the results of your research in your employment inquiries and interviews. The candidate who has been resourceful enough to learn in advance about the company and its industry makes a much better impression than one who uses the job interview to gather information.

Last, job research is cumulative. The more you do, the better will be your ability to pick good employers and make good job decisions throughout your career. You will gain a considerable financial advantage and optimize your job satisfaction.

## WHERE TO BEGIN

This book is organized in such a way as to make it easier to pinpoint the various aspects of researching for job hunting. The aspects may be lumped together in one of two categories: tools for the search or subjects of the search. We begin by reviewing the principal avenues of the hunt: the telephone and the library. Down those two avenues you will find your main sources of information: people and publications.

In advocating research we are not striking a new path through the wilderness. The adage Do your homework is as valid as it ever was. Because much of that homework will require you to talk to people, we put the chapter on interviewing right up there, in front. The interview is a recurring process so that by the time you come to the decisive one—the job interview—you have had plenty of practice. We suggest that you read that chapter before you begin so as to find out where your research will take you.

The central part of the book covers the subjects of your research. We start with careers because that is where so many people start and, increasingly, more than once in a lifetime. The chapters on researching industries help narrow the focus; the chapters on companies and prospective employers narrow it even more. Just as there is more to life than a job, there is more to a job than the work. The last section of the book, on matters geographical and cultural, covers aspects of job hunting that may be peripheral but may, in some cases, determine the casting vote.

What kind of research should you do, and how should you begin? The answer to this depends on your situation. Where you start in this book depends on where you are in your job search and in your career. For example:

- If you are in midcareer and want to make the best of your opportunities within the leading companies in your industry, start with part IV to learn how to size up the prospects of a company. You can even apply the techniques to evaluate your current employer. Your results will help you decide whether to look for advancement within that company or investigate employment elsewhere.

- If you are looking for your first job after graduating from college, you should begin with part III to target the industries that promise the most growth and prosperity, then move on to part IV to learn how to research specific companies.

- If you are committed to a particular region, begin with chapter 20.

- If you are not yet committed to a particular occupation, you might want to research the most promising career opportunities; start with part II.

# PART I

# TOOLS AND TECHNIQUES OF RESEARCH

The focus of this section is on research on profit-making companies, but the methodology and information sources are equally applicable to not-for-profit organizations, including trade associations, charitable organizations, educational institutions, and others. In fact, not-for-profits are much easier to research, as they are more likely to be open with information about themselves than are for-profit corporations.

# CHAPTER 1

# USING THE LIBRARY
# AND THE TELEPHONE

❈ ❈ ❈

## LIBRARY RESEARCH

The most effective researchers use the telephone and the library and usually concurrently. When you are starting out, the library is your best resource, especially if you need to begin by mapping out a plan. When you have enough background information, you are going to need leads—it's a job you are wanting out of this research, not an academic paper. At that point you turn to the telephone, although you may well go back to the library frequently as your leads uncover the need for more information.

Modern libraries offer many resources that make researching employers fun and easy. The library sources referred to in this book include:

- *Printed sources,* such as directories, magazines, journals, newsletters, and reports.

- *On-line databases,* accessible by a terminal in the library, which cover many of the same publications you will find in print form.

- *CD-ROM products,* compact discs that can be used with a special reader machine, usually at no cost to the job seeker—there are CDs available that contain statistics and commentary about thousands of employers.

Most libraries have a wealth of printed documents, many have on-line databases, and fewer—but increasing numbers—have CD-ROM products. Get to know your area libraries and use those with the best resources. The most helpful of the library sources are cited at appropriate points throughout this book. If your library does not have those mentioned, ask the reference librarian for alternatives.

There are several advantages to library-based research.

- *You can spend as much time as you have available with each published resource.* Your inquiry won't be confined to whatever time period the experts have to offer.

- *You won't spend money on long-distance telephone calls.*

- *You'll have a librarian there to help you if you do not know how to proceed.*

Because the information in published sources is, however, almost always outdated, it's a good idea to update what you learn at the library by talking with a few experts. The sources you find in the library will help you locate them.

## TELEPHONE RESEARCH

One of the most effective ways to research anything is to interview people who have an intimate knowledge of the subject. These experts—Wall Street analysts, trade-group executives, trade-press reporters, local business executives, company employees, and others—monitor an employer's progress and activities and can give you knowledgeable advice about a company's, or an industry's, future. They read most of what is written about the industry and can give you the highlights, along with their own assessments. They have information that you could never get from reading a company's annual report or news clippings. All in all, they can save you a lot of digging and wasted time by pointing you to the answers you need.

Face-to-face interviews are not necessary. Your telephone can link you with the best industry and company experts in the country.

There are several advantages to doing research by telephone.

- *You will get current information.* The information you get from experts is more current than anything you read in published sources. For example, a government analyst can share current industry statistics long before they are published. Likewise, a reporter for an industry's most authoritative trade journal who is working on a story about companies in the industry can give you a sneak preview weeks or months before the story is published. You can get the most current information available by talking with the people whose job requires them to stay current on your prospective employers' activities. Consider not only government analysts and reporters, but also industry consultants, the local chamber of commerce, securities analysts, and others. This is especially important if you are targeting employers in industries that either change rapidly, such as computers and other high-technology fields, or that are subject to quick declines for reasons beyond their control, such as defense contractors who, after losing a contract, may lay off thousands of employees in a day.

• *You will get information targeted to your needs.* Most published articles and reports about employers are not geared to the job hunter's interests. With a knowledgeable person on the other end of your phone line, you can ask the questions that are important to you.

• *You will get information fast.* Many times the answers you need are no more than a few phone calls away. You can spend hours in a library finding information that an individual with expertise about the employer can provide in a few minutes.

One disadvantage to doing your industry research on the telephone is your telephone bill. Nevertheless, the amount of time and effort you save doing telephone research will more than compensate for the expense.

Some job hunters feel uncomfortable asking strangers for information. If you have misgivings, shelve them until you have made a few phone calls. Most people are very willing to help you. After a few successful interviews, you should feel more comfortable with the process.

To make the telephone research process work, you simply need to know: whom to call, what to ask, and how to ask for what you want. Chapter 2 covers the topic in depth. Read it now—or whenever you are ready to start dialing—for pointers on preparations and strategy.

Jay had narrowed down his search to two companies in the data-processing industry, both of which seemed to be prospering. He researched both companies in the library, but was not satisfied with the information he found. Most of what he learned dealt with the companies' past performances, when what he really wanted to know about was their projected growth. On top of that, the information he found was more than a year old—too old for this fast changing industry. How could he learn about the companies' current developments and future prospects? Who would know where the companies were headed and where he would have the best opportunities for job growth? Jay made several telephone calls.

- *He contacted the major trade association for the industry.* The head of research at the association knew both companies well. She said the companies were profitable and currently hiring at a brisk pace. Jay also learned that Company A had recently won several large government contracts.

- *He then called a reporter at one of the major data-processing trade publications.* From the reporter, Jay learned about rumors that Company B was likely to be acquired.

- *Last, he called the local newspaper in the area where Company B is headquartered.* The business editor confirmed the acquisition rumor and named the conglomerate that was courting Company B. He also said the community was concerned that some part of Company B's operations might be relocated as a result of the acquisition.

Jay's three calls helped him focus his search. He decided not to pursue a position at Company B, because he believed that an acquisition, even if only rumored, would create a stressful work environment. He was very interested in the government contract work at Company A, and therefore decided to focus on that company.

Numerous individuals and organizations will have extremely useful insights about aspects of the job market. Listed below are some of the most helpful experts. Often as not, it will be library research that enables you to find the particular expert.

## Press Reporters

Reporters and researchers from the press and other media can be extremely good sources of information. Many types of print media cover business activities, but three of the most useful for job seekers are the trade press (publications by associations and independent publishing firms that focus on an industry or industry segment), the general business press (national business publications such as *Forbes* and *Business Week* and regional publications such as the *North Carolina Business Review*), and newspapers. Look for the reporters who are likely to have continuing interest in the particular subject of your research. Especially consider the press covering your target's industry niche and geographical region.

You can find the appropriate reporters by doing a literature search and checking bylines. Or, simply call publications you believe to have an interest, and ask for the reporter who covers the employer or the industry. If you prefer, you can visit the library to use Gale's *Directory of Publications and Broadcast Media, Editor and Publisher International Yearbook*, or the *Standard Periodical Directory*. These guides provide information about thousands of newspapers, magazines, and journals in the United States and Canada. For a global view, consult *Ulrich's International Periodicals Directory*.

Once you find the reporters who follow your target employer, ask them to clarify or expand upon points made in their stories, and learn which sources they valued most. Reporters can also provide rumors and industry gossip—information not reliable enough to print, but certainly relevant to your search.

## Trade Associations

There is an association for just about every industry and field of interest that you can imagine—more than twenty-two thousand in all. Trade associations collect a great deal of information about their members and can save you much time and energy in your research. They can provide an overview of an industry and its employers; usually they can give you good insights about the overall financial condition of particular companies; they can identify key industry experts whom you'll want to contact for more information.

There are many ways to tap these trade association sources.

- *Attend trade shows and exhibits.* These shows are huge gatherings that can serve as one-stop supermarkets for job hunters. Most of the key companies in an industry will be represented.

- *Call or visit the associations' libraries.* They have very specialized industry collections; often the collections include industry forecasts and company newsletters.

- *Call or visit the associations' executives and research directors.* They can give you a quick overview of where the industry is headed as well as its problems and strong points.

The following publications, which can be found in most libraries, list the various associations.

*Encyclopedia of Associations* (Gale Research)—This guide is published annually in three volumes. It lists the names and locations of more than twenty-two thousand organizations, their functions, number of members, number of employees, publications, and regular conventions. The key-word index helps you find the associations for any industry.

*National Trade and Professional Associations of the United States* (Columbia Books)—This directory describes seventy-three thousand organizations, arranged alphabetically. The index is arranged by subject, geographic location, and budget size.

## Labor Unions

In order to represent their members effectively, labor unions monitor the companies where their members work. They have a great deal of information, not only on unionized companies, but also on companies they hope to organize. Unions are helpful especially in answering questions about wage rates, work conditions, management attitudes toward labor, and other employee-related concerns. They are informed about company activities indirectly related to employee welfare. For example, they know about company finances, plans for growth, and other areas that ultimately affect how many, and what types of, employees are needed at the companies.

To find the unions that know about your prospective employer, simply call the employer and ask which unions are organized at the company. Most company switchboards operators will tell. Then, you can get the unions' telephone numbers from the *Encyclopedia of Associations*.

The American Federation of Labor and Congress of Industrial Organizations (AFL-CIO) in Washington is also an excellent source of information on employers. Often, the research staff can tell you which unions are organized at a particular company. The AFL-CIO publishes excellent guides on how to research companies in some specific industries.

## Special Interest Groups

Many special-interest groups either monitor employers or try to influence their activities. These groups range from support organizations, such as industry lobbies, to consumer protection associations, environmental coalitions, animal protection societies, and many other watchdog groups. Special-interest groups, particularly the ones that try to influence the activities of companies, devote considerable attention to researching particular businesses.

There are several ways to find these organizations.

- *Search through articles you have collected about your target.* You may find mention of special-interest groups that are promoting or monitoring the subject.

- *Check with the industry trade association.* It can usually tell you about special-interest groups that monitor companies in the industry.

- *Ask the local newspaper reporter* which regional groups are monitoring your target.

- *Contact the Foundation for Public Affairs,* a Washington-based organization, supported by major companies, that researches the public interest groups that are lobbying against the member companies' interests. The foundation also publishes its findings in a book called *Public Interest Profiles.*

## Securities Analysts

Securities analysts and their researchers devote a great deal of time to studying the growth and profitability prospects of public companies (companies whose stock is traded on the major exchanges or over the counter). They are constantly monitoring the winners and losers in a particular industry, and are well versed in which industries are likely, or unlikely, to be successful. If you are deciding in which industries to look for a job, or if you are interested in working for a specific public company, analysts can give you some extremely useful insights.

To find analysts who follow your target company, consult *Nelson's Directory of Investment Research* (Nelson Publications) which can be found in most libraries. This source lists industry and company analysts on Wall Street and elsewhere, and more than nine thousand companies, with a corporate profile and lists of key executives and investment analysts who follow the company. Volume 1 covers the United States. Volume 2 is international. Each volume includes alphabetical, geographical, and industry indexes. Some analysts are very busy, but others will have time to talk. If you reach an analyst who is impatient with you, do not take it personally. Just call another analyst who follows your target, or ask the busy analyst to suggest someone who may have more time to spend with you.

## Academic Institutions

Universities often collect a wide range of information on employers. If you are just starting your job search and are not sure which employer you want to target, you might want to start with your own alma mater's career-services office. That office presumably has files on many employers. Remember, however, that much of this material has been supplied by company recruiters and will probably present biased views of the companies.

Once you have identified companies you want to work for, try contacting universities near your prospective employers or schools in locations that have a particular interest in your target's industry. For example, California universities have experts on vintners in Sonoma, film-makers in Los Angeles, and computer companies in Silicon Valley. Ask the business school or library at the university for research papers or case studies prepared by faculty or students on local companies. Harvard University's business school is one prolific publisher of case studies. To order Harvard's catalog, which lists thousands of case studies, contact the Case Clearinghouse at 617-495-6117. There is a small fee for the catalog and the case studies. The school's development office, which researches employers who are prospective donors, can give you insights into your target's financial condition and philanthropic activities.

## Local Communities

If your prospective employer is important to the hometown folks, you are in luck. By taking advantage of sources in the community, you can put together a general picture of an employer with very little effort. Among the best sources of information are local newspapers and television stations, the public library, the local chamber of commerce, and local and regional economic development councils. If your interests are very specific, call sources that share that interest. For example, if you are concerned about an employer's environmental record, contact local environmental groups. Most, if not all, of these community sources can be tapped by telephone.

## The Prospective Employer

The company you hope to work for can provide you with a great deal of useful information about itself. The trick is to obtain information that has not been filtered and conditioned for job seekers. For meatier information, you will want to

- *Get the company's annual report* to stockholders from the stockholder-relations office

- *Get product and sales literature* available from the sales or marketing office

- *Consider buying a share of stock,* which will make you eligible for all stock holder mailings and regular stockholder meetings

• *Read your employer's newsletter,* copies of which may be obtained from the company's public-relations office, trade-association libraries, or the local public library.

You will also want to interview key people in your target company. The specific individuals you want to contact will depend on what you want to know. For example, if you are interested in a position in marketing, meet employees in that area. Likewise, make contact with product managers, R&D personnel, human resource professionals, or others who hold jobs that you aspire to.

# CHAPTER 2

# INTERVIEWING
# THE EXPERTS

❧ ❧ ❧

As you conduct research for your next (or first) job, you will need to interview several people who are experts on your prospective employer. This is almost a necessity, because certain information—especially about the company's plans—is rarely found in published sources. If you are hoping to work for a privately held company or a subsidiary or facility of a large corporation, firms that are not well covered by published sources, you are sure to find your best insights from people who monitor the employer's activities and performance. In other words, people you interview can give you up-to-date information you could never hope to find in a library.

Some job seekers are uncomfortable about interviewing people they do not know personally. This is just a temporary problem. Once you take the plunge and begin interviewing people you will gain self-assurance and skill. You will also find that the experience of interviewing information sources will make you more effective and confident in the job interview. This chapter is designed to provide both experienced and inexperienced interviewers with tips on how to prepare for an interview with an information source, how to ask questions and overcome objections, and how to close the interview productively. The assumption is that most of your interviews will be conducted by telephone. For in-person interviews, most of the same guidelines will apply.

# PREPARING PROPERLY

To be a successful interviewer, you need to prepare your questions and consider the source's possible responses before you make the call. Begin by determining what it is you want to learn from the source. Then think hard about the questions you are planning to ask.

**What do you want to learn about the employer? What will influence your decision about working in the industry or at the company? Are the questions appropriate for the source you are calling?**

For example, a state labor-department official is the perfect source for information about area wages and job outlooks, but would be unlikely to know how profitable your target company is. Be sure the question fits the source. There always is an appropriate source.

**Can the questions be asked in more than one way?**

*Your source may be sensitive about certain types of questions.* For example, a company's representative might avoid discussing the organization's financial performance. Instead of pressing the issue, you might want to ask about plant expansions or acquisitions—activities that usually indicate prosperity.

**How will you keep track of your questions?**

*You may be tempted to use a script when you first begin interviewing, but it is not the best approach.* When you read questions from a script, you are likely to sound a bit stilted or phony. It is much better to adopt a conversational style. Make a list of the key points you want to cover, then ask the source about each point. This approach allows the source more flexibility, and you are likely to learn far more than you would from a scripted interview.

**What do you know about the information source that will help you focus your interview and evaluate the person you are interviewing as an information source?**

*Most people whom you will interview have a biased view of the employer.* For example, an association that promotes an industry and its companies may paint a rosier picture of a company's potential than would a Wall Street analyst, whose tendency is to give conservative estimates to avoid liability. Likewise, a union official will describe top management in a very different light from that used by the company's public-relations office. Recognizing each source's biases before you make the call will help you relate to the source. Also, remember to allow for biases when you are constructing your picture of any employer.

### How will you introduce yourself and your purpose?

*You should always be honest about who you are and why you are calling.* Whether you are sizing up an industry, researching a specific company, or looking for employment opportunities, be straightforward about your purpose in calling. The only time that you may need to guard your purpose is when you are calling sources in your own industry and believe that news of your job search may get back to your current employer prematurely.

### How can you prepare yourself mentally for doing your best interview?

*If you are tired or bored, get your energy level up—sparkle!* A lackluster interviewer will not inspire anyone. Give your best so the source will have every reason to reciprocate.

*If you are distracted or tense, get yourself organized.* A disorganized interviewer wastes the source's time.

*If you are nervous about making the call, get your courage up.* What is the worst thing that can happen if you fail? If the source cannot help, you can move on to a more knowledgeable or cooperative person. In the unlikely event that someone you call is unpleasant, do not take it personally; anyone can have a bad day.

## GETTING THROUGH TO THE SOURCE

The people between you and your source—the secretaries, receptionists, and assistants (we call them filters)—can be an asset or a liability to your in your search for information. Filters themselves might be valuable sources of general information or specific job leads, so try to learn whether they can provide some of the information you need before you ask to be referred to the boss.

To reach the boss, try to establish credibility by getting a legitimate referral from a mutual acquaintance, or at least by referring to someone known. And do not be afraid to persist—pleasantly, of course. If the source is busy, ask when you might call back. If no time is suggested, offer to call back periodically. If it is important that you talk to this person, do not be afraid to keep trying. If you think that it is the filter, and not the source, who will not cooperate, try calling before and after normal hours and on the weekends. You may find your expert answering the telephone.

# INTRODUCING YOURSELF

Once you reach the people who can answer your questions, the next challenge is to make them want to help you. The best way to begin an interview is to appeal subtly to the vanity of the source. For example, by saying, "I'm told you are the best person to help me with information about this company," or, "I'm so glad to have a chance to talk with you, because I've been told you know a lot about this industry."

There are a few guidelines you might keep in mind as you begin your interview.

- *Eliminate the mystery.* Say who you are and why you are calling. Do this before the source has to ask you. Most sources will talk freely to someone who is researching a job, so you have nothing to hide.

- *Be respectful.* The source's time is a valuable gift. Acknowledge that in words and in your demeanor.

- *Be optimistic.* If you are confident of getting the information you want, and you convey that optimism in your interview style, your source will try hard to meet your expectations. Frequently sources will be only as good as you encourage them to be, so your expectations should be high.

- *Be human—be yourself.* Do not feel that you have to be aggressive to get someone's attention. You will get better results if you act naturally— even a bit vulnerable. This will put your source at ease and enable you to communicate most effectively.

- *Be humble.* Sources like to look smart and professorial. It is no fun to help a know-it-all. You will, however, want to be a quick study, so that your source does not get impatient.

- *Set the sources up for success.* Ask some initial questions that you know he or she can answer. This starts the interview off on a positive note.

To get useful answers, you must learn to ask questions in a way that will elicit the information you want. This is an art, but there are some well-tested techniques for doing that.

- *Ask questions—do not make statements.* Be sure that you do not answer your own questions. Give your source the opportunity to do so.

- *Listen—do not talk.* Listening shows your interest in the source and encourages further comment.

- *Be flexible.* Do not wed yourself to a script or to your own agenda to the extent that you hamper your source's spontaneity. Be receptive to information your source chooses to give you, and be willing to follow some tangents if they prove interesting.

- *Ask short, concise, leading questions,* such as:

    What direction is the industry taking?

    What sorts of individuals are promoted quickly in your department?

    What plans do you think the president has for this division?

    Ask yes or no questions only when you need precise information or clarification.

- *Follow up with questions and comments that encourage elaboration*

    What do you mean?

    Why do you think that's true?

    How do you believe that happened?

    That's very interesting.

    The way you explain it makes it quite clear.

- *Sense when to back off.* Not all sources will immediately trust you. For example, employer representatives might assume that you are a competitor in disguise. If a source seems distrustful, it is best to return to difficult questions later rather than try to force the issue. After you have gained the source's trust, you can ask the question again, perhaps in a different way.

- *Try to evaluate the responses during the interview.* Learn to differentiate between facts, opinions, and wild guesses. Do this by comparing each source's responses with those from other sources and looking for inconsistencies. Ask each source where the information comes from, then judge the credibility of their sources. Remember about natural biases. Companies and their trade associations, for example, may present an overly positive picture of a company's social conscience; labor unions and environmental groups may take a dimmer view.

## OVERCOMING BARRIERS

You are likely to face some obstructions when interviewing people for information about your prospective employers. It is, however, important to remember that obstruction does not mean impasse. You can tunnel over, or under, or around almost every barrier, and your tools are good interview techniques. We outline some of the obstacles you might expect to face and suggest some workable ways to overcome them. Remember to be true to your own personal style—adopt those responses that will work for you.

Your sources may claim not to know the answers to your questions, all the while knowing more than they are willing to admit. Some people are reluctant to provide information if they cannot guarantee its accuracy. You must convince them that what they know can help you—that you do not expect any guarantees or absolutes. Respond with comments such as:

☒ You might not be able to give me any guarantees, but I think your guess will be better than anything else I can find.

☒ I need to learn more about this company, and would really appreciate your educated estimate—it will certainly be better than my own.

☒ I've talked with a lot of people about this employer, and I'm convinced that you're the expert. If you had to venture a wild guess, what would it be?

You have flattered, encouraged, and freed your source to give you the benefit of his or her experience without going out on a limb.

Skilled interviewers have developed techniques to encourage responses. Try tossing out a fact, figure, theory, or rumor you have heard, and ask for the source's reaction. Many people unwilling to volunteer information will react to information provided by others. Ask them to agree or disagree—to tell you whether the information is reasonable. Ask for a range or a ballpark figure when the source does not seem to have precise answers. Often an estimate is good enough for your purposes as a job hunter. Try the indirect approach. For example, to learn if the job you are targeting provides good prospects for promotion within the company, ask what positions people who formerly held the job now hold. If you know that you are asking sensitive questions, try bundling them into less sensitive ones. For example, a company is usually more willing to provide facts about its history than its plans for the future. If you can get someone talking about the company's or the department's history, chances are you can eventually steer the conversation toward the future.

Whether or not sources provide you with information, ask for advice on how to best find the information you want:

✙ If you needed to learn about this company's commitment to this [business/ department/profession/region] how would you approach it?

✙ Have you read any articles or reports that may help me?

✙ Who do you know who might have this information?

Sometimes sources will ask you to put your request for information into writing. They may be following company policy, or they may hope you are not interested enough to follow through. Make it clear that you will follow through and ask for their commitment to respond.

✙ I'll put my letter in the mail today. May I call you next week for your response?

✙ I'll FAX my letter within the hour. May I call you this afternoon for a response?

Once learning of your serious intentions, some sources will decide that it is preferable to talk with you there and then rather than later.

Some people you call will say they do not have time to talk with you. Here are some positive ways to respond.

☒  I certainly understand and appreciate your willingness to help me. When would be a better time for me to call?

☒  I know you are very busy and I'll be happy to call back—you just name the time—but if you could give me two minutes now, I could perhaps save your time later.

Some of the people you call may say that they cannot—or will not—help you. Some organizations have policies against revealing certain information—even to prospective job hunters. You may also run into people who are just having a busy day, or who are not very generous with their time and expertise. Do not be discouraged. If you want to turn the source around, try saying:

☒  I understand. I wouldn't want you to share anything proprietary or inappropriate. I would just like to discuss some things at a very general level.

☒  I appreciate your taking my call and I certainly respect your position. Is there anyone you can suggest who might be willing to talk with me?

Your politeness may soften them up. In any event, do not get angry or take rejection personally. Preserve every source's goodwill. That way you leave the door open for future calls. You might first strike out, then come back to hit a home run.

## MAINTAINING COOPERATION

Do not let yourself get lazy during the interview. You cannot afford to lost your source's interest before getting your answers. To keep your sources interested and involved, stay enthusiastic yourself, even if you are getting tired or discouraged, reward the source along the way with compliments, gratitude, and reinforcement, and be a great listener.

# CLOSING PRODUCTIVELY

Always end the interview pleasantly, even if you are disappointed with the results. You might need to come back to those same sources and try again, and you will want to leave them feeling amiable toward you.

Go through your notes immediately after you have finished each interview, and compare what you learned with your findings from other sources. If you find inconsistencies that require clarification, it is best to call the source back immediately, while the conversation is still fresh in everyone's mind.

To acquire all the information you want to know about an employer, an industry, a profession, or a region of the country, you might have to interview a dozen or more people. Keep fresh and prepare for every interview as if it is your first. Your rewards will speak for themselves.

# PART II

# OCCUPATIONS

In this decade, economic and technological developments, compounded by global competition, are altering the face of employment. Occupations move with demographic trends and rise and fall with the industries that they support. Selecting an occupation in this environment is a challenge—one that can best be met by those armed with good information about career trends and forecasts. To ensure a successful career, you have to select an occupation that promises growth and progress. You do yourself a disservice is you simply follow a parent's career path or select an occupation because you enjoyed a particular course in college. You will find the best career opportunities if you engage in a little good, solid research.

Virtually anyone can improve his or her career opportunities by conducting some easy, basic research into the growth patterns and prospects of particular occupations. This research is especially beneficial if you are just at the point of selecting a course of study, or just starting your job search. At the early stages of your career planning, you have a great deal of flexibility to pursue the most promising choices. Even if you are in midcareer, a bit of research can help steer your course more successfully. It may convince you that it is time to make a career change.

Herman had been a production supervisor in a consumer electronics plant for five years. He had gained more responsibility in the production area, yet his financial advancement was sluggish. Finally, he began to research other career opportunities, and discovered that he could immediately increase his earning potential if he became a computer technician. In addition, his prospects for continued salary advancement and job mobility would be much better than they were in his current line of work. Even though he was in midcareer and the new field required almost a year of intensive training in night classes, the career change paid off—and the benefits should continue to increase for the remainder of his work life.

In the following chapters you learn not only about the fastest-growing careers, but also the techniques for researching any career you might have in mind. Whether you are shopping for an occupation or hoping to find out more about the prospects for your own, or any other, occupation, you'll find the help you need.

# CHAPTER 3

# WHICH OCCUPATIONS ARE GROWING, WHICH DECLINING?

Choosing—or changing—your career is a decision of great magnitude, and it deserves careful planning that has been based on reliable information. In making career decisions, the right information can lead to personal and monetary satisfaction. As you research careers, concentrate on whatever career qualities are important to you. Here we focus on qualities that are important to virtually everyone: job availability, compensation, and especially, career growth.

If you are searching for a career—whether you are a recent college graduate or dissatisfied with your present occupation—it makes good sense to aim for occupations that are expanding. Growing occupations offer the greatest variety of opportunities to new entrants, and promise the best opportunities for job growth and career mobility. These days, the greatest job growth is in the service sector, which is made up of businesses that provide services rather than manufacturing products. The service sector provides millions of clerical, sales, and other service jobs; it also creates positions for engineers, accountants, doctors, nurses, lawyers, and hundreds of other managerial, professional, and technical workers. In fact, the fastest-growing service occupations are those that require the most education.

By using the following tables that show you precisely which occupations are growing and which are declining, you can assess the potential of your own career path, as well as those of others that you may want to consider. Also, you can spot important general trends that can help you make good career decisions. For example, from the tables you will discover that almost half of the twenty fastest-growing occupations are in health-related occupations. Rapid growth is also projected for occupations related to computer technology, from operations research analysts to equipment repairers. Other fields in which employment is expected to grow are those of legal services, management and public relations, librarians, and vocational schools.

All the tables are based on data collected and analyzed by the federal government. Each table provides a different way of looking at the data. You will form the most accurate picture of various occupations if you use all the tables in conjunction.

The U.S. Department of Labor has identified two groups of outstanding growth occupations. One group represents occupations that are growing at the fastest rate, regardless of the total number of jobs represented. For example, virtually all of the thirty occupations that employed twenty-five thousand workers or more were, in 1990, concentrated in the service industries, particularly in health-related services. This trend is expected to continue. The second group represents occupations with the most actual growth, regardless of growth rate. For example, between 1990 and 2005, the retail industry is expected to provide more than five million new jobs. In these tables occupations showing the highest growth represent only a small fraction of the occupations open to you. For information about the size and growth projections for a broad cross-section of occupations, see the table beginning on page 27.

These tables record long-term projections and will provide important insights for your long-term career planning.

## TABLE 1: FASTEST GROWING OCCUPATIONS, 1990–2005

| Occupation | Number of jobs (000) | | Numerical increase | Percentage increase |
|---|---|---|---|---|
| | 1990 | 2005 | | |
| Home health aides | 287 | 550 | 263 | 91.7 |
| Paralegals | 90 | 167 | 77 | 85.2 |
| Systems analyst and computer scientists | 463 | 829 | 366 | 78.9 |
| Personal and home care aides | 103 | 183 | 79 | 76.7 |
| Physical therapists | 88 | 155 | 67 | 76.0 |
| Medical assistants | 165 | 287 | 122 | 73.9 |
| Operations research analysts | 57 | 100 | 42 | 73.2 |
| Human services workers | 145 | 249 | 103 | 71.2 |
| Radiologic technologists and technicians | 149 | 252 | 103 | 69.5 |
| Medical secretaries | 232 | 390 | 158 | 68.3 |
| Physical and corrective therapy assistants and aides | 45 | 74 | 29 | 64.0 |
| Psychologists | 125 | 204 | 79 | 63.6 |
| Travel agents | 132 | 214 | 82 | 62.3 |
| Correction officers | 230 | 372 | 142 | 61.4 |
| Data processing equipment repairers | 84 | 134 | 50 | 60.0 |
| Flight attendants | 101 | 159 | 59 | 58.5 |
| Computer programmers | 565 | 882 | 317 | 56.1 |
| Occupational therapists | 36 | 56 | 20 | 55.2 |
| Surgical technologists | 38 | 59 | 21 | 55.2 |
| Medical records technicians | 52 | 80 | 28 | 54.3 |
| Management analysts | 151 | 230 | 79 | 52.3 |
| Respiratory therapists | 60 | 91 | 31 | 52.1 |
| Child care workers | 725 | 1,078 | 353 | 48.8 |
| Marketing, advertising, and public relations managers | 427 | 630 | 203 | 47.4 |
| Legal secretaries | 281 | 413 | 133 | 47.4 |
| Receptionists and information clerks | 900 | 1,322 | 422 | 46.9 |
| Registered nurses | 1,727 | 2,494 | 767 | 44.4 |
| Nursing aides, orderlies, and attendants | 1,274 | 1,826 | 552 | 43.4 |
| Licensed practical nurses | 644 | 913 | 269 | 41.9 |
| Cooks, restaurant | 615 | 872 | 257 | 41.8 |

SOURCE: Department of Labor, Bureau of Labor Statistics, *Outlook 2000*, 1992.

## TABLE 2: OCCUPATIONS WITH THE LARGEST JOB GROWTH, 1990–2005 PROJECTION

| Occupation | Number of jobs (000) | | Numerical increase | Percentage increase |
|---|---|---|---|---|
| | 1990 | 2005 | | |
| Salesperson, retail | 3,619 | 4,506 | 887 | 24.5 |
| Registered nurses | 1,727 | 2,494 | 767 | 44.4 |
| Cashiers | 2,633 | 3,318 | 685 | 26.0 |
| General office clerks | 2,737 | 3,407 | 670 | 24.5 |
| Truck drivers, light and heavy | 2,362 | 2,979 | 617 | 26.1 |
| General managers and top executives | 3,086 | 3,684 | 598 | 19.4 |
| Janitors and cleaners, including maids and housekeeping cleaners | 3,007 | 3,562 | 555 | 18.5 |
| Nurses aides, orderlies, and attendants | 1,274 | 1,826 | 552 | 43.4 |
| Food counter, fountain, and related workers | 1,607 | 2,158 | 550 | 34.2 |
| Waiters and waitresses | 1,747 | 2,196 | 449 | 25.7 |
| Teachers, secondary school | 1,280 | 1,717 | 437 | 34.2 |
| Receptionists and information clerks | 900 | 1,322 | 422 | 46.9 |
| Systems analysts and computer scientists | 463 | 829 | 366 | 78.9 |
| Food preparation workers | 1,156 | 1,521 | 365 | 31.6 |
| Child care workers | 725 | 1,078 | 353 | 48.8 |
| Gardeners and groundskeepers, except farm | 874 | 1,222 | 348 | 39.8 |
| Accountants and auditors | 985 | 1,325 | 340 | 34.5 |
| Computer programmers | 565 | 882 | 317 | 56.1 |
| Teachers, elementary | 1,362 | 1,675 | 313 | 23.0 |
| Guards | 883 | 1,181 | 298 | 33.7 |
| Teacher aides and educational assistants | 808 | 1,086 | 278 | 34.4 |
| Licensed practical nurses | 644 | 913 | 269 | 41.9 |
| Clerical supervisors and managers | 1,218 | 1,481 | 263 | 21.6 |
| Home health aides | 287 | 550 | 263 | 91.7 |
| Cooks, restaurant | 615 | 872 | 257 | 41.8 |
| Maintenance repairers, general utility | 1,128 | 1,397 | 251 | 22.2 |
| Secretaries, except legal and medical | 3,064 | 3,312 | 248 | 8.1 |
| Cooks, short order and fast food | 743 | 989 | 246 | 33.0 |
| Lawyers | 587 | 793 | 206 | 35.1 |

SOURCE: Department of Labor, Bureau of Labor Statistics, *Outlook 2000,* 1992.

In table 3, which follows, the Department of Labor has provided estimates, for almost five hundred occupations, of the numbers of jobs likely to be available and the rates at which that availability is likely to change. The estimates are categorized as low (the most pessimistic), moderate, and high (the most optimistic).

## TABLE 3: GROWTH OR DECLINE IN JOBS, 1990–2005

| Occupation | Number of Jobs (000) | | | | Estimated change, 1990–2005 | | | | | |
| --- | --- | --- | --- | --- | --- | --- | --- | --- | --- | --- |
| | 1990 | Projected, 2005 | | | Number of jobs (000) | | | Percentage Change | | |
| | | Low | Moderate | High | Low | Moderate | High | Low | Moderate | High |
| Total, all occupations | 122,573 | 136,806 | 147,191 | 154,543 | 14,233 | 24,618 | 31,969 | 12 | 20 | 26 |
| Executive, administrative, and managerial occupations | 12,451 | 14,782 | 15,866 | 16,625 | 2,331 | 3,414 | 4,173 | 19 | 27 | 34 |
| Managerial and administrative occupations | 8,838 | 10,417 | 11,174 | 11,703 | 1,579 | 2,336 | 2,865 | 18 | 26 | 32 |
| Administrative services managers | 221 | 252 | 273 | 287 | 31 | 52 | 66 | 14 | 23 | 30 |
| Communication, transportation, and utilities operations managers | 143 | 175 | 189 | 199 | 32 | 45 | 55 | 22 | 32 | 39 |
| Construction managers | 183 | 223 | 243 | 260 | 40 | 60 | 77 | 22 | 33 | 42 |
| Education administrators | 348 | 400 | 434 | 465 | 52 | 85 | 116 | 15 | 24 | 33 |
| Engineering, mathematical, and natural science managers | 315 | 387 | 423 | 441 | 72 | 108 | 126 | 23 | 34 | 40 |
| Financial managers | 701 | 828 | 894 | 939 | 127 | 193 | 238 | 18 | 28 | 34 |
| Food service and lodging managers | 595 | 762 | 793 | 819 | 166 | 198 | 224 | 28 | 33 | 38 |
| Funeral directors and morticians | 35 | 39 | 41 | 43 | 4 | 6 | 8 | 10 | 17 | 23 |
| General managers and top executives | 3,086 | 3,409 | 3,684 | 3,871 | 323 | 598 | 784 | 10 | 19 | 25 |
| Government chief executives and legislators | 71 | 68 | 74 | 80 | -3 | 3 | 9 | -4 | 4 | 12 |
| Industrial production managers | 210 | 227 | 251 | 260 | 17 | 41 | 50 | 8 | 20 | 24 |
| Marketing, advertising, and public relations managers | 427 | 582 | 630 | 659 | 154 | 203 | 232 | 36 | 47 | 54 |
| Personnel, training, and labor relations managers | 178 | 217 | 235 | 246 | 38 | 57 | 68 | 22 | 32 | 38 |
| Property and real estate managers | 225 | 288 | 302 | 311 | 62 | 76 | 86 | 28 | 34 | 38 |
| Purchasing managers | 248 | 275 | 298 | 312 | 26 | 49 | 64 | 11 | 20 | 26 |
| All other managers and administrators | 1,850 | 2,287 | 2,412 | 2,512 | 437 | 562 | 662 | 24 | 30 | 36 |
| Management support occupations | 3,613 | 4,364 | 4,691 | 4,922 | 752 | 1,079 | 1,309 | 21 | 30 | 36 |
| Accountants and auditors | 985 | 1,235 | 1,325 | 1,385 | 250 | 340 | 400 | 25 | 34 | 41 |
| Budget analysts | 64 | 73 | 78 | 82 | 9 | 14 | 18 | 14 | 22 | 28 |
| Claims examiners, property and casualty insurance | 30 | 37 | 40 | 42 | 7 | 9 | 12 | 21 | 31 | 38 |

**TABLE 3** continued

| Occupation | Number of Jobs (000) | | | | Estimated change, 1990–2005 | | | | | |
|---|---|---|---|---|---|---|---|---|---|---|
| | 1990 | Projected, 2005 | | | Number of jobs (000) | | | Percentage Change | | |
| | | Low | Moderate | High | Low | Moderate | High | Low | Moderate | High |
| Construction and building inspectors | 60 | 65 | 71 | 76 | 6 | 11 | 16 | 9 | 19 | 27 |
| Cost estimators | 173 | 197 | 215 | 228 | 24 | 42 | 55 | 14 | 24 | 32 |
| Credit analysts | 36 | 43 | 46 | 48 | 7 | 10 | 12 | 19 | 27 | 34 |
| Employment interviewers, private or public employment service | 83 | 94 | 102 | 108 | 11 | 19 | 25 | 13 | 23 | 30 |
| Inspectors and compliance officers, except construction | 156 | 190 | 202 | 214 | 34 | 46 | 58 | 22 | 30 | 37 |
| Loan officers and counselors | 172 | 205 | 219 | 230 | 33 | 47 | 58 | 19 | 28 | 34 |
| Management analysts | 151 | 218 | 230 | 240 | 67 | 79 | 88 | 44 | 52 | 58 |
| Personnel, training, and labor relations specialists | 278 | 339 | 366 | 384 | 61 | 87 | 105 | 22 | 31 | 38 |
| Purchasing agents, except wholesale, retail, and farm products | 218 | 246 | 266 | 276 | 28 | 47 | 58 | 13 | 22 | 27 |
| Tax examiners, collectors, and revenue agents | 62 | 66 | 70 | 73 | 5 | 8 | 11 | 8 | 13 | 18 |
| Underwriters | 105 | 121 | 130 | 138 | 16 | 25 | 33 | 16 | 24 | 31 |
| Wholesale and retail buyers, except farm products | 194 | 218 | 235 | 246 | 24 | 41 | 52 | 13 | 21 | 27 |
| All other management support workers | 846 | 1,017 | 1,097 | 1,153 | 171 | 251 | 307 | 20 | 30 | 36 |
| Professional specialty occupations | 15,800 | 19,379 | 20,907 | 22,140 | 3,578 | 5,107 | 6,340 | 23 | 32 | 40 |
| Engineers | 1,519 | 1,748 | 1,919 | 2,001 | 229 | 400 | 482 | 15 | 26 | 32 |
| Aeronautical and astronautical engineers | 73 | 81 | 88 | 91 | 8 | 15 | 18 | 11 | 20 | 24 |
| Chemical engineers | 48 | 50 | 54 | 57 | 1 | 6 | 8 | 2 | 12 | 17 |
| Civil engineers, including traffic engineers | 198 | 235 | 257 | 274 | 37 | 59 | 76 | 19 | 30 | 39 |
| Electrical and electronics engineers | 426 | 519 | 571 | 593 | 93 | 145 | 167 | 22 | 34 | 39 |
| Industrial engineers, except safety engineers | 135 | 145 | 160 | 166 | 11 | 26 | 31 | 8 | 19 | 23 |
| Mechanical engineers | 233 | 263 | 289 | 301 | 30 | 56 | 68 | 13 | 24 | 29 |
| Metallurgists and metallurgical, ceramic, and materials engineers | 18 | 20 | 22 | 23 | 2 | 4 | 5 | 10 | 21 | 26 |

| Occupation | | | | | | | | | | |
|---|---|---|---|---|---|---|---|---|---|---|
| Mining engineers, including mine safety engineers | 4 | 4 | 4 | 5 | -0 | 0 | 0 | -4 | 4 | 10 |
| Nuclear engineers | 18 | 17 | 18 | 19 | -1 | -0 | 1 | -7 | -0 | 4 |
| Petroleum engineers | 17 | 16 | 18 | 18 | -2 | 0 | 1 | -10 | -1 | 3 |
| All other engineers | 347 | 397 | 436 | 454 | 50 | 89 | 107 | 14 | 26 | 31 |
| Architects and surveyors | 236 | 260 | 284 | 300 | 24 | 48 | 64 | 10 | 20 | 27 |
| Architects, except landscape and marine | 108 | 124 | 134 | 142 | 15 | 26 | 34 | 14 | 24 | 31 |
| Landscape architects | 20 | 24 | 26 | 27 | 5 | 6 | 7 | 23 | 31 | 37 |
| Surveyors | 108 | 112 | 123 | 131 | 4 | 15 | 23 | 4 | 14 | 21 |
| Life scientists | 174 | 215 | 230 | 241 | 42 | 56 | 67 | 24 | 32 | 39 |
| Agricultural and food scientists | 25 | 30 | 32 | 33 | 5 | 7 | 8 | 20 | 27 | 31 |
| Biological scientists | 62 | 78 | 83 | 87 | 16 | 21 | 25 | 26 | 34 | 39 |
| Foresters and conservation scientists | 29 | 31 | 32 | 34 | 2 | 4 | 5 | 7 | 12 | 18 |
| Medical scientists | 19 | 29 | 31 | 33 | 10 | 12 | 14 | 55 | 66 | 74 |
| All other life scientists | 39 | 47 | 51 | 55 | 8 | 12 | 16 | 21 | 32 | 41 |
| Computer, mathematical, and operations research analysts | 571 | 916 | 987 | 1,030 | 345 | 416 | 459 | 60 | 73 | 80 |
| Actuaries | 13 | 16 | 18 | 19 | 3 | 4 | 5 | 24 | 34 | 41 |
| Systems analysts and computer scientists | 463 | 769 | 829 | 864 | 306 | 366 | 401 | 66 | 79 | 87 |
| Statisticians | 16 | 16 | 18 | 18 | 1 | 2 | 3 | 5 | 12 | 16 |
| Mathematicians and all other mathematical scientists | 22 | 22 | 24 | 25 | 0 | 2 | 3 | -1 | 9 | 15 |
| Operations research analysts | 57 | 92 | 100 | 104 | 35 | 42 | 47 | 60 | 73 | 81 |
| Physical scientists | 200 | 223 | 241 | 251 | 24 | 41 | 51 | 12 | 21 | 26 |
| Chemists | 83 | 89 | 96 | 100 | 6 | 13 | 17 | 7 | 16 | 21 |
| Geologists, geophysicists, and oceanographers | 48 | 54 | 58 | 60 | 6 | 11 | 13 | 13 | 22 | 27 |
| Meteorologists | 5 | 7 | 7 | 7 | 1 | 2 | 2 | 22 | 30 | 34 |
| Physicists and astronomers | 20 | 20 | 21 | 22 | -0 | 1 | 2 | -2 | 5 | 9 |
| All other physical scientists | 44 | 54 | 59 | 62 | 11 | 15 | 18 | 24 | 34 | 41 |
| Social scientists | 224 | 301 | 320 | 336 | 77 | 96 | 112 | 34 | 43 | 50 |
| Economists | 37 | 43 | 45 | 47 | 5 | 8 | 10 | 14 | 21 | 26 |
| Psychologists | 125 | 193 | 204 | 214 | 68 | 79 | 90 | 55 | 64 | 72 |
| Urban and regional planners | 23 | 25 | 28 | 30 | 2 | 4 | 6 | 9 | 19 | 28 |
| All other social scientists | 38 | 40 | 43 | 45 | 1 | 4 | 6 | 4 | 11 | 17 |
| Social, recreational, and religious workers | 1,049 | 1,278 | 1,376 | 1,460 | 230 | 327 | 412 | 22 | 31 | 39 |
| Clergy | 209 | 214 | 228 | 240 | 5 | 19 | 31 | 2 | 9 | 15 |
| Directors, religious activities and education | 62 | 65 | 69 | 73 | 3 | 7 | 11 | 4 | 12 | 18 |
| Human services workers | 145 | 231 | 249 | 264 | 85 | 103 | 119 | 59 | 71 | 82 |
| Recreational workers | 194 | 224 | 241 | 257 | 30 | 47 | 63 | 15 | 24 | 32 |
| Social workers | 438 | 545 | 588 | 626 | 107 | 150 | 188 | 25 | 34 | 43 |
| Lawyers and judicial workers | 633 | 798 | 850 | 892 | 165 | 217 | 259 | 26 | 34 | 41 |

**TABLE 3 continued**

| Occupation | Number of Jobs (000) | | | | Estimated change, 1990–2005 | | | | | |
| --- | --- | --- | --- | --- | --- | --- | --- | --- | --- | --- |
| | 1990 | Projected, 2005 | | | Number of jobs (000) | | | Percentage Change | | |
| | | Low | Moderate | High | Low | Moderate | High | Low | Moderate | High |
| Judges, magistrates, and other judicial workers | 46 | 53 | 57 | 61 | 7 | 11 | 15 | 14 | 24 | 33 |
| Lawyers | 587 | 745 | 793 | 830 | 158 | 206 | 244 | 27 | 35 | 42 |
| Teachers, librarians, and counselors | 5,687 | 6,701 | 7,280 | 7,813 | 1,014 | 1,593 | 2,126 | 18 | 28 | 37 |
| Teachers, elementary | 1,362 | 1,538 | 1,675 | 1,803 | 176 | 313 | 441 | 13 | 23 | 32 |
| Teachers, preschool and kindergarten | 425 | 555 | 598 | 636 | 130 | 173 | 211 | 31 | 41 | 50 |
| Teachers, special education | 332 | 428 | 467 | 503 | 96 | 134 | 170 | 29 | 40 | 51 |
| Teachers, secondary school | 1,280 | 1,575 | 1,717 | 1,849 | 296 | 437 | 570 | 23 | 34 | 45 |
| College and university faculty | 712 | 776 | 846 | 911 | 64 | 134 | 200 | 9 | 19 | 28 |
| Other teachers and instructors | 757 | 895 | 963 | 1,024 | 138 | 206 | 267 | 18 | 27 | 35 |
| Farm and home management advisors | 18 | 18 | 19 | 21 | -1 | 1 | 2 | -4 | 4 | 12 |
| Instructors and coaches, sports and physical training | 221 | 254 | 274 | 293 | 32 | 53 | 72 | 15 | 24 | 32 |
| Adult and vocational education teachers | 517 | 623 | 669 | 710 | 106 | 152 | 193 | 21 | 29 | 37 |
| Instructors, adult (nonvocational) education | 219 | 273 | 289 | 304 | 54 | 70 | 85 | 25 | 32 | 39 |
| Teachers and instructors, vocational education and training | 298 | 350 | 380 | 407 | 52 | 82 | 109 | 18 | 27 | 36 |
| All other teachers and instructors | 511 | 586 | 636 | 681 | 75 | 125 | 170 | 15 | 24 | 33 |
| Librarians, archivists, curators, and related workers | 166 | 172 | 187 | 200 | 6 | 21 | 34 | 4 | 12 | 20 |
| Curators, archivists, museum technicians, and restorers | 17 | 20 | 21 | 22 | 2 | 4 | 5 | 13 | 21 | 28 |
| Librarians, professional | 149 | 152 | 165 | 177 | 4 | 17 | 29 | 3 | 11 | 19 |
| Counselors | 144 | 177 | 192 | 206 | 33 | 49 | 63 | 23 | 34 | 44 |
| Health and diagnosing occupations | 855 | 1,039 | 1,101 | 1,158 | 185 | 247 | 303 | 22 | 29 | 35 |
| Dentists | 174 | 186 | 196 | 205 | 12 | 21 | 30 | 7 | 12 | 17 |
| Optometrists | 37 | 42 | 45 | 47 | 5 | 8 | 10 | 13 | 20 | 27 |
| Physicians | 580 | 730 | 776 | 818 | 150 | 196 | 238 | 26 | 34 | 41 |
| Podiatrists | 16 | 22 | 23 | 24 | 6 | 7 | 8 | 39 | 46 | 53 |
| Veterinarians and veterinary inspectors | 47 | 59 | 62 | 64 | 12 | 14 | 17 | 26 | 31 | 35 |

| Occupation | | | | | | | | | | |
|---|---:|---:|---:|---:|---:|---:|---:|---:|---:|---:|
| Health assessment and treating occupations | 2,305 | 3,072 | 3,304 | 3,505 | 767 | 999 | 1,201 | 33 | 43 | 52 |
| Dietians and nutritionists | 45 | 52 | 56 | 59 | 7 | 11 | 14 | 16 | 24 | 32 |
| Pharmacists | 169 | 190 | 204 | 215 | 21 | 35 | 46 | 13 | 21 | 27 |
| Physician assistants | 53 | 67 | 72 | 76 | 13 | 18 | 23 | 25 | 34 | 42 |
| Registered nurses | 1,727 | 2,318 | 2,494 | 2,648 | 591 | 767 | 921 | 34 | 44 | 53 |
| Therapists | 311 | 446 | 479 | 508 | 135 | 168 | 197 | 43 | 54 | 63 |
| Occupational therapists | 36 | 52 | 56 | 60 | 16 | 20 | 24 | 44 | 55 | 65 |
| Physical therapists | 88 | 145 | 155 | 164 | 57 | 67 | 76 | 65 | 76 | 86 |
| Recreational therapists | 32 | 42 | 45 | 48 | 10 | 13 | 15 | 30 | 39 | 47 |
| Respiratory therapists | 60 | 84 | 91 | 97 | 25 | 31 | 37 | 41 | 52 | 62 |
| Speech-language pathologists and audiologists | 68 | 85 | 91 | 97 | 17 | 23 | 29 | 24 | 34 | 43 |
| All other therapists | 26 | 37 | 40 | 42 | 11 | 13 | 16 | 41 | 51 | 60 |
| Writers, artists, and entertainers | 1,542 | 1,799 | 1,915 | 1,995 | 257 | 373 | 454 | 17 | 24 | 29 |
| Artists and commercial artists | 230 | 288 | 303 | 313 | 58 | 73 | 84 | 25 | 32 | 36 |
| Athletes, coaches, umpires, and referees | 32 | 41 | 43 | 46 | 9 | 11 | 13 | 27 | 34 | 41 |
| Dancers and choreographers | 9 | 11 | 12 | 12 | 3 | 3 | 4 | 29 | 38 | 45 |
| Designers | 339 | 399 | 428 | 447 | 60 | 89 | 108 | 18 | 26 | 32 |
| Designers, except interior designers | 270 | 311 | 335 | 349 | 42 | 65 | 80 | 16 | 24 | 30 |
| Interior designers | 69 | 88 | 93 | 98 | 18 | 24 | 28 | 26 | 34 | 40 |
| Musicians | 252 | 260 | 276 | 288 | 8 | 24 | 36 | 3 | 9 | 14 |
| Photographers and camera operators | 120 | 140 | 148 | 154 | 20 | 28 | 35 | 16 | 23 | 29 |
| Camera operators, television, motion picture, video | 13 | 16 | 17 | 18 | 3 | 5 | 5 | 28 | 37 | 43 |
| Photographers | 107 | 123 | 131 | 136 | 16 | 23 | 29 | 15 | 22 | 27 |
| Producers, directors, actors, and entertainers | 95 | 125 | 134 | 139 | 31 | 39 | 45 | 32 | 41 | 47 |
| Public relations specialists and publicity writers | 109 | 121 | 130 | 137 | 12 | 21 | 28 | 11 | 19 | 25 |
| Radio and TV announcers and newscasters | 57 | 63 | 68 | 71 | 7 | 11 | 14 | 12 | 20 | 26 |
| Reporters and correspondents | 67 | 76 | 81 | 84 | 9 | 14 | 17 | 13 | 20 | 25 |
| Writers and editors, including technical writers | 232 | 274 | 292 | 303 | 42 | 60 | 71 | 18 | 26 | 31 |
| All other professional workers | 808 | 1,028 | 1,102 | 1,158 | 221 | 294 | 350 | 27 | 36 | 43 |
| Technicians and related support occupations | 4,204 | 5,317 | 5,754 | 6,063 | 1,113 | 1,550 | 1,859 | 26 | 37 | 44 |
| Health technicians and technologists | 1,833 | 2,413 | 2,595 | 2,752 | 580 | 763 | 919 | 32 | 42 | 50 |
| Clinical lab technologists and technicians | 258 | 299 | 321 | 341 | 41 | 63 | 83 | 16 | 24 | 32 |
| Dental hygienists | 97 | 127 | 137 | 145 | 30 | 40 | 48 | 31 | 41 | 50 |
| EEG technologists | 7 | 10 | 11 | 11 | 3 | 4 | 4 | 46 | 57 | 67 |

**TABLE 3** continued

| Occupation | Number of Jobs (000) | | | | Estimated change, 1990–2005 | | | | | |
| | 1990 | Projected, 2005 | | | Number of jobs (000) | | | Percentage Change | | |
| | | Low | Moderate | High | Low | Moderate | High | Low | Moderate | High |
|---|---|---|---|---|---|---|---|---|---|---|
| EKG technicians | 16 | 14 | 15 | 16 | -2 | -1 | 0 | -12 | -5 | 1 |
| Emergency medical technicians | 89 | 107 | 116 | 123 | 18 | 26 | 34 | 20 | 30 | 38 |
| Licensed practical nurses | 644 | 849 | 913 | 968 | 205 | 269 | 324 | 32 | 42 | 50 |
| Medical records technicians | 52 | 74 | 80 | 84 | 23 | 28 | 33 | 44 | 54 | 63 |
| Nuclear medicine technologists | 10 | 15 | 16 | 17 | 4 | 6 | 7 | 42 | 53 | 63 |
| Opticians, dispensing and measuring | 64 | 81 | 88 | 93 | 18 | 24 | 29 | 28 | 37 | 45 |
| Radiologic technologists and technicians | 149 | 234 | 252 | 268 | 86 | 103 | 119 | 58 | 70 | 80 |
| Surgical technologists | 38 | 55 | 59 | 63 | 17 | 21 | 25 | 44 | 55 | 65 |
| All other health professionals, paraprofessionals, and technicians | 409 | 547 | 588 | 623 | 138 | 179 | 214 | 34 | 44 | 52 |
| Engineering and science technicians and technologists | 1,327 | 1,498 | 1,640 | 1,718 | 170 | 312 | 391 | 13 | 24 | 29 |
| Engineering technicians | 755 | 881 | 965 | 1,008 | 126 | 210 | 253 | 17 | 28 | 33 |
| Electrical and electronic technicians/technologists | 363 | 444 | 488 | 508 | 81 | 125 | 145 | 22 | 34 | 40 |
| All other engineering technicians and technologists | 392 | 437 | 477 | 500 | 45 | 85 | 108 | 11 | 22 | 28 |
| Drafters | 326 | 335 | 370 | 391 | 8 | 44 | 65 | 3 | 13 | 20 |
| Science and mathematics technicians | 246 | 282 | 305 | 320 | 36 | 58 | 73 | 14 | 24 | 30 |
| Technicians, except health and engineering and science | 1,044 | 1,406 | 1,519 | 1,592 | 363 | 475 | 548 | 35 | 46 | 53 |
| Aircraft pilots and flight engineers | 90 | 111 | 120 | 126 | 21 | 31 | 37 | 24 | 34 | 41 |
| Air traffic controllers | 32 | 33 | 34 | 35 | 2 | 2 | 3 | 5 | 7 | 9 |
| Broadcast technicians | 33 | 31 | 34 | 35 | -1 | 1 | 3 | -3 | 4 | 8 |
| Computer programmers | 565 | 811 | 882 | 923 | 246 | 317 | 359 | 44 | 56 | 63 |
| Legal assistants and technicians, except clerical | 220 | 309 | 329 | 345 | 89 | 109 | 125 | 40 | 49 | 57 |
| Paralegals | 90 | 156 | 167 | 176 | 66 | 77 | 85 | 73 | 85 | 95 |
| Title examiners and searchers | 29 | 32 | 33 | 35 | 2 | 4 | 5 | 7 | 13 | 18 |
| All other legal assistants, including law clerks | 100 | 121 | 129 | 134 | 21 | 28 | 34 | 21 | 28 | 34 |
| Programmers, numerical, tool, and process control | 8 | 7 | 8 | 9 | -0 | 0 | 1 | -5 | 6 | 9 |
| Technical assistants, library | 65 | 66 | 72 | 77 | 1 | 7 | 13 | 2 | 11 | 20 |
| All other technicians | 33 | 38 | 40 | 42 | 5 | 7 | 10 | 15 | 23 | 29 |

| | | | | | | | | | | |
|---|---|---|---|---|---|---|---|---|---|---|
| Marketing and sales occupations | 14,088 | 16,288 | 17,489 | 18,313 | 2,200 | 3,401 | 4,226 | 16 | 24 | 30 |
| Cashiers | 2,633 | 3,094 | 3,318 | 3,474 | 461 | 685 | 842 | 18 | 26 | 32 |
| Counter and rental clerks | 215 | 268 | 289 | 303 | 53 | 74 | 88 | 25 | 34 | 41 |
| Insurance sales workers | 439 | 496 | 527 | 553 | 57 | 88 | 114 | 13 | 20 | 26 |
| Real estate agents, brokers, and appraisers | 413 | 471 | 492 | 508 | 58 | 79 | 95 | 14 | 19 | 23 |
| Brokers, real estate | 69 | 79 | 83 | 85 | 10 | 14 | 16 | 15 | 20 | 24 |
| Real estate appraisers | 44 | 51 | 54 | 57 | 8 | 11 | 13 | 18 | 24 | 29 |
| Sales agents, real estate | 300 | 340 | 355 | 366 | 40 | 55 | 66 | 13 | 18 | 22 |
| Salesperson, retail | 3,619 | 4,180 | 4,506 | 4,728 | 561 | 887 | 1,109 | 15 | 24 | 31 |
| Securities and financial services sales workers | 191 | 250 | 267 | 279 | 59 | 76 | 88 | 31 | 40 | 46 |
| Stock clerks, sales floor | 1,242 | 1,343 | 1,451 | 1,524 | 101 | 209 | 282 | 8 | 17 | 23 |
| Travel agents | 132 | 199 | 214 | 224 | 68 | 82 | 92 | 51 | 62 | 70 |
| All other sales and related workers | 5,204 | 5,987 | 6,426 | 6,719 | 783 | 1,222 | 1,515 | 15 | 23 | 29 |
| Administrative support occupations, including clerical | 21,951 | 22,996 | 24,835 | 26,158 | 1,044 | 2,884 | 4,207 | 5 | 13 | 19 |
| Adjusters, investigators, and collectors | 1,058 | 1,218 | 1,313 | 1,384 | 160 | 255 | 326 | 15 | 24 | 31 |
| Adjustment clerks | 320 | 360 | 390 | 409 | 40 | 70 | 89 | 12 | 22 | 28 |
| Bill and account collectors | 183 | 226 | 244 | 256 | 43 | 60 | 72 | 23 | 33 | 39 |
| Insurance claims and policy processing occupations | 423 | 486 | 521 | 550 | 62 | 98 | 127 | 15 | 23 | 30 |
| Insurance adjusters, examiners, and investigators | 147 | 177 | 189 | 200 | 29 | 42 | 52 | 20 | 28 | 35 |
| Insurance claims clerks | 104 | 119 | 128 | 135 | 15 | 24 | 31 | 15 | 23 | 30 |
| Insurance policy processing clerks | 172 | 190 | 204 | 216 | 18 | 32 | 44 | 10 | 19 | 25 |
| Welfare eligibility workers and interviewers | 93 | 102 | 111 | 119 | 9 | 18 | 26 | 10 | 19 | 28 |
| All other adjusters and investigators | 38 | 43 | 47 | 50 | 5 | 9 | 12 | 14 | 23 | 31 |
| Communications equipment operators | 345 | 219 | 236 | 248 | -126 | -108 | -96 | -37 | -31 | -28 |
| Telephone operators | 325 | 205 | 221 | 232 | -120 | -104 | -93 | -37 | -32 | -28 |
| Central office operators | 53 | 20 | 22 | 23 | -33 | -31 | -30 | -62 | -59 | -57 |
| Directory assistance operators | 26 | 10 | 11 | 11 | -16 | -16 | -15 | -62 | -59 | -57 |
| Switchboard operators | 246 | 175 | 189 | 198 | -71 | -57 | -47 | -29 | -23 | -19 |
| All other communications equipment operators | 20 | 14 | 15 | 16 | -5 | -5 | -4 | -28 | -23 | -20 |
| Computer operators and peripheral equipment operators | 320 | 334 | 361 | 379 | 14 | 42 | 59 | 4 | 13 | 19 |
| Computer operators, except peripheral equipment | 282 | 296 | 320 | 336 | 13 | 38 | 53 | 5 | 13 | 19 |

**TABLE 3** continued

| Occupation | Number of Jobs (000) | | | | Estimated change, 1990–2005 | | | | | |
| --- | --- | --- | --- | --- | --- | --- | --- | --- | --- | --- |
| | 1990 | Projected, 2005 | | | Number of jobs (000) | | | Percentage Change | | |
| | | Low | Moderate | High | Low | Moderate | High | Low | Moderate | High |
| Peripheral EDP equipment operators | 37 | 38 | 41 | 43 | 1 | 4 | 6 | 2 | 10 | 16 |
| Financial records processing occupations | 2,860 | 2,555 | 2,750 | 2,887 | -305 | -110 | 28 | -11 | -4 | 1 |
| Billing, cost, and rate clerks | 318 | 308 | 332 | 350 | -11 | 14 | 32 | -3 | 5 | 10 |
| Billing, posting, and calculating machine operators | 95 | 91 | 99 | 104 | -4 | 4 | 9 | -4 | 4 | 10 |
| Bookkeeping, accounting, and auditing clerks | 2,276 | 1,994 | 2,143 | 2,248 | -281 | -133 | -27 | -12 | -6 | -1 |
| Payroll and timekeeping clerks | 171 | 162 | 176 | 185 | -9 | 5 | 13 | -5 | 3 | 8 |
| Information clerks | 1,418 | 1,861 | 2,003 | 2,104 | 443 | 584 | 686 | 31 | 41 | 48 |
| Hotel desk clerks | 118 | 150 | 158 | 162 | 32 | 40 | 45 | 27 | 34 | 38 |
| Interviewing clerks, except personnel and social welfare | 144 | 185 | 200 | 209 | 41 | 56 | 66 | 29 | 39 | 46 |
| New accounts clerks, banking | 106 | 113 | 121 | 127 | 6 | 14 | 21 | 6 | 13 | 19 |
| Receptionists and information clerks | 900 | 1,228 | 1,322 | 1,394 | 328 | 422 | 494 | 36 | 47 | 55 |
| Reservation and transportation ticket agents and travel clerks | 150 | 186 | 202 | 212 | 36 | 52 | 62 | 24 | 34 | 41 |
| Mail clerks and messengers | 280 | 285 | 306 | 321 | 5 | 26 | 41 | 2 | 9 | 15 |
| Mail clerks, except mail machine operators and postal service | 137 | 136 | 146 | 153 | -1 | 9 | 16 | -0 | 7 | 12 |
| Messengers | 143 | 149 | 160 | 168 | 6 | 17 | 25 | 4 | 12 | 18 |
| Postal clerks and mail carriers | 439 | 479 | 519 | 548 | 40 | 80 | 109 | 9 | 18 | 25 |
| Postal mail carriers | 305 | 350 | 380 | 401 | 45 | 74 | 96 | 15 | 24 | 31 |
| Postal service clerks | 134 | 129 | 140 | 147 | -5 | 6 | 14 | -4 | 4 | 10 |
| Material recording, scheduling, dispatching, and distributing occupations | 2,513 | 2,534 | 2,754 | 2,888 | 21 | 241 | 375 | 1 | 10 | 15 |
| Dispatchers | 209 | 249 | 269 | 285 | 40 | 60 | 76 | 19 | 29 | 36 |
| Dispatchers, except police, fire, and ambulance | 138 | 168 | 181 | 191 | 30 | 43 | 53 | 22 | 31 | 38 |
| Dispatchers, police, fire, and ambulance | 71 | 80 | 87 | 94 | 10 | 17 | 23 | 14 | 24 | 33 |
| Meter readers, utilities | 50 | 35 | 37 | 39 | -15 | -12 | -10 | -30 | -25 | -20 |
| Order fillers, wholesale and retail sales | 197 | 195 | 211 | 222 | -1 | 14 | 25 | -1 | 7 | 13 |
| Procurement clerks | 56 | 48 | 51 | 53 | -8 | -4 | -2 | -14 | -8 | -4 |
| Production, planning, and expediting clerks | 237 | 217 | 239 | 248 | -20 | 1 | 10 | -9 | 1 | 4 |

| | | | | | | | | | | |
|---|---|---|---|---|---|---|---|---|---|---|
| Stock clerks, stockroom, warehouse, or yard | 752 | 726 | 786 | 824 | -26 | 34 | 72 | -4 | 4 | 10 |
| Traffic, shipping, and receiving clerks | 762 | 788 | 860 | 901 | 26 | 97 | 138 | 3 | 13 | 18 |
| Weighers, measurers, checkers, and samplers, recordkeeping | 37 | 35 | 38 | 40 | -2 | 1 | 3 | -5 | 4 | 8 |
| All other material recording, scheduling, and distribution workers | 214 | 242 | 263 | 276 | 28 | 50 | 63 | 13 | 23 | 29 |
| Records processing occupations, except financial | 949 | 966 | 1,045 | 1,100 | 17 | 96 | 151 | 2 | 10 | 16 |
| Advertising clerks | 18 | 19 | 21 | 21 | 1 | 3 | 4 | 8 | 15 | 20 |
| Brokerage clerks | 60 | 63 | 68 | 71 | 3 | 8 | 11 | 5 | 13 | 19 |
| Correspondence clerks | 30 | 34 | 37 | 39 | 4 | 7 | 9 | 13 | 22 | 29 |
| File clerks | 271 | 278 | 300 | 317 | 7 | 29 | 46 | 2 | 11 | 17 |
| Library assistants and bookmobile drivers | 117 | 119 | 130 | 139 | 2 | 13 | 23 | 2 | 11 | 19 |
| Order clerks, materials, merchandise, and service | 291 | 276 | 300 | 314 | -16 | 9 | 23 | -5 | 3 | 8 |
| Personnel clerks, except payroll and timekeeping | 129 | 145 | 155 | 162 | 16 | 27 | 34 | 13 | 21 | 26 |
| Statement clerks | 33 | 32 | 34 | 36 | -1 | 1 | 3 | -4 | 3 | 9 |
| Secretaries, stenographers, and typists | 4,680 | 4,735 | 5,110 | 5,387 | 55 | 429 | 706 | 1 | 9 | 15 |
| Secretaries | 3,576 | 3,813 | 4,116 | 4,338 | 237 | 540 | 762 | 7 | 15 | 21 |
| Legal secretaries | 281 | 385 | 413 | 435 | 104 | 133 | 154 | 37 | 47 | 55 |
| Medical secretaries | 232 | 363 | 390 | 415 | 131 | 158 | 183 | 57 | 68 | 79 |
| Secretaries, except legal and medical | 3,064 | 3,065 | 3,312 | 3,488 | 2 | 248 | 425 | 0 | 8 | 14 |
| Stenographers | 132 | 116 | 125 | 132 | -16 | -7 | 0 | -12 | -5 | 0 |
| Typists and word processors | 972 | 805 | 869 | 916 | -166 | -103 | -55 | -17 | -11 | -6 |
| Other clerical and administrative support workers | 7,090 | 7,811 | 8,439 | 8,912 | 721 | 1,349 | 1,822 | 10 | 19 | 26 |
| Bank tellers | 517 | 459 | 492 | 518 | -58 | -25 | 1 | -11 | -5 | 0 |
| Clerical supervisors and managers | 1,218 | 1,373 | 1,481 | 1,559 | 155 | 263 | 341 | 13 | 22 | 28 |
| Court clerks | 47 | 53 | 58 | 62 | 6 | 11 | 16 | 14 | 24 | 33 |
| Credit authorizers, credit checkers, and loan and credit clerks | 240 | 278 | 298 | 313 | 38 | 58 | 73 | 16 | 24 | 30 |
| Credit authorizers | 21 | 24 | 26 | 27 | 3 | 5 | 6 | 15 | 24 | 31 |
| Credit checkers | 48 | 55 | 60 | 63 | 7 | 12 | 15 | 16 | 24 | 31 |
| Loan and credit clerks | 151 | 175 | 187 | 197 | 25 | 37 | 46 | 16 | 24 | 31 |
| Loan interviewers | 20 | 23 | 25 | 26 | 3 | 4 | 6 | 13 | 21 | 27 |
| Customer service representatives, utilities | 109 | 111 | 120 | 126 | 2 | 11 | 17 | 2 | 10 | 15 |

**TABLE 3 continued**

| Occupation | Number of Jobs (000) | | | | Estimated change, 1990–2005 | | | | | |
| --- | --- | --- | --- | --- | --- | --- | --- | --- | --- | --- |
| | 1990 | Projected, 2005 | | | Number of jobs (000) | | | Percentage Change | | |
| | | Low | Moderate | High | Low | Moderate | High | Low | Moderate | High |
| Data entry keyers, except composing | 456 | 471 | 510 | 536 | 14 | 54 | 79 | 3 | 12 | 17 |
| Data entry keyers, composing | 19 | 21 | 23 | 24 | 2 | 4 | 5 | 11 | 20 | 25 |
| Duplicating, mail, and other office machine operators | 169 | 176 | 191 | 200 | 7 | 22 | 31 | 4 | 13 | 18 |
| General office clerks | 2,737 | 3,149 | 3,407 | 3,597 | 411 | 670 | 859 | 15 | 24 | 31 |
| Municipal clerks | 22 | 25 | 27 | 29 | 3 | 5 | 7 | 13 | 23 | 33 |
| Proofreaders and copy makers | 29 | 26 | 28 | 29 | -4 | -2 | -0 | -12 | -5 | -1 |
| Real estate clerks | 29 | 32 | 34 | 35 | 3 | 5 | 6 | 12 | 17 | 21 |
| Statistical clerks | 85 | 50 | 54 | 57 | -35 | -31 | -28 | -41 | -36 | -33 |
| Teacher aides and educational assistants | 808 | 999 | 1,086 | 1,165 | 192 | 278 | 358 | 24 | 34 | 44 |
| All other clerical and administrative support workers | 604 | 587 | 629 | 662 | -17 | 25 | 58 | -3 | 4 | 10 |
| Service occupations | 19,204 | 23,374 | 24,806 | 25,951 | 4,170 | 5,602 | 6,747 | 22 | 29 | 35 |
| Cleaning and building service occupations, except private household | 3,435 | 3,804 | 4,068 | 4,261 | 369 | 633 | 826 | 11 | 18 | 24 |
| Institutional cleaning supervisors | 142 | 166 | 177 | 185 | 24 | 35 | 43 | 17 | 24 | 30 |
| Janitors and cleaners, including maids and housekeeping cleaners | 3,007 | 3,332 | 3,562 | 3,728 | 326 | 555 | 721 | 11 | 18 | 24 |
| Pest controllers and assistants | 51 | 52 | 55 | 57 | 1 | 4 | 6 | 2 | 8 | 13 |
| All other cleaning and building service workers | 235 | 254 | 274 | 291 | 19 | 39 | 56 | 8 | 17 | 24 |
| Food preparation and service occupations | 7,705 | 9,582 | 10,031 | 10,387 | 1,877 | 2,325 | 2,681 | 24 | 30 | 35 |
| Chefs, cooks, and other kitchen workers | 3,069 | 3,906 | 4,104 | 4,264 | 837 | 1,035 | 1,195 | 27 | 34 | 39 |
| Cooks, except short order | 1,170 | 1,512 | 1,594 | 1,661 | 342 | 424 | 491 | 29 | 36 | 42 |
| Bakers, bread and pastry | 140 | 180 | 192 | 200 | 40 | 52 | 60 | 28 | 37 | 43 |
| Cooks, institution or cafeteria | 415 | 493 | 530 | 563 | 78 | 115 | 149 | 19 | 28 | 36 |
| Cooks, restaurant | 615 | 840 | 872 | 898 | 225 | 257 | 283 | 37 | 42 | 46 |
| Cooks, short order and fast food | 743 | 953 | 989 | 1,018 | 209 | 246 | 274 | 28 | 33 | 37 |
| Food preparation workers | 1,156 | 1,442 | 1,521 | 1,585 | 286 | 365 | 429 | 25 | 32 | 37 |
| Food and beverage service occupations | 4,400 | 5,392 | 5,623 | 5,803 | 992 | 1,223 | 1,403 | 23 | 28 | 32 |

|  |  |  |  |  |  |  |  |  |  |  |
|---|---|---|---|---|---|---|---|---|---|---|
| Bartenders | 400 | 404 | 422 | 436 | 3 | 21 | 35 | 1 | 5 | 9 |
| Dining room and cafeteria attendants and bar helpers | 461 | 592 | 619 | 641 | 131 | 158 | 180 | 28 | 34 | 39 |
| Food counter, fountain, and related workers | 1,607 | 2,067 | 2,158 | 2,229 | 459 | 550 | 622 | 29 | 34 | 39 |
| Hosts and hostesses, restaurant, lounge, or coffee shop | 184 | 220 | 229 | 235 | 36 | 44 | 51 | 19 | 24 | 28 |
| Waiters and waitresses | 1,747 | 2,110 | 2,196 | 2,262 | 363 | 449 | 515 | 21 | 26 | 29 |
| All other food preparation and service workers | 236 | 283 | 304 | 319 | 47 | 67 | 83 | 20 | 29 | 35 |
| Health service occupations | 1,972 | 2,636 | 2,832 | 3,002 | 664 | 860 | 1,030 | 34 | 44 | 52 |
| Ambulance drivers and attendants, except EMT's | 12 | 14 | 15 | 16 | 1 | 2 | 3 | 11 | 20 | 28 |
| Dental assistants | 176 | 220 | 236 | 250 | 44 | 60 | 74 | 25 | 34 | 42 |
| Medical assistants | 165 | 268 | 287 | 306 | 102 | 122 | 140 | 62 | 74 | 85 |
| Nursing aides and psychiatric aides | 1,374 | 1,824 | 1,960 | 2,077 | 450 | 587 | 703 | 33 | 43 | 51 |
| Nursing aides, orderlies, and attendants | 1,274 | 1,700 | 1,826 | 1,934 | 426 | 552 | 660 | 33 | 43 | 52 |
| Psychiatric aides | 100 | 124 | 134 | 143 | 24 | 34 | 43 | 24 | 34 | 43 |
| Occupational therapy assistants and aides | 10 | 14 | 15 | 16 | 4 | 5 | 6 | 46 | 57 | 67 |
| Pharmacy assistants | 83 | 94 | 101 | 107 | 11 | 18 | 24 | 13 | 22 | 29 |
| Physical and corrective therapy assistants and aides | 45 | 68 | 74 | 78 | 24 | 29 | 33 | 53 | 64 | 74 |
| All other health service workers | 107 | 134 | 144 | 153 | 27 | 37 | 46 | 25 | 35 | 43 |
| Personal service occupations | 2,192 | 2,983 | 3,164 | 3,316 | 790 | 972 | 1,124 | 36 | 44 | 51 |
| Amusement and recreation attendants | 184 | 213 | 228 | 241 | 29 | 44 | 57 | 16 | 24 | 31 |
| Baggage porters and bellhops | 31 | 39 | 42 | 43 | 8 | 10 | 12 | 25 | 33 | 37 |
| Barbers | 77 | 73 | 76 | 79 | -4 | -1 | 2 | -5 | -1 | 2 |
| Child care workers | 725 | 1,027 | 1,078 | 1,123 | 303 | 353 | 398 | 42 | 49 | 55 |
| Cosmetologists and related workers | 636 | 751 | 793 | 830 | 115 | 157 | 194 | 18 | 25 | 30 |
| Hairdressers, hairstylists, and cosmetologists | 597 | 703 | 742 | 775 | 106 | 145 | 178 | 18 | 24 | 30 |
| Manicurists | 25 | 33 | 35 | 37 | 8 | 10 | 11 | 30 | 38 | 45 |
| Shampooers | 14 | 16 | 17 | 18 | 2 | 3 | 4 | 13 | 21 | 29 |
| Flight attendants | 101 | 146 | 159 | 168 | 46 | 59 | 67 | 45 | 59 | 67 |
| Homemaker-home health aides | 391 | 682 | 733 | 776 | 291 | 343 | 385 | 75 | 88 | 99 |
| Home-health aides | 287 | 512 | 550 | 582 | 224 | 263 | 295 | 78 | 92 | 103 |
| Personal and home care aides | 103 | 170 | 183 | 194 | 67 | 79 | 90 | 64 | 77 | 87 |
| Ushers, lobby attendants, and ticket takers | 48 | 51 | 55 | 57 | 3 | 6 | 9 | 6 | 13 | 19 |
| Private Household workers | 782 | 514 | 555 | 584 | -268 | -227 | -198 | -34 | -29 | -25 |
| Child care workers, private household | 314 | 176 | 190 | 200 | -138 | -124 | -114 | -44 | -40 | -36 |

**TABLE 3 continued**

| Occupation | Number of Jobs (000) | | | | Estimated change, 1990–2005 | | | | | |
| --- | --- | --- | --- | --- | --- | --- | --- | --- | --- | --- |
| | 1990 | Projected, 2005 | | | Number of jobs (000) | | | Percentage Change | | |
| | | Low | Moderate | High | Low | Moderate | High | Low | Moderate | High |
| Cleaners and servants, private household | 411 | 287 | 310 | 326 | -124 | -101 | -85 | -30 | -25 | -21 |
| Cooks, private household | 12 | 9 | 10 | 11 | -3 | -2 | -1 | -22 | -16 | -12 |
| Housekeepers and butlers | 45 | 42 | 45 | 48 | -3 | 0 | 3 | -7 | 1 | 6 |
| Protective service occupations | 2,266 | 2,765 | 2,995 | 3,185 | 500 | 729 | 920 | 22 | 32 | 41 |
| Firefighting occupations | 280 | 321 | 348 | 374 | 41 | 68 | 95 | 15 | 24 | 34 |
| Firefighters | 210 | 241 | 262 | 281 | 31 | 51 | 71 | 15 | 24 | 34 |
| Firefighting and prevention supervisors | 58 | 66 | 72 | 77 | 8 | 14 | 20 | 15 | 24 | 34 |
| Fire inspection occupations | 12 | 13 | 15 | 16 | 2 | 3 | 4 | 14 | 24 | 34 |
| Law enforcement occupations | 886 | 1,093 | 1,187 | 1,277 | 208 | 302 | 392 | 23 | 34 | 44 |
| Correction officers | 230 | 342 | 372 | 400 | 112 | 142 | 170 | 49 | 61 | 74 |
| Police and detectives | 655 | 751 | 815 | 877 | 96 | 160 | 222 | 15 | 24 | 34 |
| Police and detective supervisors | 93 | 105 | 113 | 122 | 11 | 20 | 28 | 12 | 21 | 30 |
| Police detectives and investigators | 69 | 77 | 83 | 88 | 8 | 14 | 19 | 12 | 20 | 27 |
| Police patrol officers | 384 | 455 | 495 | 533 | 71 | 111 | 149 | 18 | 29 | 39 |
| Sheriffs and deputy sheriffs | 72 | 74 | 81 | 87 | 2 | 9 | 15 | 3 | 12 | 21 |
| Other law enforcement occupations | 37 | 40 | 43 | 47 | 3 | 7 | 10 | 9 | 18 | 27 |
| Other protective service workers | 1,101 | 1,352 | 1,460 | 1,534 | 251 | 359 | 433 | 23 | 33 | 39 |
| Detectives, except public | 47 | 61 | 66 | 69 | 14 | 19 | 22 | 31 | 41 | 47 |
| Guards | 883 | 1,094 | 1,181 | 1,238 | 211 | 298 | 354 | 24 | 34 | 40 |
| Crossing guards | 54 | 52 | 57 | 61 | -2 | 2 | 7 | -4 | 4 | 13 |
| All other protective service workers | 116 | 145 | 157 | 167 | 28 | 40 | 50 | 24 | 34 | 43 |
| All other service workers | 852 | 1,090 | 1,161 | 1,216 | 238 | 309 | 364 | 28 | 36 | 43 |
| Agriculture, forestry, fishing, and related occupations | 3,506 | 3,514 | 3,665 | 3,799 | 7 | 158 | 293 | 0 | 5 | 8 |
| Animal caretakers, except farm | 106 | 138 | 145 | 151 | 32 | 40 | 45 | 31 | 38 | 43 |
| Farm occupations | 901 | 802 | 828 | 853 | -99 | -73 | -48 | -11 | -8 | -5 |
| Farm workers | 837 | 723 | 745 | 766 | -114 | -92 | -71 | -14 | -11 | -8 |
| Nursery workers | 64 | 78 | 83 | 86 | 15 | 19 | 23 | 23 | 30 | 36 |
| Farm operators and managers | 1,223 | 990 | 1,023 | 1,054 | -233 | -200 | -169 | -19 | -16 | -14 |
| Farmers | 1,074 | 822 | 850 | 876 | -252 | -224 | -198 | -23 | -21 | -18 |
| Farm managers | 149 | 168 | 173 | 177 | 19 | 24 | 28 | 13 | 16 | 19 |
| Fishers, hunters, and trappers | 61 | 66 | 69 | 71 | 5 | 8 | 10 | 8 | 13 | 16 |

| Occupation | | | | | | | | | | |
|---|---|---|---|---|---|---|---|---|---|---|
| Captains and other officers, fishing vessels | 8 | 9 | 10 | 10 | 1 | 1 | 2 | 13 | 18 | 21 |
| Fishers, hunters, and trappers | 53 | 57 | 60 | 61 | 4 | 6 | 8 | 7 | 12 | 15 |
| Forestry and logging occupations | 148 | 144 | 150 | 158 | -4 | -1 | 9 | -3 | -1 | 6 |
| Forest and conservation workers | 40 | 41 | 43 | 45 | 1 | 3 | 5 | 4 | 8 | 13 |
| Timber cutting and logging occupations | 108 | 102 | 106 | 113 | -6 | -2 | 4 | -5 | -2 | 4 |
| Fallers and buckers | 36 | 34 | 35 | 37 | -2 | -1 | 1 | -6 | -3 | 2 |
| Logging tractor operators | 29 | 29 | 30 | 32 | -0 | 1 | 3 | -1 | 3 | 9 |
| Log handling equipment operators | 16 | 16 | 17 | 18 | -0 | 1 | 2 | -0 | 4 | 11 |
| All other timber cutting and related logging workers | 27 | 23 | 24 | 26 | -3 | -2 | -1 | -12 | -9 | -4 |
| Gardeners and groundskeepers, except farm | 874 | 1,158 | 1,222 | 1,275 | 284 | 348 | 401 | 33 | 40 | 46 |
| Supervisors, farming, forestry, and agricultural related occupations | 65 | 69 | 72 | 74 | 4 | 7 | 9 | 6 | 10 | 14 |
| All other agricultural, forestry, fishing, and related workers | 129 | 146 | 156 | 164 | 18 | 27 | 35 | 14 | 21 | 27 |
| Precision production, craft, and repair occupations | 14,124 | 14,710 | 15,909 | 16,698 | 586 | 1,785 | 2,574 | 4 | 13 | 18 |
| Blue-collar worker supervisors | 1,792 | 1,760 | 1,912 | 2,003 | -32 | 120 | 211 | -2 | 7 | 12 |
| Construction trades | 3,763 | 4,244 | 4,557 | 4,818 | 481 | 794 | 1,055 | 13 | 21 | 28 |
| Bricklayers and stone masons | 152 | 169 | 183 | 194 | 18 | 31 | 42 | 12 | 20 | 28 |
| Carpenters | 1,057 | 1,134 | 1,209 | 1,274 | 76 | 152 | 216 | 7 | 14 | 20 |
| Carpet installers | 73 | 84 | 88 | 92 | 11 | 15 | 19 | 15 | 21 | 26 |
| Ceiling tile installers and acoustical carpenters | 20 | 20 | 22 | 23 | 0 | 2 | 4 | 2 | 11 | 19 |
| Concrete and terrazzo finishers | 113 | 118 | 128 | 137 | 5 | 15 | 24 | 4 | 13 | 21 |
| Drywall installers and finishers | 143 | 163 | 175 | 186 | 20 | 33 | 43 | 14 | 23 | 30 |
| Electricians | 548 | 652 | 706 | 748 | 104 | 158 | 200 | 19 | 29 | 36 |
| Glaziers | 42 | 47 | 51 | 55 | 5 | 9 | 12 | 13 | 22 | 30 |
| Hard tile setters | 28 | 33 | 35 | 37 | 4 | 7 | 9 | 16 | 24 | 30 |
| Highway maintenance workers | 151 | 172 | 188 | 202 | 22 | 37 | 52 | 14 | 24 | 34 |
| Insulation workers | 70 | 80 | 87 | 93 | 10 | 17 | 23 | 15 | 24 | 33 |
| Painters and paperhangers, construction and maintenance | 453 | 533 | 564 | 590 | 80 | 111 | 137 | 18 | 24 | 30 |
| Paving, surfacing, and tamping equipment operators | 73 | 87 | 95 | 102 | 14 | 22 | 29 | 19 | 30 | 39 |
| Pipelayers and pipelaying fitters | 55 | 67 | 72 | 77 | 11 | 17 | 22 | 20 | 31 | 40 |
| Plasterers | 28 | 30 | 32 | 34 | 1 | 4 | 6 | 5 | 13 | 20 |
| Plumbers, pipefitters, and steamfitters | 379 | 426 | 459 | 485 | 47 | 80 | 106 | 12 | 21 | 28 |
| Roofers | 138 | 158 | 169 | 179 | 20 | 31 | 41 | 14 | 23 | 30 |
| Structural and reinforcing metal workers | 80 | 87 | 95 | 102 | 8 | 16 | 22 | 10 | 20 | 28 |

**TABLE 3** continued

| Occupation | Number of Jobs (000) | | | | Estimated change, 1990–2005 | | | | | |
| --- | --- | --- | --- | --- | --- | --- | --- | --- | --- | --- |
| | 1990 | Projected, 2005 | | | Number of jobs (000) | | | Percentage Change | | |
| | | Low | Moderate | High | Low | Moderate | High | Low | Moderate | High |
| All other construction trades workers | 160 | 184 | 198 | 209 | 25 | 38 | 49 | 15 | 24 | 31 |
| Extractive and related workers, including blasters | 237 | 223 | 247 | 257 | -14 | 9 | 20 | -6 | 4 | 8 |
| Oil and gas extraction occupations | 80 | 68 | 78 | 80 | -12 | -2 | -0 | -15 | -2 | -1 |
| Roustabouts | 38 | 31 | 36 | 37 | -6 | -1 | -1 | -17 | -4 | -2 |
| All other oil and gas extraction occupations | 42 | 37 | 42 | 43 | -6 | -0 | 0 | -14 | -1 | 1 |
| Mining, quarrying, and tunneling occupations | 24 | 19 | 20 | 21 | -6 | -5 | -4 | -24 | -19 | -15 |
| All other extraction and related workers | 133 | 137 | 148 | 157 | 4 | 15 | 24 | 3 | 12 | 18 |
| Mechanics, installers, and repairers | 4,900 | 5,262 | 5,669 | 5,946 | 362 | 769 | 1,046 | 7 | 16 | 21 |
| Communications equipment mechanics, installers, and repairers | 125 | 71 | 77 | 81 | -54 | -48 | -44 | -43 | -38 | -35 |
| Central office and PBX installers and repairers | 80 | 43 | 46 | 48 | -38 | -34 | -32 | -47 | -43 | -40 |
| Frame wirers, central office | 11 | 4 | 5 | 5 | -7 | -7 | -7 | -63 | -60 | -58 |
| Radio mechanics | 13 | 12 | 13 | 14 | -1 | -0 | 1 | -9 | -1 | 4 |
| Signal and track switch maintainers | 4 | 2 | 2 | 3 | -2 | -2 | -2 | -44 | -40 | -37 |
| All other communications equipment mechanics, installers, and repairers | 16 | 10 | 11 | 11 | -6 | -5 | -5 | -38 | -33 | -30 |
| Electrical and electronic equipment mechanics, installers, and repairers | 530 | 502 | 540 | 565 | -28 | 10 | 35 | -5 | 2 | 7 |
| Data processing equipment repairers | 84 | 123 | 134 | 140 | 40 | 50 | 56 | 48 | 60 | 67 |
| Electrical powerline installers and repairers | 99 | 101 | 108 | 113 | 2 | 9 | 14 | 2 | 9 | 14 |
| Electronic home entertainment equipment repairers | 41 | 43 | 46 | 48 | 2 | 5 | 7 | 5 | 13 | 18 |
| Electronics repairers, commercial and industrial equipment | 75 | 83 | 88 | 92 | 8 | 13 | 16 | 10 | 17 | 22 |

| Occupation | | | | | | | | | | |
|---|---|---|---|---|---|---|---|---|---|---|
| Station installers and repairers, telephone | 47 | 20 | 21 | 22 | -27 | -26 | -25 | -58 | -55 | -53 |
| Telephone and cable TV line installers and repairers | 133 | 85 | 92 | 98 | -48 | -40 | -35 | -36 | -30 | -26 |
| All other electrical and electronic equipment mechanics, installers, and repairers | 52 | 47 | 51 | 53 | -5 | -1 | 1 | -9 | -2 | 2 |
| Machinery and related mechanics, installers, and repairers | 1,675 | 1,834 | 1,980 | 2,074 | 159 | 305 | 400 | 9 | 18 | 24 |
| Industrial machinery mechanics | 474 | 477 | 520 | 542 | 3 | 46 | 68 | 1 | 10 | 14 |
| Maintenance repairers, general utility | 1,128 | 1,283 | 1,379 | 1,447 | 154 | 251 | 319 | 14 | 22 | 28 |
| Millwrights | 73 | 75 | 82 | 86 | 2 | 9 | 13 | 2 | 12 | 18 |
| Vehicle and mobile equipment mechanics and repairers | 1,568 | 1,762 | 1,892 | 1,987 | 194 | 324 | 419 | 12 | 21 | 27 |
| Aircraft mechanics and engine specialists | 122 | 140 | 151 | 158 | 18 | 29 | 36 | 15 | 24 | 29 |
| Aircraft engine specialists | 17 | 19 | 21 | 21 | 2 | 4 | 4 | 15 | 22 | 27 |
| Aircraft mechanics | 105 | 121 | 131 | 136 | 16 | 26 | 31 | 15 | 24 | 30 |
| Automotive body and related repairers | 219 | 249 | 267 | 281 | 30 | 48 | 62 | 14 | 22 | 28 |
| Automotive mechanics | 757 | 861 | 923 | 969 | 104 | 166 | 212 | 14 | 22 | 28 |
| Bus and truck mechanics and diesel engine specialists | 268 | 302 | 326 | 343 | 34 | 58 | 76 | 13 | 22 | 28 |
| Farm equipment mechanics | 48 | 49 | 52 | 55 | 1 | 4 | 7 | 3 | 9 | 14 |
| Mobile heavy equipment mechanics | 104 | 109 | 117 | 123 | 5 | 13 | 19 | 5 | 13 | 18 |
| Motorcycle, boat, and small engine mechanics | 50 | 51 | 55 | 58 | 1 | 5 | 7 | 3 | 10 | 15 |
| Motorcycle repairers | 12 | 12 | 13 | 13 | 0 | 1 | 2 | 4 | 11 | 16 |
| Small engine specialists | 39 | 39 | 42 | 44 | 1 | 4 | 6 | 2 | 9 | 14 |
| Other mechanics, installers, and repairers | 1,002 | 1,093 | 1,180 | 1,240 | 91 | 177 | 237 | 9 | 18 | 24 |
| Bicycle repairers | 15 | 16 | 17 | 18 | 1 | 2 | 2 | 5 | 11 | 16 |
| Camera and photographic equipment repairers | 7 | 8 | 9 | 9 | 1 | 1 | 2 | 10 | 17 | 21 |
| Coin and vending machine servicers and repairers | 26 | 24 | 26 | 27 | -2 | -0 | 1 | -8 | -1 | 4 |
| Electric meter installers and repairers | 14 | 15 | 16 | 17 | 1 | 2 | 3 | 11 | 18 | 24 |
| Electromedical and biomedical equipment repairers | 8 | 11 | 12 | 13 | 3 | 4 | 5 | 40 | 51 | 60 |
| Elevator installers and repairers | 19 | 20 | 22 | 23 | 1 | 3 | 5 | 7 | 17 | 24 |

**TABLE 3 continued**

| Occupation | Number of Jobs (000) | | | | Estimated change, 1990–2005 | | | | | |
| | 1990 | Projected, 2005 | | | Number of jobs (000) | | | Percentage Change | | |
| | | Low | Moderate | High | Low | Moderate | High | Low | Moderate | High |
|---|---|---|---|---|---|---|---|---|---|---|
| Heat, air conditioning and refrigeration mechanics and installers | 219 | 246 | 266 | 280 | 27 | 46 | 61 | 12 | 21 | 28 |
| Home appliance and power tool repairers | 71 | 65 | 70 | 73 | -6 | -1 | 3 | -8 | -1 | 4 |
| Musical instrument repairers and tuners | 9 | 8 | 9 | 9 | -0 | 0 | 1 | -4 | 2 | 7 |
| Office machine and cash register servicers | 73 | 76 | 82 | 86 | 3 | 9 | 14 | 5 | 13 | 19 |
| Precision instrument repairers | 50 | 50 | 54 | 56 | -0 | 4 | 6 | -0 | 8 | 12 |
| Riggers | 14 | 13 | 14 | 15 | -1 | -0 | 1 | -6 | -0 | 4 |
| Tire repairers and changers | 81 | 88 | 95 | 100 | 7 | 14 | 19 | 9 | 17 | 23 |
| Watchmakers | 7 | 4 | 5 | 5 | -3 | -2 | -2 | -37 | -33 | -30 |
| All other mechanics, installers, and repairers | 390 | 447 | 484 | 508 | 57 | 94 | 118 | 15 | 24 | 30 |
| Production occupations, precision | 3,134 | 2,928 | 3,208 | 3,338 | -206 | 74 | 204 | -7 | 2 | 7 |
| Assemblers, precision | 352 | 209 | 236 | 243 | -143 | -116 | -109 | -41 | -33 | -31 |
| Aircraft assemblers, precision | 32 | 31 | 34 | 35 | -1 | 2 | 3 | -3 | 6 | 9 |
| Electrical and electronic equipment assemblers, precision | 171 | 78 | 90 | 92 | -93 | -81 | -79 | -55 | -48 | -46 |
| Electromechanical equipment assemblers, precision | 49 | 27 | 31 | 32 | -21 | -18 | -17 | -44 | -37 | -35 |
| Fitters, structural metal, precision | 15 | 12 | 13 | 14 | -3 | -2 | -1 | -21 | -14 | -9 |
| Machine builders and other precision machine assemblers | 50 | 37 | 42 | 43 | -13 | -8 | -7 | -25 | -17 | -14 |
| All other precision assemblers | 34 | 23 | 26 | 27 | -11 | -8 | -7 | -32 | -24 | -21 |
| Food workers, precision | 301 | 271 | 286 | 297 | -30 | -15 | -4 | -10 | -5 | -1 |
| Bakers, manufacturing | 34 | 32 | 32 | 33 | -2 | -1 | -0 | -6 | -4 | -1 |
| Butchers and meatcutters | 234 | 207 | 220 | 229 | -27 | -14 | -4 | -12 | -6 | -2 |
| All other precision food and tobacco workers | 34 | 33 | 34 | 35 | -1 | 0 | 1 | -2 | 1 | 3 |
| Inspectors, testers, and graders, precision | 668 | 592 | 659 | 683 | -77 | -9 | 15 | -11 | -1 | 2 |
| Metal workers, precision | 936 | 930 | 1,021 | 1,065 | -6 | 85 | 129 | -1 | 9 | 14 |
| Boilermakers | 22 | 21 | 23 | 24 | -1 | 1 | 2 | -4 | 3 | 9 |
| Jewelers and silversmiths | 40 | 44 | 48 | 50 | 4 | 8 | 10 | 9 | 20 | 24 |
| Machinists | 386 | 389 | 427 | 444 | 3 | 41 | 58 | 1 | 10 | 15 |

| Occupation | | | | | | | | | | |
|---|---|---|---|---|---|---|---|---|---|---|
| Sheet metal workers and duct installers | 233 | 242 | 263 | 278 | 9 | 30 | 44 | 4 | 13 | 19 |
| Shipfitters | 13 | 12 | 12 | 13 | -1 | -0 | -0 | -9 | 4 | -1 |
| Tool and die makers | 141 | 130 | 145 | 150 | -11 | 4 | 9 | -7 | 3 | 6 |
| All other precision metal workers | 101 | 92 | 103 | 106 | -9 | 2 | 6 | -9 | 2 | 6 |
| Printing workers, precision | 161 | 181 | 195 | 203 | 20 | 33 | 41 | 12 | 21 | 26 |
| Bookbinders | 7 | 8 | 8 | 8 | 0 | 1 | 1 | 5 | 13 | 18 |
| Compositors and typesetters, precision | 14 | 13 | 14 | 15 | -1 | -0 | 0 | -8 | -2 | 1 |
| Job printers | 15 | 17 | 18 | 19 | 2 | 3 | 4 | 14 | 23 | 28 |
| Paste-up workers | 30 | 32 | 34 | 36 | 2 | 4 | 5 | 5 | 13 | 18 |
| Electronic pagination systems workers | 12 | 14 | 16 | 16 | 3 | 4 | 5 | 24 | 33 | 39 |
| Photoengravers | 8 | 9 | 9 | 10 | 0 | -1 | -1 | 5 | 13 | 17 |
| Camera operators | 17 | 19 | 20 | 21 | 2 | 4 | 4 | 13 | 21 | 26 |
| Strippers, printing | 32 | 40 | 43 | 44 | 8 | 11 | 13 | 25 | 34 | 40 |
| Platemakers | 14 | 16 | 17 | 18 | 2 | 3 | 4 | 15 | 23 | 29 |
| All other printing workers, precision | 12 | 14 | 15 | 16 | 2 | 3 | 3 | 15 | 23 | 28 |
| Textile, apparel, and furnishings workers, precision | 272 | 274 | 302 | 313 | 2 | 29 | 41 | 1 | 11 | 15 |
| Custom tailors and sewers | 116 | 129 | 137 | 143 | 13 | 21 | 27 | 11 | 18 | 23 |
| Patternmakers and layout workers, fabric and apparel | 16 | 12 | 15 | 15 | -4 | -1 | -0 | -23 | -4 | -2 |
| Shoe and leather workers and repairers, precision | 27 | 16 | 22 | 23 | -11 | -5 | -4 | -40 | -19 | -15 |
| Upholsterers | 64 | 65 | 70 | 72 | 1 | 6 | 8 | 1 | 10 | 13 |
| All other precision textile, apparel, and furnishings workers | 50 | 52 | 57 | 60 | 2 | 7 | 10 | 5 | 15 | 20 |
| Woodworkers, precision | 213 | 223 | 240 | 251 | 10 | 27 | 39 | 5 | 13 | 18 |
| Cabinetmakers and bench carpenters | 107 | 114 | 122 | 128 | 7 | 14 | 21 | 6 | 13 | 19 |
| Furniture finishers | 34 | 35 | 38 | 39 | 1 | 4 | 6 | 3 | 12 | 17 |
| Wood machinists | 46 | 48 | 51 | 54 | 1 | 5 | 8 | 3 | 12 | 17 |
| All other precision woodworkers | 25 | 26 | 29 | 30 | 1 | 3 | 4 | 3 | 13 | 17 |
| Other precision workers | 231 | 249 | 270 | 283 | 18 | 39 | 52 | 8 | 17 | 23 |
| Dental lab technicians, precision | 57 | 56 | 59 | 63 | -1 | 3 | 6 | -2 | 4 | 10 |
| Optical goods workers, precision | 19 | 22 | 25 | 26 | 3 | 6 | 6 | 14 | 29 | 34 |
| Photographic process workers, precision | 18 | 19 | 21 | 22 | 2 | 3 | 4 | 8 | 16 | 21 |
| All other precision workers | 137 | 152 | 165 | 173 | 15 | 28 | 36 | 11 | 21 | 26 |
| Plant and system occupations | 297 | 294 | 317 | 335 | -4 | 19 | 37 | -1 | 6 | 12 |

**TABLE 3 continued**

| Occupation | Number of Jobs (000) | | | | Estimated change, 1990–2005 | | | | | |
| --- | --- | --- | --- | --- | --- | --- | --- | --- | --- | --- |
| | 1990 | Projected, 2005 | | | Number of jobs (000) | | | Percentage Change | | |
| | | Low | Moderate | High | Low | Moderate | High | Low | Moderate | High |
| Chemical plant and system operators | 35 | 28 | 30 | 31 | -7 | -5 | -3 | -21 | -14 | -10 |
| Electric power generating plant operators, distributors, and dispatchers | 44 | 45 | 48 | 50 | 1 | 4 | 6 | 2 | 9 | 14 |
| Power distributors and dispatchers | 18 | 18 | 19 | 20 | -0 | 1 | 2 | -1 | 6 | 11 |
| Power generation and reactor plant operators | 26 | 27 | 29 | 31 | 1 | 3 | 4 | 3 | 11 | 17 |
| Gas and petroleum plant and system occupations | 31 | 25 | 27 | 28 | -5 | -3 | -3 | -18 | -11 | -9 |
| Stationary engineers | 35 | 33 | 36 | 37 | -2 | 0 | 2 | -5 | 1 | 7 |
| Water and liquid waste treatment plant and system operators | 78 | 93 | 101 | 109 | 15 | 23 | 30 | 19 | 29 | 39 |
| All other plant and system operators | 74 | 69 | 75 | 79 | -5 | 1 | 4 | -7 | 1 | 6 |
| Operators, fabricators, and laborers | 17,245 | 16,448 | 17,961 | 18,796 | -797 | 716 | 1,550 | -5 | 4 | 9 |
| Machine setters, set-up operators, operators, and tenders | 4,905 | 4,104 | 4,579 | 4,754 | -800 | -326 | -151 | -16 | -7 | -3 |
| Numerical control machine tool operators and tenders, metal and plastic | 70 | 78 | 87 | 90 | 7 | 16 | 19 | 11 | 23 | 27 |
| Combination machine tool setters, set-up operators, operators, and tenders | 93 | 102 | 113 | 118 | 10 | 21 | 25 | 11 | 23 | 27 |
| Machine tool cut and form setters, operators, and tenders, metal and plastic | 765 | 529 | 585 | 609 | -236 | -179 | -156 | -31 | -23 | -20 |
| Drilling and boring machine tool setters and set-up operators, metal and plastic | 52 | 35 | 39 | 40 | -17 | -13 | -12 | -33 | -26 | -23 |
| Grinding machine setters and set-up operators, metal and plastic | 72 | 49 | 54 | 56 | -24 | -18 | -16 | -33 | -25 | -22 |
| Lathe and turning machine tool setters and set-up operators, metal and plastic | 80 | 55 | 61 | 63 | -26 | -20 | -17 | -32 | -24 | -22 |

| Occupation | | | | | | | | | | |
|---|---|---|---|---|---|---|---|---|---|---|
| Machine forming operators and tenders, metal and plastic | 174 | 119 | 131 | 137 | -55 | -43 | -37 | -32 | -25 | -21 |
| Machine tool cutting operators and tenders, metal and plastic | 145 | 93 | 104 | 107 | -52 | -42 | -38 | -36 | -29 | -26 |
| Punching machine setters and set-up operators, metal and plastic | 52 | 38 | 42 | 44 | -14 | -10 | -8 | -27 | -18 | -15 |
| All other machine tool cutting and forming, etc. | 189 | 140 | 155 | 161 | -49 | -34 | -28 | -26 | -18 | -15 |
| Metal fabricating machine setters, operators, and related workers | 140 | 136 | 149 | 156 | -5 | 9 | 16 | -3 | 6 | 11 |
| Metal fabricators, structural metal products | 34 | 35 | 37 | 40 | 1 | 4 | 6 | 2 | 11 | 18 |
| Soldering and brazing machine operators and tenders | 11 | 10 | 11 | 11 | -1 | -0 | 0 | -12 | -1 | 2 |
| Welding machine setters, operators, and tenders | 95 | 92 | 101 | 105 | -4 | 6 | 10 | -4 | 6 | 10 |
| Metal and plastic processing machine setters, operators, and related workers | 393 | 355 | 396 | 411 | -38 | 3 | 18 | -10 | 1 | 5 |
| Electrolytic plating machine operators and tenders, setters and set-up operators, metal and plastic | 43 | 34 | 38 | 39 | -10 | -6 | -4 | -22 | -13 | -10 |
| Foundry mold assembly and shakeout workers | 10 | 6 | 7 | 7 | -3 | -3 | -2 | -33 | -26 | -23 |
| Furnace operators and tenders | 22 | 19 | 21 | 22 | -3 | -0 | 0 | -12 | -2 | 2 |
| Heaters, metal and plastic | 5 | 4 | 5 | 5 | -0 | 0 | 0 | -9 | 1 | 6 |
| Heating equipment setters and set-up operators, metal and plastic | 7 | 6 | 7 | 7 | -1 | -0 | 0 | -10 | -0 | 4 |
| Heat treating machine operators and tenders, metal and plastic | 21 | 19 | 21 | 22 | -2 | 0 | 1 | -10 | 0 | 4 |
| Metal molding machine operators and tenders, setters, and set-up operators | 38 | 28 | 31 | 32 | -10 | -7 | -6 | -26 | -18 | -15 |
| Nonelectrolytic plating machine operators and tenders, settlers, and set-up operators | 7 | 5 | 6 | 6 | -2 | -1 | -1 | -22 | -15 | -11 |

**TABLE 3 continued**

| Occupation | Number of Jobs (000) | | | | Estimated change, 1990–2005 | | | | | |
| | 1990 | Projected, 2005 | | | Number of jobs (000) | | | Percentage Change | | |
| | | Low | Moderate | High | Low | Moderate | High | Low | Moderate | High |
| --- | --- | --- | --- | --- | --- | --- | --- | --- | --- | --- |
| Plastic molding machine operators and tenders, settlers, and set-up operators | 143 | 155 | 173 | 180 | 12 | 31 | 37 | 8 | 21 | 26 |
| All other metal and plastic machine settlers, operators, and related workers | 99 | 79 | 88 | 91 | -20 | -11 | -8 | -20 | -11 | -8 |
| Printing, binding, and related workers | 393 | 430 | 466 | 484 | 37 | 72 | 90 | 9 | 18 | 23 |
| Bindery machine operators and set-up operators | 71 | 73 | 79 | 82 | 2 | 8 | 11 | 3 | 11 | 16 |
| Printing press operators | 224 | 249 | 268 | 279 | 24 | 44 | 54 | 11 | 19 | 24 |
| Letterpress operators | 16 | 13 | 14 | 15 | -3 | -2 | -1 | -16 | -10 | -6 |
| Offset lithographic press operators | 91 | 113 | 122 | 127 | 22 | 31 | 36 | 25 | 34 | 39 |
| Printing press machine setters, operators and tenders | 104 | 106 | 115 | 120 | 3 | 12 | 16 | 3 | 11 | 16 |
| All other printing press setters and set-up operators | 14 | 16 | 17 | 17 | 2 | 3 | 3 | 13 | 20 | 25 |
| Photoengraving and lithographing machine operators, and photographers | 98 | 108 | 119 | 123 | 10 | 21 | 25 | 10 | 21 | 25 |
| Photoengraving and lithographic machine operators and tenders | 6 | 6 | 7 | 7 | 1 | 1 | 1 | 11 | 20 | 25 |
| Screen printing machine setters and set-up operators | 26 | 28 | 31 | 32 | 2 | 5 | 6 | 6 | 19 | 22 |
| Typesetting and composing machine operators and tenders | 26 | 30 | 32 | 33 | 4 | 6 | 7 | 14 | 23 | 28 |
| All other printing, binding, and related workers | 40 | 44 | 48 | 50 | 4 | 8 | 10 | 11 | 21 | 26 |
| Textile and related setters, operators, and related workers | 1,090 | 751 | 912 | 936 | -339 | -178 | -153 | -31 | -16 | -14 |

| Occupation | | | | | | | | | | |
|---|---|---|---|---|---|---|---|---|---|---|
| Extruding and forming machine operators and tenders, synthetic or glass fibers | 21 | 18 | 20 | 21 | -3 | -1 | 0 | -12 | -3 | 1 |
| Pressing machine operators and tenders, textile, garment, and related materials | 84 | 85 | 96 | 100 | 0 | 12 | 16 | 0 | 14 | 19 |
| Sewing machine operators, garment | 585 | 368 | 469 | 478 | -217 | -116 | -106 | -37 | -20 | -18 |
| Sewing machine operators, nongarment | 131 | 121 | 138 | 142 | -10 | 7 | 11 | -8 | 5 | 8 |
| Textile bleaching and dyeing machine operators and tenders | 28 | 17 | 20 | 21 | -11 | -8 | -7 | -39 | -28 | -26 |
| Textile draw-out and winding machine operators and tenders | 199 | 116 | 138 | 142 | -82 | -61 | -57 | -41 | -31 | -29 |
| Textile machine setters and set-up operators | 42 | 26 | 30 | 31 | -16 | -11 | -10 | -38 | -27 | -25 |
| Woodworking machine setters, operators, and other related workers | 136 | 142 | 152 | 160 | 6 | 16 | 24 | 4 | 12 | 17 |
| Head sawyers and sawing machine operators and tenders, setters, and set-up operators | 72 | 75 | 80 | 85 | 3 | 8 | 13 | 4 | 11 | 17 |
| Woodworking machine operators and tenders, setters, and set-up operators | 64 | 67 | 72 | 75 | 3 | 8 | 11 | 4 | 12 | 18 |
| Other machine setters, set-up operators, operators, and tenders | 1,825 | 1,582 | 1,718 | 1,790 | -243 | -106 | -35 | -13 | -6 | -2 |
| Boiler operators and tenders, low pressure | 21 | 20 | 22 | 23 | -2 | 0 | 1 | -7 | 0 | 6 |
| Cement and gluing machine operators and tenders | 35 | 25 | 28 | 29 | -10 | -7 | -6 | -28 | -20 | -16 |
| Chemical equipment controllers, operators, and tenders | 75 | 56 | 61 | 63 | -19 | -14 | -11 | -25 | -19 | -15 |
| Cooking and roasting machine operators and tenders, food and tobacco | 31 | 26 | 26 | 27 | -6 | -5 | -4 | -18 | -16 | -14 |
| Crushing and mixing machine operators and tenders | 135 | 134 | 145 | 151 | -1 | 10 | 16 | -1 | 7 | 12 |
| Cutting and slicing machine setters, operators, and tenders | 88 | 81 | 89 | 92 | -7 | 1 | 4 | -8 | 1 | 5 |
| Dairy processing equipment operators, including setters | 18 | 15 | 16 | 16 | -3 | -2 | -2 | -15 | -13 | -11 |

**TABLE 3 continued**

| Occupation | Number of Jobs (000) | | | | Estimated change, 1990–2005 | | | | | |
| | 1990 | Projected, 2005 | | | Number of jobs (000) | | | Percentage Change | | |
| | | Low | Moderate | High | Low | Moderate | High | Low | Moderate | High |
|---|---|---|---|---|---|---|---|---|---|---|
| Electronic semiconductor processors | 32 | 19 | 22 | 22 | -13 | -10 | -10 | -41 | -31 | -30 |
| Extruding and forming machine setters, operators, and tenders | 94 | 85 | 93 | 97 | -9 | -1 | 3 | -10 | -1 | 3 |
| Furnace, kiln, or kettle operators and tenders | 56 | 48 | 53 | 55 | -8 | -4 | -1 | -15 | -6 | -2 |
| Laundry and drycleaning machine operators and tenders, except pressing | 173 | 198 | 212 | 223 | 26 | 39 | 50 | 15 | 23 | 29 |
| Motion picture projectionists | 13 | 11 | 12 | 12 | -2 | -1 | -1 | -15 | -9 | -5 |
| Packaging and filling machine operators and tenders | 324 | 278 | 297 | 308 | -46 | -27 | -16 | -14 | -8 | -5 |
| Painting and coating machine operators | 160 | 143 | 158 | 165 | -16 | -2 | 5 | -10 | -1 | 3 |
| Coating, painting, and spraying machine operators, tenders, setters, and set-up operators | 117 | 103 | 115 | 119 | -14 | -3 | 2 | -12 | -2 | 2 |
| Painters, transportation equipment | 42 | 40 | 43 | 45 | -2 | 1 | 3 | -4 | 3 | 8 |
| Paper goods machine setters and set-up operators | 59 | 53 | 57 | 59 | -6 | -2 | 1 | -10 | -3 | 1 |
| Photographic processing machine operators and tenders | 58 | 64 | 69 | 73 | 6 | 11 | 15 | 11 | 20 | 25 |
| Separating and still machine operators and tenders | 26 | 19 | 21 | 21 | -6 | -5 | -4 | -25 | -20 | -17 |
| Shoe sewing machine operators and tenders | 18 | 5 | 10 | 10 | -13 | -8 | -8 | -71 | -46 | -43 |
| Tire building machine operators | 14 | 8 | 9 | 9 | -6 | -5 | -5 | -45 | -38 | -34 |
| All other machine operators, tenders, setters, and set-up operators | 396 | 294 | 320 | 334 | -102 | -75 | -62 | -26 | -19 | -16 |
| Hand workers, including assemblers and fabricators | 2,675 | 2,100 | 2,307 | 2,394 | -575 | -368 | -281 | -21 | -14 | -11 |
| Cannery workers | 78 | 70 | 73 | 74 | -8 | -6 | -4 | -10 | -7 | -5 |
| Coil winders, tapers, and finishers | 20 | 11 | 13 | 13 | -8 | -6 | -6 | -41 | -33 | -31 |
| Cutters and trimmers, hand | 59 | 48 | 55 | 57 | -11 | -4 | -2 | -19 | -6 | -3 |

| Occupation | | | | | | | | | | |
|---|---|---|---|---|---|---|---|---|---|---|
| Electrical and electronic assemblers | 232 | 112 | 128 | 131 | -121 | -105 | -101 | -52 | -45 | -44 |
| Grinders and polishers, hand | 84 | 59 | 65 | 67 | -25 | -19 | -16 | -30 | -23 | -20 |
| Machine assemblers | 50 | 40 | 44 | 46 | -11 | -6 | -4 | -21 | -12 | -9 |
| Meat, poultry, and fish cutters, and trimmers, hand | 121 | 132 | 136 | 140 | 11 | 15 | 19 | 9 | 12 | 15 |
| Metal pourers and casters, basic shapes | 12 | 10 | 11 | 11 | -2 | -1 | -1 | -18 | -9 | -6 |
| Painting, coating, and decorating workers, hand | 46 | 46 | 50 | 52 | 0 | 4 | 6 | 0 | 9 | 14 |
| Portable machine cutters | 13 | 10 | 12 | 13 | -3 | -0 | -0 | -24 | -4 | -2 |
| Pressers, hand | 17 | 15 | 18 | 19 | -2 | 1 | 1 | -14 | 4 | 8 |
| Sewers, hand | 16 | 11 | 15 | 15 | -5 | -1 | -1 | -28 | -7 | -5 |
| Solderers and brazers | 28 | 21 | 24 | 24 | -7 | -5 | -4 | -25 | -16 | -13 |
| Welders and cutters | 332 | 317 | 344 | 360 | -15 | 13 | 29 | -4 | 4 | 9 |
| All other assemblers and fabricators | 1,192 | 888 | 980 | 1,018 | -304 | -212 | -173 | -26 | -18 | -15 |
| All other hand workers | 375 | 311 | 339 | 352 | -64 | -36 | -23 | -17 | -10 | -6 |
| Transportation and material moving machine and vehicle operators | 4,730 | 5,329 | 5,743 | 6,043 | 599 | 1,013 | 1,312 | 13 | 21 | 28 |
| Motor vehicle operators | 3,417 | 3,997 | 4,301 | 4,522 | 580 | 883 | 1,105 | 17 | 26 | 32 |
| Bus drivers | 561 | 680 | 738 | 789 | 118 | 177 | 228 | 21 | 32 | 41 |
| Bus drivers, school | 402 | 497 | 541 | 579 | 95 | 138 | 177 | 24 | 34 | 44 |
| Taxi drivers and chauffeurs | 108 | 132 | 140 | 146 | 24 | 32 | 38 | 22 | 29 | 35 |
| Truckdrivers | 2,701 | 3,126 | 3,360 | 3,522 | 425 | 659 | 821 | 16 | 24 | 30 |
| Driver/sales workers | 339 | 359 | 381 | 397 | 20 | 42 | 58 | 6 | 12 | 17 |
| Truckdrivers, light and heavy | 2,362 | 2,767 | 2,979 | 3,125 | 405 | 617 | 763 | 17 | 26 | 32 |
| All other motor vehicle operators | 47 | 58 | 62 | 65 | 12 | 16 | 18 | 25 | 33 | 40 |
| Rail transportation workers | 107 | 95 | 102 | 108 | -12 | -5 | 1 | -11 | -4 | 2 |
| Locomotive engineers | 16 | 14 | 15 | 16 | -2 | -1 | -0 | -12 | -6 | -0 |
| Railroad brake, signal, and switch operators | 35 | 27 | 29 | 31 | -8 | -6 | -4 | -23 | -18 | -13 |
| Railroad conductors and yardmasters | 28 | 22 | 24 | 25 | -6 | -4 | -3 | -20 | -14 | -9 |
| Rail yard engineers, dinkey operators, and hostlers | 8 | 7 | 8 | 8 | -1 | -0 | -0 | -12 | -5 | 1 |
| Subway and streetcar operators | 14 | 21 | 23 | 24 | 7 | 9 | 10 | 53 | 66 | 79 |
| All other rail vehicle operators | 6 | 3 | 3 | 4 | -2 | -2 | -2 | -42 | -38 | -35 |
| Water transportation and related workers | 140 | 135 | 144 | 153 | -5 | 4 | 13 | -4 | 3 | 10 |
| Able seamen, ordinary seamen, and marine oilers | 22 | 16 | 17 | 18 | -6 | -5 | -4 | -28 | -24 | -18 |
| Captains and pilots, ship | 14 | 13 | 14 | 15 | -1 | 0 | 1 | -4 | 1 | 9 |

**TABLE 3 continued**

| Occupation | Number of Jobs (000) | | | | Estimated change, 1990–2005 | | | | | |
| | 1990 | Projected, 2005 | | | Number of jobs (000) | | | Percentage Change | | |
| | | Low | Moderate | High | Low | Moderate | High | Low | Moderate | High |
|---|---|---|---|---|---|---|---|---|---|---|
| Mates, ship, boat, and barge | 7 | 6 | 7 | 7 | -1 | -0 | 0 | -9 | -4 | 4 |
| Ship engineers | 7 | 5 | 5 | 6 | -1 | -1 | -1 | -23 | -19 | -13 |
| All other transportation and related workers | 91 | 94 | 102 | 108 | 4 | 11 | 17 | 4 | 12 | 18 |
| Material moving equipment operators | 1,019 | 1,053 | 1,142 | 1,202 | 34 | 123 | 183 | 3 | 12 | 18 |
| Crane and tower operators | 51 | 50 | 54 | 57 | -1 | 4 | 6 | -2 | 7 | 13 |
| Excavation and loading machine operators | 74 | 77 | 83 | 88 | 2 | 9 | 14 | 3 | 12 | 19 |
| Grader, dozer, and scraper operators | 93 | 96 | 104 | 110 | 2 | 11 | 17 | 3 | 11 | 18 |
| Hoist and winch operators | 11 | 12 | 13 | 13 | 1 | 1 | 2 | 4 | 13 | 19 |
| Industrial truck and tractor operators | 431 | 433 | 469 | 492 | 2 | 38 | 60 | 0 | 9 | 14 |
| Operating engineers | 157 | 186 | 201 | 214 | 28 | 44 | 57 | 18 | 28 | 36 |
| All other material moving equipment operators | 201 | 200 | 218 | 227 | -0 | 17 | 26 | -0 | 8 | 13 |
| All other transportation and material moving equipment operators | 47 | 50 | 54 | 57 | 3 | 7 | 10 | 5 | 14 | 21 |
| Helpers, laborers, and material movers, hand | 4,935 | 4,914 | 5,332 | 5,606 | -21 | 396 | 670 | -0 | 8 | 14 |
| Freight, stock, and material movers, hand | 884 | 912 | 990 | 1,037 | 28 | 106 | 153 | 3 | 12 | 17 |
| Hand packers and packagers | 667 | 685 | 744 | 774 | 18 | 77 | 107 | 3 | 12 | 16 |
| Helpers, construction trades | 552 | 583 | 636 | 679 | 32 | 84 | 128 | 6 | 15 | 23 |
| Machine feeders and offbearers | 255 | 229 | 249 | 260 | -26 | -6 | 5 | -10 | -2 | 2 |
| Parking lot attendants | 50 | 57 | 61 | 64 | 7 | 11 | 15 | 14 | 23 | 29 |
| Refuse collectors | 124 | 120 | 129 | 137 | -4 | 5 | 13 | -4 | 4 | 10 |
| Service station attendants | 246 | 212 | 229 | 240 | -34 | -17 | -6 | -14 | -7 | -2 |
| Vehicle washers and equipment cleaners | 240 | 274 | 295 | 310 | 34 | 55 | 70 | 14 | 23 | 29 |
| All other helpers, laborers, and material movers, hand | 1,918 | 1,842 | 1,999 | 2,103 | -76 | 80 | 185 | -4 | 4 | 10 |

SOURCE: United States Department of Labor, Bureau of Labor Statistics, *Outlook 2000*, 1992.

# CHAPTER 4

# RESEARCHING
# THE PROFESSIONS

In this chapter we outline effective ways to research any job or profession—your own or ones you may be considering. You will learn which government agencies, private-sector offices, and publications can help you evaluate the prospects of a career in any field. By making a few phone calls, you can steer your way into a promising career—and away from fields with fewer opportunities.

As you begin your research into the job market in general, or into your specific occupation, you will benefit by keeping the following points in mind.

- *Occupations with large numbers of jobs usually have more job openings* and offer more flexibility and geographic mobility than do occupations with few jobs.

- *An occupational field, however large, that is declining in size will generate more competition for the decreasing number of jobs.* Be sure to compare several years' data to spot growth or decline trends in an occupation.

- *Remember that statistical studies, which often are based on representative samples, can be misleading.* A particular region may offer much better prospects for an occupation than the national sample would suggest.

Consequently, you will want to double-check statistical data with experts on the profession.

• *Projections about employment, even those made by the country's leading labor experts, can be wrong if industry growth has been miscalculated.* For example, U.S. Department of Labor studies overestimated the growth of jobs connected with the electronic mail industry. They failed to predict the tremendous growth of the facsimile machine industry, which quickly outpaced electronic mail. Job hunters who consulted a variety of sources rather than relying solely on government statistics would have been aware of these conditions and prepared to take advantage of the opportunities in the facsimile industry.

• *Try to get the most current data available.* With fierce competition in business and growth of new people-replacing technology, the outlook for an occupation can change rapidly. Current information is essential to good career decision making.

• *Watch the newspaper and other current publications for news about events and conditions—such as changes in industries, technologies, and government regulations—that may affect your occupation.* The effects may be negative or positive. Affordable computer technology quickly displaced old-fashioned accountants but created exciting new opportunities for accountants with experience in computers and systems design. President Reagan's reduction in the federal bureaucracy during the early 1980s created a glut of highly skilled government workers in the Washington area, greatly increasing job competition. The Rehabilitation Act passed by Congress in 1974 guaranteed disabled people the right to work, thereby creating a whole array of new jobs for professionals helping the disabled to become active in the workplace.

## GOVERNMENT PUBLICATIONS

Usually, the first step in evaluating an occupation is to study its history and outlook. There is no shortage of information about occupations in the United States. In fact, you may feel overwhelmed by the amount of information that is available to you. The most valuable sources of occupational information are listed in this chapter. The primary source of labor-market statistics in the United States is the U.S.

Department of Labor (DOL). Many job studies that you see come directly, or indirectly, from figures generated by the DOL's Bureau of Labor Statistics or Employment and Training Administration. Most information about the labor market at the state and local level is developed by state employment agencies in cooperation with the U.S. Department of Labor. The best DOL publications are described below and are easy to find. Most are available in large public libraries, U.S. government depository libraries (see page 101) and career counseling offices at universities and community job centers. Also included on pages 56 and 57 are the addresses of regional offices located throughout the United States where these publications can be found, and where labor statistics experts can assist you. You can order copies of these publications through the Government Printing Office and obtain a free list of additional publications by writing to the department. For the national picture, the DOL's publications are a good place to start, but you should not feel limited to these. Professional associations, industry groups, and for-profit publishers study national and regional occupational outlooks. Be creative and adventuresome in your search for occupational statistics if you are not satisfied with what the DOL studies provide.

You will get the best available information by using a combination of published studies and the opinions of job-market experts. For every publication listed in this chapter, you will find in appendix VI, the address and telephone number of the publishing agency or organization, so you can contact it directly. In each organization, there are analysts who can assist you in understanding the statistics. They can often provide additional information from their research—information that was not published. You may telephone these agencies from anywhere in the country, but you may prefer to call or visit an office in your own vicinity. Where available, the names of state or regional offices of the organizations are provided.

Before you begin studying reports or talking with occupational experts, you need to understand the way occupations are classified. Most state agencies and all federal agencies have a common system for organizing occupations. You can find the key to the classification system, and to the occupational statistics, in the following publication, which can be found in most libraries.

*Dictionary of Occupational Titles, 1991* (U.S. Department of Labor)— Covers more than twenty thousand occupations; lists nine-digit occupation code numbers, titles, related industries, alternate titles, descriptions of tasks performed, and related occupations.

*Occupational Outlook Handbook* (Bureau of Labor Statistics)—This is the single best guide for learning about particular occupations. Published annually, it provides data on occupational characteristics and training, as well as the outlook for approximately two hundred occupations. Each section usually includes data on employment, unemployment and personal income, with an emphasis on occupational supply and demand. After each section is a list of sources for further information.

*Occupational Outlook Quarterly* (Bureau of Labor Statistics)—A Supplement to *Occupational Outlook Handbook,* this is a periodical to help job seekers, employment planners, and guidance counselors keep abreast of current occupational and employment developments between editions of the *Handbook.*

*Monthly Labor Review* (Bureau of Labor Statistics)—A periodical covering employment in the United States, it contains articles on the labor force, wages, prices, and productivity. Regular features profile current labor statistics.

*The Job Outlook Handbook 1990–2005* (Bureau of Labor Statistics)— Summaries of employment data for each occupation listed in the *Occupational Outlook Handbook,* consisting of occupation title, number of jobs in 1990, projections through 2005, and summary of job prospects.

*Occupational Projections and Training Data* (Bureau of Labor Statistics)—An annual, this publication provides projections of individual occupations for the next twenty years and data on employment and unemployment, including current and projected employment, and annual job openings due to growth and replacement for about fifty-five occupational categories.

The Department of Labor also publishes guides on occupations. These are taken from the *Occupational Outlook Handbook* and focus on the nature of the work, conditions of employment, training, qualifications, advancement, job outlook, and earnings. Here is a sample of what you might find. (S/N: stock number, to be quoted when ordering from the Government Printing Office.)

*Business and Managerial Occupations*
S/N 029-001-03094-1

*Computer and Mathematics-Related Occupations*
S/N 029-001-03096-7

*Education and Social Service Occupations and Clergy*
S/N 029-001-03098-3

*Engineering, Scientific, and Related Occupations*
S/N 029-001-03095-9

*Sales Occupations*
S/N 029-001-03104-1

Information about earnings projections is published periodically.

*Employment and Earnings* (Bureau of Labor Statistics)—This publication is made up of current data on employment, hours, and earnings for the United States as a whole, for states and for more than two hundred local areas. Supplements present revised data for recent years from surveys of business establishments.

*Occupational Projects and Training Data* (Bureau of Labor Statistics)—A ranking of occupations by growth rate, earnings, and other measures useful in evaluating employment prospects.

*Wage Surveys* (available only through Bureau of Labor Statistics, Publications Sales Center, P.O. Box 2145, Chicago IL 60690; 312-353-1880)—The following surveys of various industries may be used to supplement the *National Survey.*

**Banking (1989)**
Bulletin 2371

**Computer and Data Processing Services (1987)**
Bulletin 2318

**Hospitals (August 1989)**
Bulletin 2364

**Life and Health Insurance Carriers (1986)**
Bulletin 2293

**Meat Products (1990)**
Bulletin 2416

**Millwork (1984)**
Bulletin 2244

▣ Motor Vehicles and Parts (1989)
▣ Bulletin 2384

Synthetic Fibers (1985)
Bulletin 2268

▣ Nursing and Personal Care
▣ Facilities (1985)
▣ Bulletin 2275

Textile Mills (1985)
Bulletin 2265

# Clearinghouses

The Bureau of Labor Statistics operates regional offices throughout the United States. Each office maintains a full collection of reports published by the bureau, and has a staff of statistical experts to assist you. The Employment and Training Administration operates ten regional offices, many of them in the same building in each region as those of the Bureau of the Bureau of Labor Statistics. Each regional office has a Regional Administrator who coordinates activities and is an excellent source of information about local occupational statistics and programs.

## Bureau of Labor Statistics Offices

*Region I* (Maine, Vermont, New Hampshire, Massachusetts, Connecticut, Rhode Island)
1 Congress Street, 10th floor
Boston, MA 02114
617-565-2331

*Region II* (New York, New Jersey, Puerto Rico, Virgin Islands)
Room 808
201 Varick Street
New York, NY 10014
212-337-2500

*Region III* (Pennsylvania, West Virginia, Delaware, Maryland, District of Columbia)
3535 Market Street
Philadelphia, PA 19104
215-596-1151

*Region IV* (Florida, Georgia, Mississippi, Alabama, Tennessee, Kentucky, North Carolina, South Carolina)
1371 Peachtree Street, NE
Atlanta, GA 30367
404-347-2161

*Region V* (Minnesota, Wisconsin, Michigan, Indiana, Illinois, Ohio)
Federal Office Building, 9th Floor
230 S. Dearborn Street
Chicago, IL 60604
312-353-7226

*Region VI* (New Mexico, Texas, Oklahoma, Arkansas, Louisiana)
Federal Building
525 Griffin Street, Room 221
Dallas, TX 75202
214-767-6953

*Regions VII and VIII* (Colorado, Iowa,
Kansas, Missouri, Montana, Nebraska,
North Dakota, South Dakota, Utah,
Wyoming)
911 Walnut Street
Kansas City, MO 64106
816-426-2378

*Regions IX and X* (Alaska, Washington,
Oregon, Idaho, California, Nevada,
Arizona, Hawaii, Guam,
American Samoa)
71 Stevenson Street
P.O. Box 193766
San Francisco, CA 94119
415-744-7166

## Employment and Training Administration Offices

*Region I* (Maine, Vermont, New Hampshire,
Massachusetts, Connecticut,
Rhode Island, Puerto Rico,
Virgin Islands)
1 Congress Street
Boston, MA 02203
617-565-3630

*Region II* (New York, New Jersey)
201 Varick Street
New York, NY 10014
212-337-2139

*Region III* (Pennsylvania, West Virginia,
Virginia, Delaware,
District of Columbia)
3535 Market Street
Philadelphia, PA 19104
215-596-6336

*Region IV* (Florida, Georgia, Mississippi,
Alabama, Tennessee, Kentucky,
North Carolina, South Carolina)
1375 Peachtree Street, NE
Atlanta, GA 30367
404-347-4411

*Region V* (Minnesota, Wisconsin,
Michigan, Indiana, Illinois, Ohio)
230 S. Dearborn Street
Chicago, IL 60604
312-353-0313

*Region VI* (New Mexico, Texas,
Oklahoma, Arkansas, Louisiana)
525 Griffin Square
Dallas, TX 75202
214-767-8263

*Region VII* (Nebraska, Kansas,
Missouri, Iowa)
911 Walnut Avenue
Kansas City, KS 64106
816-426-3796

*Region VIII* (Montana, North Dakota,
South Dakota, Wyoming, Utah,
Colorado)
1961 Stout Street
Denver, CO 80294
303-844-4401

*Region IX* (California, Nevada, Arizona, Hawaii)
71 Stevenson Street
San Francisco, CA 94102
415-744-6650

*Region X* (Alaska, Washington, Oregon, Idaho)
1111 3rd Avenue
Seattle, WA 98101
206-553-7700

The Educational Resources Information Center (ERIC) serves as a clearinghouse for government and private-industry reports in a variety of educational and training areas. In addition to a national computerized information system, ERIC maintains a network of offices specializing in particular aspects of education. You can write to those offices and request a list of sources relevant to your occupation. These sources can include books, journal articles, private-industry studies, and published and unpublished government reports.

The two ERIC clearinghouses most relevant to career and labor market information are:

ERIC/Adult, Career, and Vocational Education
Ohio State University
1960 Kenny Road
Columbus, OH 43210

ERIC/Counseling and Student Services
University of North Carolina
Greensboro, NC 27412

## OTHER USEFUL PUBLICATIONS

The following books provide a national overview of various occupations. Many can be found in college career-counseling offices and large public libraries. Local and state employment offices may also have copies.

- *Career Information Center* (Glencoe Publishing)—Thirteen volumes; each volume focuses on particular types of occupations, for example, Agribusiness, Communications and the Arts.

- *Opportunities in...* (VGM Career Horizons) and dozens of other single-volume books on specific occupations.

- *Equal Opportunity Publications* (Equal Opportunity Publications)— Each issue highlights career opportunities for women, minorities, and the handicapped; published three times a year.

Krants, Les, ed., *The Jobs Rated Almanac* (Pharos Books)—There is a section on the outlook for each profession.

Wright, John W., *Almanac of Jobs and Salaries* (Avon Books)—Provides salary (including geographic breakdown) and outlook information on hundreds of occupations.

Also available are newsletters that focus on employment opportunities in a particular occupation or area.

*Artsearch* (Theater Communications Group)—Classified listings for jobs in the performing arts, in particular dance, music, educational institutions and theater; biweekly.

*Employment Information in the Mathematical Sciences* (American Mathematical Society)—Listings by state for positions for mathematicians beyond the Bachelor's degree level; six issues a year.

*Employment Opportunities for Business Economists* (National Association of Business Economics)—Job openings for business economists and analysts; quarterly.

*Environmental Opportunities* (Environmental Opportunities)—Each issue includes between eighty and 120 full-time positions for environmental jobs in administration, agriculture, consulting, teaching, research, and preservation; monthly.

*International Employment Hotline* (Cantrell)—Current overseas job openings listed by country; job title, description, and contact information; monthly.

*Rocky Mountain Employment Newsletter* (Intermountain Referral Service)—Listing of jobs, including job title, description, requirements and employer's name and address for: Colorado, Idaho, Montana, Arizona, New Mexico, Washington, Oregon, and Wyoming; semi-monthly.

# JOB LISTINGS

Job listings and advertisements for specific professions are carried in publications that cater to those professions. For example, *The Chronicle of Higher Education* posts jobs in colleges and universities, and *Association Trends* lists job openings in associations. Others list regional jobs. *The Nursing Spectrum* gives biweekly listings of positions in nursing in the Washington area, and on Tuesdays in the Health section the *Washington Post* carries job listings in the health care field.

Ask your library and college career services center which listings are available.

PART III

# INDUSTRIES

Companies do not operate in a vacuum—they are part of a larger industry environment. You should find out where the specific industry you are interested in is headed. Is it growing or declining? Are the salaries commensurate with those in other industries that might hire you? If the outlook for the industry is disappointing, you may want to look for opportunities in other industries. You will want to make the most of your opportunities by working in an industry on the upswing—an industry that is likely to offer the maximum job growth and better-than-average compensation. Learn which industries are growing the fastest and achieving the best profits. These will likely have the most jobs and the greatest opportunities for job growth in the next decade.

Industries can be defined in many ways. For example, within the broadly defined prerecorded-music industry are smaller industries, including those for compact discs, tapes, and LPs. This is an important concept for job hunters who want to work in particular industries but also maximize their opportunities. A job hunter who wants to work in the prerecorded music industry will do much better to go into the compact discs sector, which is growing, than into the declining LP sector.

# CHAPTER 5

# QUICK REFERENCE
# TO HIGH-GROWTH
# INDUSTRIES

Fast growth in an industry is generally good news for the job hunter. Industry growth means job opportunity and mobility and often higher salaries than are available in stagnant or declining industries. For example, industries with a healthy growth rate, such as semiconductors or medical instruments, offer far better odds for the job hunter than would an industry such as leather goods, which is in a decline.

Regardless of the state of the economy, there are always industries that are booming and many more that are holding their own. This chapter, in a series of tables, gives you a quick resource for identifying boom and bust industries. It also enables you to compare the growth patterns and forecasts for 156 manufacturing industries that represent more than 75 percent of all manufactured goods as well as for selected service industries.

In the tables below, adapted from originals produced by the U.S. Department of Commerce (DOC), you will discover which U.S. industries are forecast to have the greatest rates of growth and decline. For example, in table 4, you will see that high-technology industries dominate the list.

## TABLE 4: FASTEST GROWING MANUFACTURING INDUSTRIES IN 1993

| SIC code | Industry | Percentage increase |
|---|---|---|
| 3674 | Semiconductors | 12.0 |
| 3841 | Surgical and medical instruments | 8.5 |
| 3842 | Surgical appliances and supplies | 8.5 |
| 357A | Computers and peripherals (SIC 3571, 3572, 3575, 3577) | 8.2† |
| 3845 | Electromedical equipment | 7.8 |
| 3711 | Motor vehicle and car bodies | 6.8 |
| 3633 | Household laundry equipment | 6.7 |
| 3632 | Household refrigerator and freezers | 6.5 |
| 371A | Automobile parts and accessories | 6.1 |
| 3844 | X-ray apparatus and tubes | 5.6 |

\* SIC codes are explained on page 91.        † In current dollars

SOURCE: United States Department of Commerce, International Trade Administration, *U.S. Industrial Outlook, 1993*, 1993.

From table 5, one might conclude that information and health-related industries should be leading performers.

## TABLE 5: TRENDS IN SELECTED SERVICE INDUSTRIES, 1990–1993 (in billions of current dollars)

| Industry | Unit of measure | 1993 value | Percentage change (1990–1993) | | |
|---|---|---|---|---|---|
| | | | 1990–1991 | 1991–1992* | 1992–1993† |
| Accounting | Receipts | 37.5 | 2.2 | 2.9 | 4.2 |
| Advertising | Receipts | 21.5 | 1.5 | 2.5 | 3.6 |
| Banks | Assets | 3,788.0 | 4.0 | 3.0 | 4.0 |
| Computer professional services | Revenues | 61.0 | 12.2 | 9.9 | 9.3 |
| Credit unions | Assets | 274.5 | 14.5 | 12.0 | 8.0 |
| Data processing | Revenues | 45.7 | 14.1 | 12.9 | 13.7 |
| Electronic information services | Revenues | 13.5 | 13.2 | 13.7 | 16.4 |
| Equipment leasing | Original equipment cost | 126.3 | -3.3 | 0.0 | 5.0 |
| Health services | Revenues | 939.9 | 11.4 | 11.5 | 12.1 |
| Home entertainment | Revenues | 26.7 | 7.6 | 7.7 | 7.7 |
| Legal services | Receipts | 106.5 | 4.3 | 5.3 | 6.5 |
| Life insurance | Premiums | 284.8 | -0.1 | 3.3 | 4.5 |
| Management consulting | Receipts | 70.0 | 3.8 | 4.7 | 5.3 |
| Motion picture theaters | Receipts | 4.7 | -4.4 | -1.3 | 0.0 |
| Prerecorded music | Manufacturers' value | 9.4 | 3.9 | 7.5 | 11.3 |
| Property/casualty insurance | Net premiums written | 239.3 | 2.4 | 3.2 | 4.0 |
| Railroad (class 1) | Revenue ton-miles | 29.5 | 0.6 | 2.4 | 3.3 |
| Retail sales, total | Sales | 2,038.0 | 0.9 | 4.9 | 5.4 |
| Apparel and accessories stores | Sales | 106.0 | 1.1 | 4.2 | 7.1 |
| Department stores | Sales | 196.0 | 3.5 | 6.2 | 3.7 |
| Eating and drinking places | Sales | 219.0 | 4.3 | 5.7 | 6.8 |
| Food retailing | Sales | 395.9 | 2.5 | 1.6 | 2.3 |
| Savings institutions | Assets | 800.0 | -12.9 | -7.0 | -1.8 |
| Space commerce | Revenues | 4.9 | 24.7 | 14.1 | 2.0 |
| Telecommunications | Revenues | 176.4†† | 5.3 | 4.0 | 6.3 |
| Travel services | Expenditures | 393.0 | 3.1 | 8.0 | 5.7 |
| Trucking | Cargo ton-miles | 296.0 | 3.1 | 1.6 | 1.9 |
| Venture capital | Capital commitments | 3.2 | -31.2 | 96.7 | 28.0 |

\* Estimate.        † Forecast.        †† In billions of constant dollars.

SOURCE: United States Department of Commerce, International Trade Administration, *U.S. Industrial Outlook, 1993*, 1993.

In table 6, ten industries that job hunters should avoid are ranked. As the industries with the greatest declines they are likely to offer relatively meager hiring and promotion opportunities.

### TABLE 6: DECLINING MANUFACTURING INDUSTRIES

| SIC code* | Industry | Percentage decline 1992–1993 |
|-----------|----------|------------------------------|
| 3172 | Personal leather goods | -3.4 |
| 3171 | Women's handbags and purses | -3.6 |
| 2386 | Leather and sheep-lined clothing | -3.8 |
| 3724 | Aircraft engines and engine parts | -3.8 |
| 3728 | Aircraft parts and equipment | -4.8 |
| 3764 | Space propulsion units and parts | -5.0 |
| 3554 | Paper industries machinery | -5.2 |
| 3761 | Guided missiles and space vehicles | -5.7 |
| 3769 | Space vehicles equipment | -6.0 |
| 3721 | Aircraft | -6.0 |

\* SIC codes are explained on page 91.

SOURCE: United States Department of Commerce, International Trade Administration, *U.S. Industrial Outlook, 1993,* 1993.

From table 7, the size and growth rates for 156 manufacturing industries may be compared. The SIC code, explained on page 91, will be useful when you research these industries.

## TABLE 7: FORECAST GROWTH RATES FOR 156 MANUFACTURING INDUSTRIES

| SIC code | Industry | Outlook chapter | Shipments 1993 ($000,000)† | Shipments Percentage growth (1992-1993) | Shipments Rank | Growth 1988-1993 Compound annual percentage rate | Growth 1988-1993 Rank |
|---|---|---|---|---|---|---|---|
| 2015 | Poultry slaughtering and processing | 31 | 21.500 | 3.5 | 47 | 6.7 | 7 |
| 201A | Red meat | 31 | 64.350 | 1.9 | 104 | 0.0 | 82 |
| 2021 | Creamery butter | 31 | 1.913 | 1.6 | 113 | 0.7 | 74 |
| 2022 | Cheese, natural and processed | 31 | 14.619 | 1.6 | 112 | 2.3 | 38 |
| 2023 | Dry, condensed, and evaporated products | 31 | 5.003 | 0.9 | 123 | -4.2 | 144 |
| 2024 | Ice cream and frozen desserts | 31 | 4.916 | 3.5 | 50 | 2.7 | 34 |
| 2026 | Fluid milk | 31 | 19.364 | -1.3 | 134 | -1.8 | 122 |
| 203A | Canned foods | 31 | 27.055 | 1.7 | 108 | 1.8 | 48 |
| 203B | Frozen foods | 31 | 14.185 | 1.8 | 107 | 3.3 | 24 |
| 2051 | Bread, cake, and related products | 31 | 14.423 | 0.8 | 124 | -1.1 | 110 |
| 2052 | Cookies and crackers | 31 | 6.689 | 1.5 | 116 | 1.6 | 53 |
| 2053 | Frozen bakery products, except bread | 31 | 1.014 | -1.5 | 135 | -4.4 | 147 |
| 2064 | Candy and other confectionery products | 31 | 8.082 | 2.9 | 73 | 2.2 | 42 |
| 2082 | Malt beverages | 31 | 15.730 | 1.5 | 114 | 2.7 | 33 |
| 2084 | Wines, brandy, and brandy spirits | 31 | 3.213 | 0.4 | 127 | -1.4 | 114 |
| 2085 | Distilled and blended liquors | 31 | 2.735 | -1.6 | 137 | -4.3 | 145 |
| 2086 | Bottled and canned soft drinks | 31 | 22.896 | 1.3 | 119 | 0.0 | 80 |
| 2386 | Leather and sheep-lined clothing | 33 | 0.127 | -3.8 | 149 | -9.3 | 155 |
| 2411 | Logging | 6 | 9.065 | -1.0 | 133 | -2.7 | 135 |
| 2421 | Sawmills and planing mills, general | 6 | 16.259 | 2.0 | 97 | -1.7 | 120 |
| 2431 | Millwork | 6 | 8.915 | 2.5 | 83 | -0.4 | 93 |
| 2435 | Hardwood veneer and plywood | 6 | 1.885 | 1.9 | 105 | -1.5 | 116 |
| 2436 | Softwood veneer and plywood | 6 | 4.630 | 4.4 | 30 | -0.4 | 94 |
| 2448 | Wood pallets and skids | 6 | 1.863 | 2.5 | 85 | 2.9 | 27 |
| 2451 | Mobile homes | 5 | 4.100 | 5.1 | 16 | 0.3 | 78 |
| 2493 | Reconstituted wood products | 6 | 3.115 | 3.7 | 46 | 1.4 | 60 |
| 2511 | Wood household furniture | 36 | 7.237 | 3.5 | 49 | -1.8 | 121 |
| 2512 | Upholstered household furniture | 36 | 5.410 | 4.6 | 25 | 0.9 | 70 |
| 2514 | Metal household furniture | 36 | 1.991 | 3.9 | 45 | -1.6 | 119 |
| 2515 | Mattresses and bedsprings | 36 | 2.715 | 4.5 | 27 | 2.8 | 29 |
| 2611 | Pulp mills | 10 | 5.204 | 4.0 | 39 | 4.0 | 19 |
| 2653 | Corrugated and solid fiber boxes | 10 | 18.735 | 4.0 | 40 | 2.7 | 31 |
| 2657 | Folding paperboard boxes | 10 | 5.965 | 1.2 | 121 | 0.5 | 75 |
| 2676 | Sanitary paper products | 10 | 13.850 | 3.5 | 53 | 3.2 | 25 |
| 2677 | Envelopes | 10 | 2.578 | 2.8 | 76 | -0.2 | 88 |
| 26PM | Paper and paperboard mills | 10 | 48.790 | 4.5 | 28 | 1.8 | 50 |
| 2711 | Newspapers | 24 | 24.495 | -1.8 | 139 | -4.5 | 148 |
| 2721 | Periodicals | 24 | 16.623 | 2.4 | 86 | -1.1 | 107 |
| 2731 | Book publishing | 24 | 14.035 | 3.4 | 55 | 1.9 | 46 |
| 2732 | Book printing | 24 | 3.955 | 2.7 | 78 | 3.0 | 26 |
| 2741 | Miscellaneous publishing | 24 | 8.315 | 3.2 | 57 | 3.0 | 58 |
| 275 | Commercial printing | 24 | 49.725 | 3.0 | 62 | 1.5 | 56 |
| 2761 | Manifold business forms | 24 | 6.686 | -1.0 | 132 | -1.5 | 117 |

**TABLE 7 continued**

| SIC code | Industry | Outlook chapter | Shipments | | | Growth 1988–1993 | |
|---|---|---|---|---|---|---|---|
| | | | 1993 ($000,000)† | Percentage growth (1992–1993) | Rank | Compound annual percentage rate | Rank |
| 2771 | Greeting cards | 24 | 3.822 | 5.0 | 19 | 5.8 | 13 |
| 2782 | Blankbooks and looseleaf binders | 24 | 2.860 | 2.7 | 79 | -0.5 | 95 |
| 2789 | Bookbinding and related work | 24 | 1.305 | 2.0 | 103 | 2.1 | 43 |
| 2791 | Typesetting | 24 | 1.988 | 3.5 | 52 | 1.3 | 65 |
| 2796 | Platemaking services | 24 | 2.802 | 3.5 | 48 | 2.3 | 40 |
| 281A | Industrial inorganic chemicals, except pigments | 11 | 21.938 | 3.0 | 70 | 3.8 | 22 |
| 2821 | Plastics materials and resins | 12 | 28.737 | 3.0 | 63 | 1.3 | 62 |
| 2822 | Synthetic rubber | 12 | 3.900 | 4.0 | 37 | 1.6 | 55 |
| 2833 | Medicinals and botanicals | 43 | 4.538 | 3.0 | 65 | 2.8 | 30 |
| 2834 | Pharmaceutical preparations | 43 | 37.737 | 5.2 | 14 | 2.7 | 32 |
| 2835 | Diagnostic substances | 43 | 2.432 | 3.0 | 69 | 1.7 | 52 |
| 2836 | Biological products, except diagnostic | 43 | 2.174 | 3.0 | 68 | 4.4 | 17 |
| 2841 | Soap and other detergents | 34 | 15.622 | 2.5 | 82 | 5.8 | 12 |
| 2842 | Polishes and sanitation goods | 34 | 5.537 | 2.0 | 95 | -0.3 | 89 |
| 2843 | Surface active agents | 34 | 2.917 | 4.5 | 26 | -1.1 | 109 |
| 2844 | Toilet preparations | 34 | 17.178 | 2.3 | 89 | 1.5 | 59 |
| 2851 | Paints and allied products | 11 | 11.961 | 1.5 | 117 | -1.6 | 118 |
| 2873 | Nitrogenous fertilizers | 11 | 2.621 | -1.5 | 136 | 2.1 | 44 |
| 2874 | Phosphatic fertilizers | 11 | 5.195 | 5.0 | 20 | 5.7 | 14 |
| 2879 | Agricultural chemicals, NEC | 11 | 8.006 | 2.0 | 99 | 3.6 | 23 |
| 2891 | Adhesives and sealants | 11 | 5.117 | 3.0 | 64 | 2.6 | 35 |
| 2911 | Petroleum refining | 4 | 122.827 | 0.4 | 126 | -0.2 | 86 |
| 3011 | Tires and inner tubes | 12 | 11.588 | 4.0 | 36 | 1.3 | 63 |
| 3069 | Fabricated rubber products, NEC | 12 | 6.443 | 3.0 | 66 | 1.6 | 54 |
| 3088 | Plastic plumbing fixtures | 7 | 1.100 | 1.9 | 106 | 6.3 | 9 |
| 308A | Miscellaneous plastic products, except bottles and plumbing | 12 | 66.500 | 2.9 | 71 | 2.4 | 37 |
| 3111 | Leather tanning and finishing | 33 | 2.151 | 5.0 | 23 | 0.0 | 81 |
| 3142 | House slippers | 33 | 0.249 | 2.0 | 93 | 1.8 | 49 |
| 3143 | Men's footwear, except athletic | 33 | 1.724 | 3.0 | 67 | -3.2 | 138 |
| 3144 | Women's footwear, except athletic | 33 | 1.079 | 0.0 | 129 | -4.2 | 143 |
| 3149 | Footwear, except rubber, NEC | 33 | 0.273 | -2.8 | 143 | -9.4 | 156 |
| 3151 | Leather gloves and mittens | 33 | 0.118 | -3.3 | 146 | -7.7 | 154 |
| 3161 | Luggage | 33 | 0.953 | 0.0 | 130 | 1.0 | 67 |
| 3171 | Women's handbags and purses | 33 | 0.407 | -3.6 | 148 | -5.4 | 150 |
| 3172 | Personal leather goods, NEC | 33 | 0.282 | -3.4 | 147 | -6.3 | 151 |
| 3211 | Flat glass | 7 | 2.050 | 2.0 | 101 | -3.0 | 136 |
| 3241 | Cement, hydraulic | 7 | 4.175 | 3.3 | 56 | -0.2 | 87 |
| 3253 | Ceramic wall and floor tile | 7 | 0.747 | 5.4 | 12 | 0.4 | 77 |
| 3261 | Vitreous plumbing fixtures | 7 | 0.750 | 1.4 | 118 | -3.9 | 142 |
| 3275 | Gypsum products | 7 | 3.076 | 3.9 | 44 | 2.5 | 36 |

| SIC | Industry | | | | | | |
|---|---|---|---|---|---|---|---|
| 331A | Steel mill products (SIC 3312, 3315–17) | 13 | 54.860 | 2.4 | 87 | -1.1 | 111 |
| 3431 | Metal sanitary ware | 7 | 0.875 | 0.6 | 125 | -0.6 | 98 |
| 3432 | Plumbing fixture fittings and trim | 7 | 2.250 | 2.3 | 90 | -0.7 | 99 |
| 3441 | Fabricated structural metal | 7 | 7.510 | -2.0 | 140 | -2.5 | 132 |
| 3451 | Screw machine products | 14 | 2.892 | 4.0 | 41 | -1.0 | 105 |
| 3452 | Bolts, nuts, rivets, and washers | 14 | 5.127 | 3.5 | 51 | -0.8 | 101 |
| 349A | Valves and pipe fittings | 14 | 7.210 | -2.5 | 81 | 0.0 | 83 |
| 3523 | Farm machinery and equipment | 17 | 8.266 | 3.2 | 141 | -0.6 | 96 |
| 3524 | Lawn and garden equipment | 36 | 4.291 | 3.0 | 58 | -2.0 | 127 |
| 3531 | Construction machinery | 17 | 14.650 | 3.1 | 61 | 0.7 | 72 |
| 3532 | Mining machinery | 17 | 1.675 | 2.0 | 60 | 2.0 | 45 |
| 3533 | Oil and gas field machinery | 17 | 4.488 | 4.3 | 100 | 6.5 | 8 |
| 3541 | Machine tools, metal cutting types | 16 | 2.864 | 5.0 | 33 | -1.0 | 104 |
| 3542 | Machine tools, metal forming types | 16 | 1.229 | 2.8 | 17 | -6.4 | 152 |
| 3544 | Special dies, tools, jigs and fixtures | 16 | 7.932 | 4.2 | 74 | 0.0 | 84 |
| 3546 | Power-driven handtools | 16 | 2.602 | 2.8 | 34 | 1.2 | 66 |
| 3552 | Textile machinery | 17 | 1.300 | -5.2 | 75 | -1.9 | 126 |
| 3554 | Paper industries machinery | 17 | 2.235 | 2.0 | 153 | 2.9 | 28 |
| 3555 | Printing trades machinery | 17 | 2.786 | 4.4 | 94 | -2.5 | 130 |
| 3556 | Food products machinery | 17 | 2.083 | 4.5 | 32 | 0.8 | 71 |
| 3562 | Ball and roller bearings | 14 | 3.675 | 5.0 | 29 | -1.3 | 113 |
| 3565 | Packaging machinery | 17 | 2.569 | | 22 | 3.8 | 21 |
| 357A | Computers and peripherals (SIC 3571, 3572, 3575, 3577) | 26 | 65.000†† | 8.2 | 4 | 0.7 | 73 |
| 3585 | Refrigeration and heating equipment | 17 | 17.334 | 4.0 | 35 | -1.0 | 106 |
| 3612 | Transformers, except electronic | 18 | 3.317 | -1.7 | 138 | -2.5 | 131 |
| 3613 | Switchgear and switchboard apparatus | 18 | 4.715 | 2.0 | 102 | -2.2 | 128 |
| 3621 | Motors and generators | 18 | 6.351 | 1.0 | 122 | -2.6 | 134 |
| 3625 | Relays and industrial controls | 18 | 6.950 | 2.7 | 77 | 1.4 | 61 |
| 3631 | Household cooking equipment | 36 | 3.205 | 4.0 | 42 | -3.2 | 140 |
| 3632 | Household refrigerators and freezers | 36 | 4.195 | 6.5 | 8 | 1.5 | 57 |
| 3633 | Household laundry equipment | 36 | 3.395 | 6.7 | 7 | 1.7 | 51 |
| 3634 | Electric housewares and fans | 36 | 2.845 | 1.6 | 111 | 0.4 | 76 |
| 3635 | Household vacuum cleaners | 36 | 1.925 | 5.4 | 11 | 5.8 | 11 |
| 3639 | Household appliances, NEC | 36 | 2.955 | 5.2 | 15 | 5.6 | 15 |
| 3643 | Current-carrying wiring devices | 8 | 4.358 | 2.5 | 84 | 0.9 | 68 |
| 3644 | Noncurrent-carrying wiring devices | 8 | 2.790 | -0.5 | 131 | -1.9 | 125 |
| 364A | Lighting fixtures (SIC 3645, 3646, 3648) | 8 | 5.937 | 1.5 | 115 | -1.1 | 108 |
| 3651 | Household audio and video equipment | 36 | 7.856 | 1.7 | 110 | 4.0 | 20 |
| 3661 | Telephone and telegraph apparatus | 29 | 17.075 | 2.0 | 98 | -1.4 | 115 |
| 3663 | Radio and TV communications equipment | 29 | 19.100 | 2.0 | 96 | 4.2 | 18 |
| 3674 | Semiconductors | 15 | 35.571 | 12.0 | | 9.5 | 4 |
| 367A | Electronic parts, except semiconductors (SIC 3671–2, 3675–9) | 15 | 35.071 | 3.9 | 43 | 0.9 | 69 |
| 3711 | Motor vehicles and car bodies | 35 | 137.500 | 6.8 | 6 | -0.4 | 92 |
| 3715 | Truck trailers | 35 | 3.219 | 5.0 | 21 | -1.8 | 124 |
| 371A | Automotive parts and accessories | 35 | 96.311 | 6.1 | 9 | -0.8 | 100 |
| 3721 | Aircraft | 20 | 41.416 | -6.0 | 156 | 0.3 | 79 |
| 3724 | Aircraft engines and engine parts | 20 | 17.878 | -3.8 | 150 | -1.8 | 123 |
| 3728 | Aircraft parts and equipment, NEC | 20 | 16.443 | -4.8 | 151 | -0.6 | 97 |

**TABLE 7 continued**

| SIC code | Industry | Outlook chapter | Shipments 1993 ($000,000)†† | Shipments Percentage growth (1992–1993) | Shipments Rank | Growth 1988–1993 Compound annual percentage rate | Growth 1988–1993 Rank |
|---|---|---|---|---|---|---|---|
| 3731 | Ship building and repairing | 21 | 9,554 | -3.2 | 145 | 2.2 | 41 |
| 3732 | Boat building and repairing | 37 | 4,113 | 2.6 | 80 | -6.5 | 153 |
| 3751 | Motorcycles, bicycles, and parts | 37 | 1,461 | 3.4 | 54 | 7.5 | 5 |
| 3761 | Guided missiles and space vehicles | 20 | 22,927 | -5.7 | 154 | -0.3 | 90 |
| 3764 | Space propulsion units and parts | 20 | 3,145 | -5.0 | 152 | -4.4 | 146 |
| 3769 | Space vehicle equipment, NEC | 20 | 1,390 | -6.0 | 155 | -4.8 | 149 |
| 3812 | Search and navigation equipment | 29 | 30,768 | -3.1 | 144 | -3.2 | 139 |
| 3821 | Laboratory apparatus and furniture | 22 | 1,892 | 3.2 | 59 | -1.0 | 103 |
| 3822 | Environmental controls | 22 | 2,213 | 0.3 | 128 | -0.3 | 91 |
| 3823 | Process control instruments | 22 | 5,419 | 1.7 | 109 | 1.3 | 64 |
| 3824 | Fluid meters and counting devices | 22 | 1,399 | -2.8 | 142 | -3.0 | 137 |
| 3825 | Instruments to measure electricity | 22 | 8,636 | 5.0 | 18 | 1.8 | 47 |
| 3826 | Analytical instruments | 22 | 5,052 | 4.7 | 24 | 6.0 | 10 |
| 3827 | Optical instruments and lenses | 22 | 1,915 | 2.2 | 91 | -0.8 | 102 |
| 3829 | Measuring and controlling devices, NEC | 22 | 4,052 | 2.3 | 88 | 2.3 | 39 |
| 3841 | Surgical and medical instruments | 44 | 13,133 | 8.5 | 2 | 10.0 | 3 |
| 3842 | Surgical appliances and supplies | 44 | 13,449 | 8.5 | 3 | 6.9 | 6 |
| 3843 | Dental equipment and supplies | 44 | 1,489 | 5.3 | 13 | -0.2 | 85 |
| 3844 | X-ray apparatus and tubes | 44 | 3,252 | 5.6 | 10 | 16.0 | 1 |
| 3845 | Electromedical equipment | 44 | 7,269 | 7.8 | 5 | 11.9 | 2 |
| 3861 | Photographic equipment and supplies | 23 | 17,000 | 1.2 | 120 | -3.7 | 141 |
| 3911 | Jewelry, precious metal | 37 | 3,900 | 4.0 | 38 | -1.2 | 112 |
| 3931 | Musical instruments | 37 | 0.736 | 2.9 | 72 | -2.5 | 133 |
| 3949 | Sporting and athletic goods, NEC | 37 | 7,014 | 4.4 | 31 | 4.7 | 16 |
| 3961 | Costume jewelry | 37 | 1,210 | 2.1 | 92 | -2.3 | 129 |

NOTE: NEC = not elsewhere classified.
* The chapter in U.S. *Industrial Outlook 1993* in which the industry is covered.
† 1987 dollars.
†† Current dollars.

SOURCE: United States Department of Commerce, International Trade Administration, U.S. *Industrial Outlook 1993*, 1993.

Employment in the United States economy is projected to increase by almost 25 million jobs between 1990 and 2005, rising from 122.6 million jobs to 147.2 million. Most of this projected growth will come in the service industries; increase in manufacturing output should be offset by greater labor productivity. In table 8 below, we provide a breakdown of the projected total employment by selected industries through the year 2005. (A table showing the growth or decline for particular occupations begins on page 27.)

## TABLE 8: EMPLOYMENT, BY INDUSTRY, 1975, 1990, AND PROJECTED TO 2005

| SIC code[1] | Industry | Employment (000) | | Projection for 2005 | | | Annual growth rate[2] | |
|---|---|---|---|---|---|---|---|---|
| | | 1975 | 1990 | Low | Moderate | High | Employment, 1990–2005 | Output, 1990–2005 [4] |
| | Nonfarm wage and salary[3] | 76,680 | 109,319 | 122,755 | 132,647 | 139,531 | 1.3 | 1.3 |
| 10–14 | Mining | 752 | 711 | 598 | 668 | 690 | -.4 | -0.1 |
| 10 | Metal mining | 94 | 59 | 57 | 64 | 68 | -.6 | .6 |
| 12 | Coal mining | 213 | 148 | 108 | 113 | 119 | -1.8 | 1.4 |
| 131,132 | Crude petroleum, natural gas, and gas liquids | 155 | 196 | 153 | 172 | 174 | .9 | -.9 |
| 138 | Oil and gas field services | 174 | 198 | 176 | 205 | 208 | .2 | .4 |
| 14 | Nonmetallic minerals, except fuels | 117 | 111 | 105 | 114 | 120 | .2 | 1.5 |
| 15,16,17 | Construction | 3,525 | 5,136 | 5,552 | 6,059 | 6,484 | 1.1 | 1.8 |
| 20–39 | Manufacturing | 18,323 | 19,111 | 16,727 | 18,514 | 19,189 | -.2 | 2.3 |
| 24,25,32–39 | Durable manufacturing | 10,662 | 11,115 | 9,467 | 10,517 | 10,915 | -.4 | 2.9 |
| 24 | Lumber and wood products | 627 | 741 | 690 | 722 | 777 | -.2 | 1.9 |
| 241 | Logging | 74 | 85 | 79 | 82 | 88 | -.3 | 1.4 |
| 242 | Sawmills and planing mills | 202 | 200 | 167 | 175 | 189 | -.9 | 1.7 |
| 2431,4,9 | Millwork and structural wood members, n.e.c. | 109 | 208 | 233 | 239 | 259 | .9 | 2.6 |
| 2435,6 | Veneer and plywood | 62 | 57 | 44 | 46 | 50 | -1.3 | 1.7 |
| 244,9 | Wood containers and miscellaneous wood products | 117 | 131 | 112 | 122 | 128 | -.5 | 2.1 |
| 2451 | Mobile homes | 44 | 42 | 35 | 35 | 39 | -1.1 | .7 |
| 2452 | Prefabricated wood buildings | 20 | 19 | 21 | 22 | 24 | .9 | 1.4 |
| 25 | Furniture and fixtures | 417 | 510 | 554 | 618 | 636 | 1.3 | 2.8 |
| 251 | Household furniture | 284 | 291 | 291 | 328 | 332 | .8 | 1.9 |
| 254 | Partitions and fixtures | 51 | 80 | 99 | 108 | 115 | 2.1 | 1.9 |
| 252,3,9 | Office and miscellaneous furniture and fixtures | 82 | 139 | 164 | 182 | 190 | 1.8 | 4.0 |
| 32 | Stone, clay, and glass products | 598 | 557 | 480 | 516 | 545 | -.5 | 1.3 |
| 321,2,3 | Glass and glass products | 180 | 160 | 119 | 128 | 132 | -1.5 | 1.1 |
| 324,327 | Cement, concrete, gypsum, and plaster products | 222 | 226 | 218 | 230 | 247 | .1 | 1.7 |
| 325,6,8,9 | Stone, clay, and miscellaneous mineral products | 196 | 172 | 142 | 158 | 166 | -.6 | .8 |
| 33 | Primary metal industries | 1,139 | 756 | 581 | 643 | 671 | -1.1 | .6 |
| 331 | Blast furnace and basic steel products | 548 | 275 | 198 | 222 | 232 | -1.4 | .2 |
| 332 | Iron and steel foundries | 230 | 132 | 109 | 120 | 125 | -.6 | .2 |
| 333 | Primary nonferrous metals | 66 | 46 | 35 | 39 | 41 | -1.0 | .1 |
| 334,9 | Miscellaneous primary and secondary metals. | 38 | 46 | 36 | 40 | 42 | -.8 | 1.6 |
| 335 | Nonferrous rolling and drawing | 181 | 172 | 129 | 141 | 148 | -1.3 | 1.0 |
| 336 | Nonferrous foundries | 76 | 84 | 73 | 81 | 84 | -.3 | 2.2 |

| Code | Industry | | | | | | | |
|---|---|---|---|---|---|---|---|---|
| 34 | Fabricated metal products | 1,453 | 1,423 | 1,138 | 1,238 | 1,298 | -.9 | 1.0 |
| 341 | Metal cans and shipping containers | 79 | 50 | 35 | 35 | 36 | -2.3 | -.6 |
| 342 | Cutlery, handtools, and hardware | 153 | 131 | 98 | 106 | 110 | -1.4 | 1.2 |
| 343 | Plumbing and nonelectrical heating equipment | 61 | 60 | 54 | 56 | 60 | -.4 | 1.2 |
| 344 | Fabricated structural metal products | 449 | 427 | 338 | 365 | 389 | -1.0 | 1.1 |
| 345 | Screw machine products, bolts, rivets, etc. | 93 | 96 | 79 | 89 | 92 | -.5 | .7 |
| 3462,3 | Forgings | 58 | 40 | 26 | 29 | 29 | -2.3 | .0 |
| 3465 | Automotive stampings | 82 | 101 | 81 | 90 | 94 | -.8 | 2.5 |
| 3466,9 | Stampings, except automotive | 106 | 84 | 54 | 59 | 61 | -2.3 | .4 |
| 347 | Metal services, n.e.c. | 84 | 121 | 129 | 143 | 148 | 1.1 | 2.6 |
| 3482,3484 | Small arms and small arms ammunition | 29 | 23 | 16 | 17 | 17 | -2.1 | 1.2 |
| 3483,3489 | Ammunition and ordnance, except small arms | 38 | 52 | 28 | 30 | 30 | -3.8 | -2.0 |
| 349 | Miscellaneous fabricated metal products | 222 | 237 | 202 | 221 | 231 | -.5 | .8 |
| 35 | Industrial machinery and equipment | 2,076 | 2,095 | 1,728 | 1,941 | 2,009 | -1.4 | 5.2 |
| 351 | Engines and turbines | 120 | 89 | 65 | 72 | 74 | .4 | .9 |
| 352 | Farm and garden machinery | 161 | 106 | 101 | 113 | 118 | -1.5 | 1.0 |
| 3531 | Construction machinery | 162 | 86 | 61 | 69 | 72 | -.7 | 2.2 |
| 3532,3 | Mining and oil field machinery | 94 | 60 | 50 | 54 | 57 | .5 | 2.6 |
| 3534,5,6,7 | Materials handling machinery and equipment | 86 | 82 | 79 | 89 | 93 | -.3 | 2.0 |
| 354 | Metalworking machinery | 329 | 330 | 282 | 316 | 327 | -.6 | .5 |
| 355 | Special industry machinery | 173 | 159 | 128 | 145 | 149 | -1.1 | 1.7 |
| 356 | General industrial machinery | 268 | 248 | 183 | 212 | 217 | -.9 | 1.0 |
| 3571,2,5,7 | Computer equipment | (5) | 396 | 297 | 345 | 353 | -1.9 | 7.6 |
| 3578,9 | Office and accounting machines | (5) | 43 | 28 | 33 | 33 | .8 | .1 |
| 358 | Refrigeration and service industry machinery | 144 | 177 | 183 | 200 | 209 | -.5 | 1.4 |
| 359 | Industrial machinery n.e.c. | 263 | 317 | 271 | 295 | 307 | -.4 | 1.4 |
| 36 | Electronic and other electric equipment | 1,442 | 1,673 | 1,345 | 1,567 | 1,603 | -1.0 | 3.1 |
| 361 | Electric distributing equipment | 109 | 97 | 76 | 84 | 88 | -1.2 | .8 |
| 362 | Electrical industrial apparatus | 203 | 169 | 125 | 141 | 145 | -1.9 | 1.3 |
| 363 | Household appliances | 160 | 125 | 85 | 94 | 95 | .1 | 2.0 |
| 364 | Electric lighting and wiring equipment | 182 | 189 | 174 | 191 | 199 | -.8 | 1.8 |
| 365 | Household audio and video equipment | 112 | 83 | 39 | 74 | 75 | -1.0 | 2.9 |
| 3661 | Telephone and telegraph apparatus | (5) | 128 | 96 | 110 | 114 | -1.1 | 2.5 |
| 3663,9 | Broadcasting and communications equipment | (5) | 135 | 101 | 115 | 117 | -.1 | 2.6 |
| 3674 | Semiconductors and related devices | 122 | 238 | 201 | 235 | 236 | .4 | 5.6 |
| 3671,2,5-9 | Miscellaneous electronic components | (5) | 343 | 302 | 363 | 366 | -.1 | 3.7 |
| 3691,4 | Storage batteries and engine electrical parts | 87 | 100 | 89 | 98 | 102 | -.5 | 2.8 |
| 3692,5,9 | Electrical equipment and supplies, n.e.c. | (5) | 67 | 56 | 62 | 65 | -.3 | 3.7 |
| 37 | Transportation equipment | 1,700 | 1,980 | 1,719 | 1,889 | 1,950 | -.6 | 1.8 |
| 371 | Motor vehicles and equipment | 792 | 809 | 668 | 744 | 771 | -1.0 | 2.5 |
| 3711 | Motor vehicles and car bodies | 375 | 328 | 220 | 246 | 258 | -1.1 | 2.7 |
| 3714 | Motor vehicle parts and accessories | 353 | 397 | 359 | 400 | 409 | -.1 | 2.0 |
| 3713,5,6 | Truck and bus bodies, trailers, and motor homes | 65 | 84 | 89 | 98 | 105 | 1.0 | 3.4 |
| 3721 | Aircraft | 293 | 377 | 331 | 360 | 373 | -.3 | .4 |
| 3724,3764 | Aircraft and missile engines | 134 | 180 | 171 | 190 | 193 | .4 | 1.4 |
| 3728,3769 | Aircraft and missile parts and equipment, n.e.c. | 90 | 202 | 212 | 230 | 238 | .9 | 1.2 |
| 3761 | Guided missiles and space vehicles | 79 | 134 | 91 | 98 | 100 | -2.0 | -.4 |
| 3731 | Ship building and repairing | 154 | 129 | 98 | 104 | 106 | -1.4 | -1.7 |

**TABLE 8** continued

| SIC code [1] | Industry | Employment (000) | | | | | Annual growth rate [2] | |
| --- | --- | --- | --- | --- | --- | --- | --- | --- |
| | | 1975 | 1990 | Projection for 2005 | | | Employment, 1990–2005 | Output, 1990–2005 |
| | | | | Low | Moderate | High | | |
| 3732 | Boat building and repairing | 40 | 58 | 70 | 76 | 80 | 1.8 | 2.5 |
| 374 | Railroad equipment | 57 | 33 | 31 | 34 | 35 | .1 | .3 |
| 375,9 | Miscellaneous transportation equipment | 65 | 58 | 47 | 52 | 55 | -.7 | 1.7 |
| 38 | Instruments and related products | 804 | 1,004 | 923 | 1,018 | 1,054 | .1 | 3.1 |
| 381 | Search and navigation equipment | (5) | 284 | 268 | 295 | 303 | .3 | 3.6 |
| 382,387 | Measuring and controlling devices, watches | (5) | 334 | 240 | 271 | 279 | -1.4 | 1.8 |
| 385 | Ophthalmic goods | 36 | 42 | 38 | 45 | 46 | .5 | 3.7 |
| 3841–3 | Medical instruments and supplies | 109 | 206 | 264 | 282 | 296 | 2.1 | 4.6 |
| 3844–5 | X-ray and other electromedical apparatus | (5) | 39 | 44 | 49 | 51 | 1.6 | 4.0 |
| 386 | Photographic equipment and supplies | 121 | 100 | 69 | 76 | 79 | -1.8 | 2.3 |
| 39 | Miscellaneous manufacturing industries | 407 | 377 | 312 | 364 | 372 | -.2 | 1.1 |
| 391 | Jewelry, silverware, and plated wire | 52 | 53 | 35 | 50 | 51 | -.3 | .8 |
| 394 | Toys and sporting goods | 116 | 104 | 76 | 94 | 95 | -.7 | 1.1 |
| 393,5,6,9 | Manufactured products, n.e.c. | 239 | 220 | 201 | 221 | 226 | .0 | 1.1 |
| 20–23,26–31 | Nondurable manufacturing | 7,661 | 7,995 | 7,260 | 7,998 | 8,274 | .0 | 1.6 |
| 20 | Food and kindred products | 1,658 | 1,668 | 1,515 | 1,560 | 1,598 | -.4 | 1.2 |
| 201 | Meat products | 336 | 426 | 430 | 443 | 454 | .3 | .9 |
| 202 | Dairy products | 194 | 155 | 120 | 123 | 126 | -1.5 | 1.0 |
| 203 | Preserved fruits and vegetables | 232 | 247 | 243 | 250 | 255 | .1 | 2.2 |
| 204,7 | Grain mill products, fats and oils | 179 | 158 | 125 | 130 | 135 | -1.3 | 1.4 |
| 205 | Bakery products | 236 | 212 | 176 | 180 | 184 | -1.1 | .3 |
| 206 | Sugar and confectionery products | 110 | 101 | 98 | 100 | 103 | -.1 | .2 |
| 2082,3,4,5 | Alcoholic beverages | 87 | 65 | 51 | 52 | 53 | -1.4 | 1.0 |
| 2086,7 | Soft drinks and flavorings | 135 | 121 | 89 | 92 | 94 | -1.8 | 1.3 |
| 209 | Miscellaneous foods and kindred products | 146 | 183 | 184 | 190 | 195 | .3 | 1.7 |
| 21 | Tobacco manufactures | 76 | 49 | 32 | 34 | 35 | -2.5 | -.2 |
| 22 | Textile mill products | 868 | 691 | 499 | 596 | 613 | -1.0 | 1.9 |
| 221,2,3,4,6,8 | Weaving, finishing, yarn, and thread mills | 521 | 372 | 239 | 286 | 293 | -1.7 | 1.7 |
| 225 | Knitting mills | 228 | 206 | 156 | 195 | 198 | -.4 | 1.6 |
| 227 | Carpets and rugs | 55 | 62 | 67 | 75 | 80 | 1.3 | 2.6 |
| 229 | Miscellaneous textile goods | 64 | 51 | 36 | 40 | 42 | -1.6 | 2.5 |
| 23 | Apparel and other textile products | 1,243 | 1,043 | 667 | 848 | 863 | -1.4 | 2.1 |
| 231–8 | Apparel | 1,087 | 839 | 479 | 638 | 649 | -1.8 | 1.8 |
| 239 | Miscellaneous fabricated textile products | 157 | 205 | 188 | 210 | 214 | .2 | 3.1 |
| 26 | Paper and allied products | 633 | 699 | 674 | 727 | 757 | .3 | 2.1 |
| 261,2,3 | Pulp, paper, and paperboard mills | 249 | 245 | 213 | 229 | 242 | -.4 | 2.3 |
| 265 | Paperboard containers and boxes | 194 | 210 | 199 | 216 | 223 | .2 | 1.2 |

| Code | Industry | | | | | | | |
|---|---|---:|---:|---:|---:|---:|---:|---:|
| 267 | Converted paper products except containers | 191 | 244 | 262 | 282 | 292 | 1.0 | 2.4 |
| 27 | Printing and publishing | 1,083 | 1,574 | 1,767 | 1,900 | 1,976 | 1.3 | 2.4 |
| 271 | Newspapers | 377 | 476 | 488 | 519 | 538 | .6 | 1.2 |
| 272 | Periodicals | 68 | 129 | 169 | 180 | 187 | 2.2 | 2.1 |
| 273 | Books | 98 | 122 | 130 | 143 | 149 | 1.1 | 2.0 |
| 274 | Miscellaneous publishing | 39 | 82 | 114 | 123 | 128 | 2.7 | 4.3 |
| 275,6 | Commercial printing and business forms | 384 | 603 | 679 | 733 | 764 | 1.3 | 2.9 |
| 277 | Greeting card publishing | 22 | 25 | 29 | 30 | 30 | 1.1 | 1.7 |
| 278 | Blankbooks and bookbinding | 55 | 72 | 81 | 89 | 92 | 1.4 | 1.8 |
| 279 | Printing trade services | 41 | 64 | 78 | 84 | 87 | 1.8 | 1.8 |
| 28 | Chemicals and allied products | 1,015 | 1,093 | 1,022 | 1,098 | 1,146 | .0 | 2.0 |
| 281,6 | Industrial chemicals | 298 | 297 | 229 | 246 | 261 | -1.2 | 1.1 |
| 282 | Plastics materials and synthetics | 218 | 181 | 159 | 175 | 185 | -.2 | 2.7 |
| 283 | Drugs | 167 | 238 | 275 | 293 | 301 | 1.4 | 3.2 |
| 284 | Soap, cleaners, and toilet goods | 122 | 160 | 172 | 179 | 184 | .8 | 1.5 |
| 285 | Paints and allied products | 62 | 62 | 52 | 56 | 59 | -.6 | 2.2 |
| 287 | Agricultural chemicals | 65 | 56 | 37 | 38 | 41 | -2.5 | 1.6 |
| 289 | Miscellaneous chemical products | 82 | 100 | 100 | 109 | 115 | .6 | 2.6 |
| 29 | Petroleum and coal products | 194 | 158 | 114 | 122 | 126 | -1.7 | .3 |
| 291 | Petroleum refining | 153 | 118 | 79 | 85 | 86 | -2.2 | .2 |
| 295,9 | Miscellaneous petroleum and coal products | 42 | 40 | 35 | 37 | 39 | -.4 | 1.9 |
| 30 | Rubber and miscellaneous plastics products | 643 | 889 | 933 | 1,043 | 1,085 | 1.1 | 3.4 |
| 301 | Tires and inner tubes | 124 | 86 | 57 | 65 | 68 | -1.8 | 1.0 |
| 302,5,6 | Rubber products, plastic hose and footwear | 185 | 176 | 138 | 158 | 164 | -.7 | 1.2 |
| 308 | Miscellaneous plastics products, n.e.c. | 334 | 627 | 738 | 820 | 852 | 1.8 | 4.3 |
| 31 | Leather and leather products | 248 | 132 | 36 | 72 | 75 | -4.0 | -1.4 |
| 313,4 | Footwear except rubber and plastic | 167 | 80 | 18 | 41 | 44 | -4.3 | -2.5 |
| 311,5,6,7,9 | Luggage, handbags, and leather products, n.e.c. | 81 | 52 | 18 | 31 | 31 | -3.5 | -.6 |
| 40-42,44-49 | Transportation, communications, utilities | 4,542 | 5,826 | 6,203 | 6,689 | 7,019 | .9 | 2.2 |
| 40-42,44-47 | Transportation | 2,634 | 3,554 | 4,092 | 4,427 | 4,651 | 1.5 | 2.3 |
| 40 | Railroad transportation | 548 | 280 | 212 | 227 | 240 | -1.4 | .7 |
| 41 | Local and interurban passenger transit | 270 | 343 | 392 | 424 | 446 | 1.4 | .5 |
| 42 | Trucking and warehousing | 1,108 | 1,638 | 1,895 | 2,048 | 2,144 | 1.5 | 3.0 |
| 44 | Water transportation | 194 | 174 | 144 | 153 | 166 | -.9 | .8 |
| 45 | Air transportation | 363 | 751 | 942 | 1,027 | 1,079 | 2.1 | 2.6 |
| 46 | Pipelines, except natural gas | 18 | 19 | 18 | 19 | 19 | .1 | .3 |
| 47 | Transportation services | 134 | 350 | 277 | 530 | 557 | 2.8 | 3.8 |
| 472 | Passenger transportation arrangement | — | 192 | 277 | 299 | 315 | 3.0 | 3.5 |
| 473,4,8 | Miscellaneous transportation services | | 158 | 213 | 230 | 243 | 2.5 | 4.0 |
| 48 | Communications | 1,176 | 1,311 | 1,058 | 1,143 | 1,200 | -.9 | 2.9 |
| 481,2,9 | Communications, except broadcasting | 1,015 | 947 | 669 | 724 | 762 | -1.8 | 2.8 |
| 483,4 | Radio and television broadcasting, cable TV | 160 | 364 | 389 | 419 | 439 | .9 | 3.1 |
| 49 | Electric, gas, and sanitary services | 733 | 961 | 1,053 | 1,119 | 1,167 | 1.0 | 1.8 |
| 491,pt. 493 | Electric utilities including combined services | 434 | 571 | 571 | 604 | 629 | .4 | 2.1 |
| 492,pt. 493 | Gas utilities, including combined services | 218 | 206 | 204 | 216 | 224 | .3 | .8 |
| 494,5,6,7,pt.493 | Water and sanitation, including combined services | 81 | 184 | 278 | 299 | 314 | 3.3 | 3.5 |

**TABLE 8** continued

| SIC code [1] | Industry | Employment (000) | | | | | | Annual growth rate [2] | |
| --- | --- | --- | --- | --- | --- | --- | --- | --- | --- |
| | | 1975 | 1990 | Projection for 2005 | | | | Employment, 1990–2005 | Output, 1990–2005 |
| | | | | Low | Moderate | High | | | |
| 50,51 | Wholesale trade | 4,430 | 6,205 | 6,669 | 7,210 | 7,585 | | 1.0 | 2.2 |
| 52–59 | Retail trade | 12,630 | 19,683 | 23,306 | 24,804 | 25,856 | | 1.6 | 2.5 |
| 52–57,59 | Retail trade, except eating and drinking places | 9,251 | 13,118 | 14,888 | 16,092 | 16,903 | | 1.4 | 2.8 |
| 58 | Eating and drinking places | 3,380 | 6,565 | 8,418 | 8,712 | 8,953 | | 1.9 | 1.8 |
| 60–67 | Finance, insurance, and real estate | 4,165 | 6,739 | 7,599 | 8,129 | 8,525 | | 1.3 | 2.1 |
| 60 | Depository institutions | (5) | 2,278 | 2,339 | 2,510 | 2,642 | | .6 | 1.7 |
| 61,7 | Nondepository; holding and investment offices | (5) | 596 | 819 | 871 | 911 | | 2.6 | 2.7 |
| 62 | Security and commodity brokers | 170 | 427 | 502 | 541 | 568 | | 1.6 | 3.7 |
| 63 | Insurance carriers | 1,085 | 1,453 | 1,574 | 1,693 | 1,791 | | 1.0 | 1.4 |
| 64 | Insurance agents, brokers, and service | 357 | 665 | 824 | 886 | 937 | | 1.9 | 2.1 |
| 65 | Real estate | 760 | 1,319 | 1,542 | 1,626 | 1,676 | | 1.4 | 2.9 |
| 70–87,89 | Services [3] | 13,627 | 27,588 | 36,223 | 39,058 | 41,109 | | 2.3 | |
| 70 | Hotels and other lodging places | 898 | 1,649 | 2,062 | 2,174 | 2,232 | | 1.9 | 1.8 |
| 72 | Personal services | 782 | 1,113 | 1,244 | 1,338 | 1,416 | | 1.2 | 2.0 |
| 721,5 | Laundry, cleaning, and shoe repair | (5) | 440 | 464 | 499 | 526 | | .8 | .5 |
| 722,9 | Personal services, n.e.c. | (5) | 199 | 256 | 275 | 292 | | 2.2 | 3.6 |
| 723,4 | Beauty and barber shops | 292 | 391 | 434 | 468 | 496 | | 1.2 | 1.8 |
| 726 | Funeral services and crematories | 70 | 83 | 90 | 97 | 102 | | 1.0 | .7 |
| 73 | Business services | 1,697 | 5,241 | 7,029 | 7,623 | 7,964 | | 2.5 | 3.5 |
| 731 | Advertising | 122 | 238 | 320 | 345 | 359 | | 2.5 | 2.2 |
| 734 | Services to buildings | 391 | 809 | 930 | 995 | 1,035 | | 1.4 | 2.5 |
| 735 | Miscellaneous equipment rental and leasing | — | 211 | 298 | 324 | 339 | | 2.9 | 1.2 |
| 736 | Personnel supply services | 242 | 1,559 | 1,901 | 2,068 | 2,165 | | 1.9 | 3.2 |
| 737 | Computer and data processing services | 143 | 784 | 1,368 | 1,494 | 1,556 | | 4.4 | 4.5 |
| 7381,2 | Detective, guard, and security services | — | 503 | 648 | 706 | 739 | | 2.3 | 3.4 |
| 7334,5,6; 7384 732; 7331, 8; 7383,9 | Photocopying, commercial art, photofinishing | — | 200 | 270 | 293 | 308 | | 2.6 | 3.1 |
| | Business services, n.e.c. | — | 937 | 1,295 | 1,397 | 1,463 | | 2.7 | 4.4 |
| 75 | Auto repair, services, and garages | 439 | 928 | 1,152 | 1,245 | 1,315 | | 2.0 | 2.0 |
| 751 | Automotive rentals, without drivers | 81 | 180 | 249 | 271 | 284 | | 2.8 | 2.5 |
| 752,3,4 | Automotive parking, repair, and services | 358 | 748 | 903 | 975 | 1,031 | | 1.8 | 1.8 |
| 76 | Miscellaneous repair shops | 218 | 390 | 441 | 480 | 504 | | 1.4 | 1.2 |
| 762 | Electrical repair shops | 66 | 116 | 141 | 153 | 161 | | 1.8 | 1.2 |
| 763,4 | Watch, clock, jewelry, and furniture repair | 26 | 31 | 26 | 28 | 29 | | -.7 | 1.2 |
| 769 | Miscellaneous repair shops and related services | 125 | 243 | 275 | 300 | 314 | | 1.4 | 1.1 |
| 78 | Motion pictures | (5) | 408 | 444 | 476 | 497 | | 1.0 | 3.2 |

| Code | Industry | | | | | | | |
|---|---|---|---|---|---|---|---|---|
| 784 | Video tape rental | — | 132 | 139 | 150 | 157 | .8 | 1.7 |
| 79 | Amusement and recreation services | (5) | 1,089 | 1,331 | 1,428 | 1,511 | 1.8 | 3.2 |
| 792 | Producers, orchestras, and entertainers | 58 | 146 | 188 | 201 | 211 | 2.1 | 3.3 |
| 793 | Bowling centers | 67 | 93 | 79 | 85 | 90 | -.6 | .4 |
| 794 | Commercial sports | (5) | 99 | 111 | 119 | 126 | 1.2 | 1.3 |
| 791,9 | Amusement and recreation services, n.e.c. | | 751 | 953 | 1,024 | 1,084 | 2.1 | 3.6 |
| 80 | Health services | 4,134 | 7,844 | 10,727 | 11,519 | 12,212 | 2.6 | 3.3 |
| 801,2,3,4 | Offices of health practitioners | (5) | 2,180 | 3,231 | 3,470 | 3,688 | 3.1 | 3.2 |
| 805 | Nursing and personal care facilities | 759 | 1,420 | 2,031 | 2,182 | 2,311 | 2.9 | 3.5 |
| 806 | Hospitals, private | 2,274 | 3,547 | 4,289 | 4,605 | 4,871 | 1.8 | 3.0 |
| 807,8,9 | Health services, n.e.c. | (5) | 697 | 1,177 | 1,262 | 1,342 | 4.0 | 4.8 |
| 81 | Legal services | 341 | 919 | 1,327 | 1,427 | 1,500 | 3.0 | 2.7 |
| 82 | Educational services | 1,001 | 1,652 | 2,151 | 2,326 | 2,458 | 2.3 | 2.1 |
| 821 | Elementary and secondary schools | 233 | 457 | 641 | 689 | 735 | 2.8 | 1.8 |
| 822 | Colleges and universities | 673 | 988 | 1,200 | 1,302 | 1,368 | 1.9 | 1.9 |
| 823–9 | Libraries, vocational and other schools | (5) | 207 | 311 | 335 | 355 | 3.3 | 2.8 |
| 83 | Social services | 690 | 1,811 | 2,673 | 2,874 | 3,031 | 3.1 | 3.7 |
| 832,9 | Individual and miscellaneous social services | (5) | 638 | 923 | 991 | 1,046 | 3.0 | 3.4 |
| 833 | Job training and related services | 94 | 247 | 295 | 320 | 335 | 1.7 | 3.3 |
| 835 | Child day care services | 199 | 457 | 607 | 652 | 689 | 2.4 | 3.3 |
| 836 | Residential care | 146 | 469 | 848 | 911 | 961 | 4.5 | 5.0 |
| 84,86,8733 | Museums, zoos, and membership organizations | (5) | 2,149 | 2,315 | 2,488 | 2,628 | 1.0 | 1.9 |
| 84; 865,9; 8733 | Museums and noncommercial organizations, n.e.c. | (5) | 314 | 391 | 421 | 445 | 2.0 | 2.5 |
| 861,2 | Business and professional associations | 103 | 158 | 178 | 192 | 202 | 1.3 | 2.1 |
| 863,4 | Labor, civic, and social organizations | 435 | 559 | 581 | 624 | 662 | .7 | .7 |
| 866 | Religious organizations [6] | 856 | 1,117 | 1,165 | 1,250 | 1,319 | .8 | 2.0 |
| 87 (less 8733), 89 | Engineering, management, and services, n.e.c. | | 2,396 | 3,326 | 3,660 | 3,843 | 2.9 | 2.6 |
| 871 | Engineering and architectural services | 382 | 793 | 964 | 1,083 | 1,163 | 2.1 | 2.1 |
| 8731,2,4 | Research and testing services | — | 407 | 551 | 609 | 625 | 2.7 | 2.5 |
| 874 | Management and public relations | — | 622 | 1,006 | 1,097 | 1,146 | 3.9 | 4.1 |
| 872,89 | Accounting, auditing, and services, n.e.c. | (5) | 575 | 805 | 871 | 910 | 2.8 | .9 |
| | Government | 14,686 | 18,322 | 19,899 | 21,515 | 23,074 | 1.1 | 1.4 |
| | Federal government | 2,748 | 3,085 | 3,089 | 3,184 | 3,266 | .2 | .6 |
| | Federal enterprises | 882 | 1,040 | 1,089 | 1,174 | 1,236 | .8 | 2.4 |
| | U.S. Postal Service | 697 | 819 | 874 | 948 | 1,001 | 1.0 | 3.1 |
| | Federal electric utilities | 32 | 39 | 31 | 33 | 34 | -1.2 | -1.0 |
| | Federal government enterprises, n.e.c. | 153 | 182 | 184 | 193 | 201 | .4 | .4 |
| | Federal general government | 1,866 | 2,045 | 2,000 | 2,010 | 2,030 | -.1 | .0 |
| | State and local government | 11,937 | 15,237 | 16,810 | 18,331 | 19,808 | 1.2 | 1.8 |
| | State and local enterprises | 674 | 928 | 1,104 | 1,185 | 1,244 | 1.6 | 2.2 |
| | Local government passenger transit | 112 | 205 | 254 | 275 | 289 | 2.0 | .7 |
| | State and local electric utilities | 60 | 83 | 93 | 98 | 102 | 1.1 | -.6 |
| | State and local government enterprises, n.e.c. | 502 | 640 | 757 | 812 | 853 | 1.6 | 3.0 |

**TABLE 8 continued**

| SIC code [1] | Industry | Employment (000) | | Projection for 2005 | | | Annual growth rate [2] | |
|---|---|---|---|---|---|---|---|---|
| | | 1975 | 1990 | Low | Moderate | High | Employment, 1990-2005 | Output, 1990-2005 |
| | State and local general government | 11,263 | 14,309 | 15,706 | 17,146 | 18,563 | 1.2 | 1.8 |
| | State and local government hospitals | 992 | 1,084 | 1,188 | 1,298 | 1,405 | 1.2 | .9 |
| | State government education | 1,323 | 1,724 | 1,875 | 2,047 | 2,216 | 1.1 | 1.6 |
| | Local government education | 4,834 | 6,064 | 6,761 | 7,383 | 7,991 | 1.3 | 1.9 |
| | State and local general government, n.e.c. | 4,115 | 5,438 | 5,882 | 6,419 | 6,952 | 1.1 | 1.9 |
| 01,02,07,08,09 | Agriculture [7] | 3,459 | 3,276 | 2,969 | 3,080 | 3,181 | -.4 | 1.8 |
| pt.01,pt.02 | Livestock and livestock products | 1,410 | 1,096 | 843 | 864 | 885 | -1.6 | .8 |
| pt.01,pt.02 | Other agricultural products | 1,552 | 1,097 | 757 | 781 | 807 | -2.2 | 2.7 |
| 07 | Agricultural services | 428 | 975 | 1,245 | 1,304 | 1,353 | 2.0 | 2.2 |
| 08 | Forestry | 15 | 35 | 41 | 42 | 45 | 1.2 | 1.6 |
| 09 | Fishing, hunting, and trapping | 35 | 73 | 83 | 89 | 91 | 1.3 | 2.8 |
| 88 | Private households | 1,362 | 1,014 | 648 | 700 | 736 | -2.4 | .1 |
| | Nonagricultural self-employed and unpaid family [8] | 6,165 | 8,961 | 10,415 | 10,763 | 11,095 | 1.2 | (4) |
| | Total [9] | 87,666 | 122,570 | 136,807 | 147,190 | 154,543 | 1.2 | 2.2 |

Notes: Dash = data not available.   pt. = part.   n.e.c. = not elsewhere classified.

[1] SIC codes are explained on page 91.
[2] Rates based on moderate case scenario.
[3] Excludes SIC 074,5,8 (agricultural services) and 99 (nonclassifiable establishments). The data therefore are not exactly comparable with data published in *Employment and Earnings.*
[4] Comparable estimate of output growth not available.
[5] Current employment statistics figures not available. Estimates were produced by the Bureau's Office of Employment Projections for these projections.
[6] Does not meet usual publication criteria of SIC Current Employment Statistics program.
[7] Excludes government wage and salary workers, and includes private SIC 08,09 (forestry and fisheries).
[8] Excludes SIC 08,09 (forestry and fisheries).
[9] Wage and salary data are from the Current Employment Statistics (payroll) survey, which counts jobs, whereas self-employed, unpaid family worker, agricultural, and private household data are from Current Population Survey (household survey), which counts workers.

SOURCE: U.S. Department of Labor, *Outlook: 1990–2005,* Historical output data are from the U.S. Department of Commerce, Bureau of Economic Analysis.

# CHAPTER 6

# EVALUATING
# AN INDUSTRY

It is easy to learn about the history and the outlook of any industry. If you find the answers to most of the questions outlined below, you will find out whether an industry offers a promising work environment. All the information sources you need are described in the following chapters.

**How large is the industry?**
Bigger industries generally mean more jobs.

**How fast has the industry grown?**
Look at the percentage increase in growth over the past five years. Compare this figure with the same measure for the top-ten growth industries listed on page 25. Is the growth rate going up or down? Steady or increasing growth rates are good news for the job hunter. Industries do experience slower growth rates as they mature. If an industry has been around for many years and appears to be solid and profitable, you should not be discouraged by low growth rates.

Get estimates for sales in both dollars and units sold. This will help you understand the nature of the growth. For example, if units decline while dollars rise, the growth in dollars may be due to inflation.

**What is the industry's potential for growth? What are the one-year and five-year sales forecasts for the industry?**
Historical trends in an industry are important, but, as a job hunter in the field, you are even more interested in what the future holds. Watch the newspapers

for news about industries. Also look for news about matters that are likely to affect industries. For example, a big increase or decrease in the federal defense budget will cause waves throughout the defense industry.

**What are the products or services of the industry?**
Most industries can be divided into smaller industry or market segments. You may need to study some of the segments to target the best career opportunities for yourself. For example, the emerging private-sector space industry includes not only machinery to be hurled into space, but also satellite communications, space insurance, materials research and processing in space, and space-based industrial facilities. From the job hunter's perspective these market segments have different qualities and outlooks. The demand for satellite services is increasing rapidly, but the space insurance industry was unprepared for the unprecedented number of launch failures in the mid-1980s, when claims jumped to $400 million. According to the U.S. Department of Commerce, these losses resulted in an insurance crisis with a worldwide reduction in availability and sharply higher premiums.

**Is the industry based on a particular product technology that may soon be obsolete? If so, is the industry responding with new technologies?**
If twenty years ago, you had researched the keypunch equipment industry, you might have been favorably impressed with job opportunities. Within a few years, punched cards were, however, replaced by other methods of data entry. It is likely that many young people today are unaware that keypunch technology ever existed.

**What changes in production technology are expected to occur in the industry?**
The importance of technological overhaul depends on your particular job. For example, in an industry that is being automated, marketing managers may feel little effect, whereas plant managers may be replaced by others who have experience in plant process conversion; personnel directors may not risk losing their jobs but may face the unhappy prospect of laying off substantial numbers of manufacturing workers.

**Is the industry's product or service an important part of domestic or industrial life? Will its usefulness continue?**
All things considered, the job hunter is likely to feel more secure in an industry made up of established products rather than of fads.

### Is the industry fiercely competitive?

Companies that are barely surviving tough competition do not usually make good employers. Highly competitive industries are not necessarily undesirable, but make sure to identify, and eliminate from your list of prospective employers the companies that are most likely to suffer from the competitive battle.

### Are supplies needed by the industry available in sufficient quantity at reasonably consistent prices?

If supplies, such as raw materials and labor, are scarce or their prices volatile, the industry's performance may be erratic.

### Is the customer base for the industry growing or shrinking?

Industries are dependent upon their customers, so it is important to know the trends in the market. For example, industries supported by the middle-aged and elderly, such as leisure activities and supported-living communities, will have a growing customer base as the postwar baby boomers grow older. The young adult market is shrinking, casting a pall over industries such as construction of so-called starter homes.

### What are the prospects for the industry in your target region?

If you are already committed to a particular region of the country, find out how your target industry is faring in that area.

### What are the prospects for your profession or field of interest within the industry?

If you already know the type of job you want to have, find out the prospects for that job within the industry.

These are the most important questions to ask about the industry you are targeting for your job hunt. As you learn more about the industry, you may discover other areas about which you need information. Whatever information you are seeking, you will want to employ an efficient research strategy. For best results, use a combination of telephone and library research techniques. For example, you might want to begin your research in the library, reading about the industry, in preparation for making calls to industry experts. Also, use the library to help you find industry experts to interview.

In 1988, Sarah, a recent materials engineering graduate, had limited time to do employment research. She wanted to work in plastics but was not sure which industries offered the best opportunities. Her career counselor and faculty advisor suggested the container industry or the aerospace industry. Sarah decided to do a few hours of research on each.

First, she visited a U.S. government depository library near her home and consulted the *Monthly Catalog of U.S. Government Publications.* She found citations to several publications and studies published by the U.S. Department of Commerce relating to her areas of interest (*U.S. Industrial Outlook, Statistics for Industry Groups and Industries, Plastic Bottles, New Complete Aircraft and Aircraft Engines,* and *Backlog of Orders for Aerospace Companies*), and was able to read them in the library. From these studies, she learned that the immediate future of the plastics container industry looked most promising—current-year shipments were expected to increase by about 7.6 percent over the previous year, while orders for the aerospace industry were expected to increase by only 1.2 percent.

Although this was encouraging, she wanted to learn if there were more current information available. The *Encyclopedia of Associations,* also in the federal depository library, led her to four organizations: Aerospace Industries Association, General Aviation Manufacturers Association, The Society of the Plastics Industry, and Can Manufacturers Institute. The industry experts at these organizations talked with her about the industries, discussing both the past and the future. From the association executives, Sarah learned that the U.S. Congress and some state legislatures were considering bans on certain types of plastic containers because of waste disposal problems. These experts felt "uncertain" about the long-term prospects of the plastic container industry. Steadily increasing backlogs of orders in the aerospace industry, and the increasing average age of the world jet-transport fleet suggested that the aerospace industry would have a healthy future replacing old planes. Based on what she learned from the industry experts, Sarah decided to target the aerospace industry. Had she consulted only published sources, her decision would have been quite different.

Her choice of aircraft over plastic bottles was a good one, as subsequent growth rates in the industry show. More important, Sarah had learned the value of staying in touch with people who monitor industry trends. By 1992, when growth of the aircraft industry was softening, she had already begun interviewing for positions in industries with a more optimistic future.

## CHAPTER 7

# TAPPING THE EXPERTS
# IN THE PRIVATE SECTOR

Finding experts on industries is simple. Below we have outlined several types of experts and the tools you need to find them. Each directory of experts is available in most public or academic libraries. Most of the individuals described below are accustomed to being contacted by the public for information, so do not be reluctant to call them.

Before you begin your interviews, review the questions outlined on pages 77-79. Use them as a guideline. Also review the telephone research techniques described on pages 12-20. Knowing how to interview people can increase your success exponentially. Remember, for best results, do not turn those interviews into job inquiries. Save those for later interviews, when you have completed your research on industries and employers. For now, just make a note of which industry experts seem most knowledgeable and cooperative.

## ESTABLISHED INDUSTRIES

### Association Executives

Hundreds of industry associations gather and disseminate information about their industry for their members. Because of these activities, trade associations have industry experts on staff and most also publish pamphlets and books discussing the state and the future of the industry. Many of their publications are free of charge. Because associations' studies are often prepared for lobbying purposes, you can expect that they will have certain biases. For example, if an industry study is seeking tax relief or import restrictions, it may present a pessimistic picture of the industry. Keep this in mind, and look at the story the numbers tell rather than simply relying on the association's interpretations. Are overall sales decreasing or increasing? What about profits? Are there more or fewer firms in the industry than there were several years ago? Compare the industry to the high-performance industries discussed on pages 61-63.

When you call the association, ask to speak with the executive director. The director normally has the broadest view of the industry. He or she may refer you to someone who has specialized expertise. Alternative sources are the association's research director or librarian. Both will know about all the studies conducted or sponsored by the association as well as other significant industry reports.

Industry experts working for trade associations can help you understand their entire industry and any of its segments, as Mark, a life-insurance salesman, discovered. Mark sold insurance to industrial clients for their employees, and thought that it might be more lucrative to sell to individuals instead. A quick call to the American Council on Life Insurance revealed that sales to individuals had actually dropped dramatically in the past five years, and that Mark was selling insurance in the fastest growing segment of the insurance industry. He decided to stay put, and set more ambitious goals for himself.

To find the trade associations that track your industry, visit your library and use either of the following association directories: *Encyclopedia of Associations* or *National Trade and Professional Associations of the United States.* They will acquaint you with thousands of associations on every imaginable industry.

## Securities Analysts

Securities analysts, the individuals who monitor the performance of particular stocks on the world's stock exchanges, are well informed about the industries they track. If there are public companies in your industry (companies whose stocks are traded on one of the stock exchanges), chances are that several stock analysts will be tracking that industry. Some are on Wall Street; others are located in large cities throughout the country and around the world.

When you contact securities analysts, remember that they, like associations, may be biased. In many cases, they will make conservative estimates about the industry, so that their clients do not rely on exaggerated information. Use their opinions in conjunction with the information you learn from other knowledgeable sources. Because securities analysts are often short on time, prepare your questions carefully and make your interviews as streamlined as possible. Use the interviewing tips outlined on pages 240-246 to help you prepare for your interviews.

To find analysts who track companies and industries in the United States and abroad, visit your library to consult *Nelson's Directory of Investment Research*. Most brokerage houses, investment banks, and other financial institutions also have information centers, the staff and resources of which can be very useful for job hunters. Give them a try.

## Trade Journalists

Most industries have journals and newsletters that are written for industry participants. The researchers, reporters, and editors of these trade publications can be excellent sources of industry information. In many cases they have very detailed, impartial data. They can also make referrals to other industry contacts. Call them directly and ask your questions about the industry you are targeting.

To learn which trade publications cover your target industry, contact the industry trade association librarian or check one of the following periodicals directories:

Gale's *Directory of Publications and Broadcast Media* (Gale Research)

*Standard Periodical Directory* (Oxbridge Communications)

*Ulrich's International Periodicals Directory* (Reed Reference)

Reporters from business magazines or newspapers, such as *Business Week* and *The Wall Street Journal,* can also be helpful. As you find good articles about the industries that interest you, call the reporters who are cited in bylines. Many will talk to you if you are willing to wait until they have a little spare time between deadlines.

## EXPERTS IN INDUSTRY

It is always worthwhile to get a firsthand overview from companies in the industry. This step becomes almost mandatory when you are interested in a new, obscure, or changing industry, because few people outside the industry are well informed.

Because he devoted a few hours to interviewing people in the industry, Joe made a terrific long-term career decision. Many years ago, he knew he wanted to get into banking and favored the savings and loan institutions (S&Ls). Because he also had some interest in commercial banking, he decided to research both industries. His literature revealed a few failed S&Ls, but it was his interviews with people in both industries that convinced Joe that commercial banking would have a more promising future. Through the years, he has watched the decline of the S&L industry, and congratulates himself for doing a little homework to put his career on the right track.

Industry participants have a vantage point and can give you first-hand insights into their industry. Finding names of companies in the industry is simple. Once you know the SIC code for the industry (refer to page 91), check *Ward's Business Directory of U.S. Private and Public Companies,* which is in most larger libraries. It lists thousands of companies, arranged by SIC code. An alternative source is *Dun's Business Rankings,* which may be available in your library.

Once you are ready to contact a company, who do you talk to? The company president will normally have the best overview of the industry. You may want to start with his or her office. If the president is too busy to talk with you (to be expected in a large company), his or her assistant or secretary will likely find someone who can. The marketing department is also an excellent source of industry information, because it is marketing's job to know—and project—the market for the industry's products or services.

Of course, it is useful to talk with people who do the kind of work you hope to do. There are several ways to contact them. You might ask the president's office to refer you to your professional counterparts in the company. Also, most professional associations have a membership directory. Get the directory for your profession and scan it for members who are in your target industries. If the association will not send you a directory, or wants to charge you for it, ask the staff for the names of just a few members in industries that interest you. Keep in mind that although professionals may not have the most informed or objective view of an industry, they can certainly give you a real-world view of how industry trends are affecting their own jobs—information that is important to you.

## Regional Industry Experts

Sometimes an industry is very successful in one part of the country and sagging in others. For example, construction can be very healthy in Atlanta and Orlando while it withers in New Orleans and Flint, Michigan. If you are committed to a particular state or region, you will want to focus on the regional health of industries. The following offices gather information on local or regional industries.

*State and county economic development offices.* As the name implies, these offices are responsible for monitoring the area's economy, including the future of local industries. Often they have published reports on the area's star industries or industries that are being given special business incentives to locate in the area.

*Chambers of commerce.* State and local chambers of commerce promote area business, and will certainly be conversant in industry trends and events.

*State-level industry regulators.* States regulate a variety of industries, collecting and compiling industry statistics. The industries regulated vary from state to state, but often include insurance, banking, food and drugs, health care, and public utilities. Check your governor's office or state public-relations office to learn which industries are regulated and how to contact the offices you need. Begin with directory assistance in your state capital.

*State libraries.* Call the state library to ask about industry reports and studies published by the state. You can also ask the librarian which state agencies are most appropriate for your research.

There are three directories that list the economic development offices, libraries, and other state and local agencies. You are likely to find at least one of them in your local library.

*Federal Executive Directory* and *State Executive Directory* (Carroll Publishing)—Covers thirty-five thousand federal government and thirty-seven thousand state government officials.

*How to Find Information about Companies, Part I* (Washington Researchers Publishing)—Covers twenty key offices in all fifty states, including complete contact information.

*Municipal Yearbook* (International City and County Management Association)—Provides contact information on county executives and municipal employees in hundreds of localities throughout the United States.

## EMERGING INDUSTRIES

The future of emerging industries may be less secure than that for established ones, but getting in on the ground floor can be both exciting and profitable for the adventurous job hunter. Usually statistics and information are easy to find for established industries. Emerging industries may be a different story. Some industries are so new that they have merited little attention from the press and fostered no industry association.

One extremely new business is that of cattle cloning. Although the business-related aspects of biotechnology are gaining recognition, some specific applications are in their infancy. Cattle cloning is designed to provide optimal quality and weight of beef. It produces cattle with identical genetic materials and nearly carbon-copy carcasses with the same weight and fat content. According to experts, this process could revolutionize the meat-packing industry, allowing for increased standardization of packing plants. As yet, only a few companies are studying the process. Consequently, little has been reported by the government or the general press on the business.

To learn about the prospects of new industries you will have to tap different kinds of sources from those you might use for more established industries. Here are some key sources that you should try.

## University Researchers

Very often university-affiliated research laboratories are on the cutting edge of new technology and industries. Professors are usually willing to discuss the future of the industry spawned by the technology they are studying. They may also provide insights about various industries that will be affected, perhaps even revolutionized, by the technology. For example, robotics experts know not only about the robotics industry, but also about industries that are using robotics in the manufacturing process.

Ask the relevant trade association or the Office of Technology Assessment (see page 98) for the names of those universities at which the technologies that interest you are being studied and for the names and locations of the people involved in research. Call the universities directly. Because the professors working intimately with new technologies may have an overly optimistic view of their impact and growth, you will want to balance your research by talking with other sources such as those mentioned below.

## Future-Oriented Publications

Publications such as *Omni,* published monthly by Omni Publications International, and *The Futurist,* published bimonthly by the World Future Society, specialize in forecasting life in the twenty-first century. At times, they profile emerging technologies that may change the nature of our society. If you are interested in working in an emerging industry, use these publications to get ideas. If you are interested in a specific emerging industry that these publications have not profiled, ask the editors for suggestions of sources and leads for information.

### Future-Oriented Organizations

Several organizations in the public and private sectors specialize in peering into the future. The following groups are worth a phone call if you are interested in learning more about emerging industries:

◇ *World Future Society*—A non-profit organization, can be reached at 7910 Woodmont Avenue, Suite 450, Bethesda, MD 20814, 301-656-8274.

◇ *Office of Technology Assessment*—See page 98 for a description and contact information for this government organization.

◇ *Congressional Clearinghouse on the Future*—This organization, supported by the U.S. Congress, can be reached at 555 House Office Building, Annex 2, Washington, DC 20515, 202-226-3434.

Trade-association gatherings and records of proceedings often focus on new technologies or processes. Ask relevant trade associations for information about their past and future conferences and publications. The business press, which includes *The Wall Street Journal, Business Week,* and *Forbes,* regularly report on emerging technologies and the industries they are spawning.

## SPECIALIZED INFORMATION

If you have not managed to find experts on your target industry from the sources describe above, use the following directories to find leads to specialized organizations and agencies that may have the information.

◇ *Directory of Special Libraries and Information Centers* (Gale Research)— Contains descriptions and contact information for research libraries, information centers, archives, and data centers maintained by government agencies, business, industries, newspapers, and other organizations. Look for those libraries that specialize, or have a particular interest, in your target industry.

*Directories in Print* (Gale Research)—Lists approximately fourteen thousand business and industrial directories of all kinds, professional and scientific rosters, and other lists and guides. These can help you locate directories that highlight companies in a particular industry.

*Business Organizations, Agencies, and Publications Directory* (Gale Research)—Includes references to government agencies, commodity and stock exchanges, unions, chambers of commerce, publishers, databases, and business libraries and information centers. Here you will need to use your imagination to identify sources that would know about your target industry.

# CHAPTER 8

# TAPPING THE EXPERTS
# IN GOVERNMENT

Analysts within the federal government are excellent sources of industry information. Some are accustomed to providing data to the public, but few are called on by job hunters who wish to size up an industry. Keep this in mind as you contact the experts described below. Although they will be eager to assist you, and delighted that you have an interest in the industry they study, their focus is on the government's need for the data, rather than on the particular interests that you may have. Never mind—they have great data that you can use to your advantage in selecting industries for employment. Just be prepared to help the analysts focus on your particular interests.

There are two great advantages to using government analysts for industry insights. First, they are very willing to help you find the information you need. Second, in many cases they are the most knowledgeable and impartial sources of information that you will find. Federal agencies that have considerable industry expertise are listed on pages 93-100. Good information may lurk elsewhere in unexpected places within the government bureaucracy. Be sure to ask for referrals to other agencies and private-sector organizations that are likely to have information about your target industries.

If the agency provides a personnel directory to the public, we have identified it for you and given you ordering information. Because such lists are designed for in-house use, they are not always easy to interpret. For a user-friendly directory of industry experts in the federal government, visit your library and use *Who Knows: A Guide to Washington Experts.* It lists the experts by industry of expertise and is quick and easy to use.

In using government experts and their reports, it is helpful to understand how the government defines industries. Although most industry reports are easy to understand, sometimes you will run across information that is organized by code number and requires decoding. In order to classify thousands of industries, the federal government created Standard Industrial Classification (SIC) Codes. General industry groupings are categorized by the first two digits of the code. For example, the SIC codes for products and services in the category chemicals and allied products all begin with a 28. Products under this category are designated by the 28 as a base number and additional numbers are supplied for further classification: alkalies and chlorine are all SIC number 2812; industrial gases are SIC number 2813. Most government reports use SIC codes to group statistics and text within standardized areas, and many private-sector reports adopt the government system. If you find reports that use SIC codes with more than four digits, recognize that each digit to the right simply gives further definition to the industry. For example, no matter how many digits are tacked on after the 2813 code, the products are still in the industrial gases industry group.

Finding the classification number of your industry or market segment is easy. Most of the federal agencies mentioned below are willing to tell you which SIC codes apply to the industries you are interested in. Most libraries carry the Department of Commerce's *Standard Industrial Classification Manual,* which defines all the SIC codes. A word of warning: Do not limit yourself to SIC codes. If you ask for information strictly by SIC code, you may miss many good insights into your target industry. The SIC system is far from perfect, and it is especially weak in emerging industries. Describe your interests to the experts but talk in terms of SIC codes only when you are required to do so.

# LIBRARY RESEARCH

The directories listed below give you additional contact information for the agencies we have listed above, as well as other agencies and committees that are

useful to job hunters doing industry research. The first two books are free or inexpensive. The rest are expensive; you will want to review them in the library.

◇ *United States Government Manual* (GPO)—Provides descriptions and
contact information for the legislative, judicial, and executive branches,
as well as information on quasi-official agencies and selected international organizations.

◇ *Federal Information Centers* (Federal Information Center)—A free
directory of federally funded information centers in more than seventy
metropolitan areas nationwide. These centers assist the public in
securing specific answers to questions involving federal government
offices and services. These centers do not have expertise in industry
information, but may be able to put you in touch with someone who
can help you.

◇ *Encyclopedia of Governmental Advisory Organizations* (Gale Research)—
A reference guide to interagency committees, government-related
boards, panels, task forces, commissions, conferences, and other bodies.

◇ *Federal Executive Directory* and *State Executive Directory* (Carroll
Publishing)—Contact information for thirty-five thousand federal and
thirty-seven thousand state government officials.

◇ *Federal Yellow Book* (Washington Monitor)—Covers the White House,
Executive Office of the President, and departments and agencies of the
executive branch.

◇ *How to Find Business Intelligence in Washington* (Washington
Researchers)—Identifies sources of business information, including
key experts, throughout the federal government.

◇ *Washington Information Directory* (Congressional Quarterly Books)—
An excellent all-around directory providing names and descriptions of
governmental, quasi-governmental, and private groups focusing on
particular subjects and industries.

◇ *Who Knows: A Guide to Washington Experts* (Washington Researchers)—
This book gives the names and direct telephone numbers of eleven

thousand industry, country, and data experts in the government. It is organized in alphabetical order by subject/topic area, so you can quickly find experts for the industries that interest you.

# TELEPHONE RESEARCH

The ranks of the government's bureaucracy are filled with experts of all stripes. Being public servants, they are quite prepared, as part of their job, to provide information. The sources we list below will help you find them.

## Departments and Agencies

The executive department and regulatory agencies are good places to start looking for industry experts. You will likely have the most success with the following:

*International Trade Administration (ITA) Industry Analysts.* ITA is the single best source for industry information. Industry analysts within ITA track both domestic and foreign industries and markets. These analysts have enormous amounts of data. There are three ways to reach them: call ITA at 202-482-3808 and ask for the name and telephone number for the analyst for your industry; get the names, along with industry reports, from *U.S. Industrial Outlook* or purchase the *U.S. Department of Commerce Telephone Directory* (U.S. Government Printing Office), which lists key industry analysts with the Department of Commerce. To obtain a copy of the directory, write or call the Superintendent of Documents, U.S. Government Printing Office, Washington, DC 20402, 202-512-2051.

*Bureau of the Census Industry Specialists.* Industry experts at the Bureau of the Census have raw data that you can use in your comparisons between industries. (To discuss what the data mean, it is better to talk to ITA analysts.) To find the expert for your industry, order the following directory, *Telephone Contacts for Data Users.* It covers key personnel in the Bureau of the Census. To order, call 301-763-4100.

*International Trade Commission (ITC).* You will probably find at least one analyst at ITC who knows about the industries you are investigating.

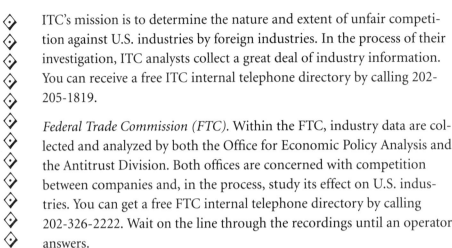

ITC's mission is to determine the nature and extent of unfair competition against U.S. industries by foreign industries. In the process of their investigation, ITC analysts collect a great deal of industry information. You can receive a free ITC internal telephone directory by calling 202-205-1819.

*Federal Trade Commission (FTC).* Within the FTC, industry data are collected and analyzed by both the Office for Economic Policy Analysis and the Antitrust Division. Both offices are concerned with competition between companies and, in the process, study its effect on U.S. industries. You can get a free FTC internal telephone directory by calling 202-326-2222. Wait on the line through the recordings until an operator answers.

## Congressional Staff and Research Organizations

The U.S. Congress and its various ancillary services study hundreds of industries. The studies, which may relate to import restrictions, taxation, safety, and many other issues, often contain excellent information about industry structure, operations, and trends. The following offices have the best information about industries.

### Caucuses

Congress has special interest groups, some of which study or support industries. Below are the caucuses you will find useful in industry research. In most cases the caucus telephone number is the main number for the congressional representative. You may have to persist in order to reach someone knowledgeable about the activities of the caucus.

| Senate | House |
|---|---|
| Beef Caucus: 202-224-6441 | Arts Caucus: 202-226-2456 |
| Coal Caucus: 202-224-4343 | Automotive Caucus: 202-225-3611 |
| Copper Caucus: 202-224-6621 | Environmental Study: 202-226-3300 |
| Rail Caucus: 202-224-3244 | Export Task Force: 202-226-3480 |
| Rural Health Caucus: 202-224-2551 | Space Caucus: 202-225-2631 |
| Steel Caucus: 202-224-6472 | Textile Caucus: 202-225-5501 |
| Tourism Caucus: 202-224-2644 | Travel and Tourism Caucus: 202-225-3935 |
| Wine Caucus: 202-224-3841 | |

## The Congressional Budget Office

The Congressional Budget Office (CBO) studies the way in which industries affect the national economy. Consequently, the reports often contain good information about industry growth and profits—information important to job hunters. CBO also conducts special industry studies from time to time. CBO industry experts are listed below.

| Industry | Specialist | Telephone (202) |
|---|---|---|
| Aerospace | David Moore | 226-2940 |
| Agriculture | Roger Hitchner | 226-2940 |
| Automotive | Elliot Schwartz | 226-2940 |
| Aviation | Mitchell Rosenfeld | 226-2860 |
| Banking | Elliot Schwartz | 226-2940 |
| Computers | Philip Webre | 226-2940 |
| Education | Jay Noell | 226-2672 |
| | Constance Rhind | 226-2672 |
| Electronics | Philip Webre | 226-2940 |

| | | |
|---|---|---|
| Energy | Richard Farmer | 226-2951 |
| Housing | Carla Pedone | 226-2665 |
| Materials | Elliot Schwartz | 226-2940 |
| Medicaid | Linda Bilheimer | 226-2673 |
| Medicare | Sandra Christensen | 226-2665 |
| | Harriet Komisar | 226-2655 |
| Municipal finance | vacant | |
| Petroleum | Richard Farmer | 226-2951 |
| Recreation | Deborah Reis | 226-2860 |
| Semiconductors | Philip Webre | 226-2940 |
| Service industries | Elliot Schwartz | 226-2940 |
| Space technology | Mark Grabowicz | 226-2860 |
| Steel | Elliot Schwartz | 226-2940 |
| Technology | Mark Grabowicz | 226-2860 |
| Transportation | Marjorie Miller | 226-2860 |
| Weapons systems | R. William Thomas | 226-2909 |

## Congressional Research Service

The Congressional Research Service (CRS) issues a variety of reports on industries and markets. Because CRS exists primarily to conduct research for Congress, you will have to get a list of the reports and order those you want from the office of your senator or representative.

Several years ago, Jerry wanted to learn more about the airline industry, but he did not want to spend time doing a lot of research. He had contacted CRS before when he was writing a term paper and knew they did research on a variety of topics. He decided to call CRS to determine if the staff there had already done the research for him. The CRS staff cited a new research report and gave him the report identification numbers. With the report number in hand, he then called his senator to get a copy of the report. Less than three weeks later, he had a free, comprehensive study entitled "Airlines Under Deregulation at Mid-Decade: Trends and Policy Implications." The report contained estimates of industry growth and a discussion of various market segments. Jerry learned that airline profits had been slight or negative in three of the past five years. Based on this information, Jerry decided to target more stable and profitable industries. History has proven his decision to be a good one.

CRS industry areas are listed below. If the experts in these offices are reluctant to spend time with you, place your request for assistance through your members of Congress.

| Industry | Telephone (202) | Industry | Telephone (202) |
|---|---|---|---|
| Apparel | 707-7577 | Defense | 707-5064 |
| | | | 707-7800 |
| Automotive industry | 707-7577 | | |
| | 707-7800 | Electronics, consumer | 707-7067 |
| Aviation | 707-7033 | Vocational education, | |
| | | science, and | |
| Banking | 707-7800 | mathematics | 707-7055 |
| | 707-6006 | | 707-6228 |
| Cable television | 707-7800 | | |
| | 707-6006 | Energy | 707-7039 |
| | | | 707-7040 |
| Chemical industries | 707-7577 | safety | 707-7012 |
| Computer industries | 707-7577 | Fruit and vegetable | |
| | | industries | 707-7232 |
| Computer software | 707-6006 | Geosciences | 707-7078 |
| Construction | 707-7800 | High-tech industries | 707-7577 |

| | | | | |
|---|---|---|---|---|
| Highways, mass transportation | 707-7581 | Services | 707-7800 | |
| Insurance | 707-7800 | Software | 707-6006 | |
| | 707-6228 | Space programs | 707-7040 | |
| | 707-7577 | Steel | 707-7577 | |
| Mining industries | 707-7577 | Strategic Defense Initiative | 707-1432 | |
| Nuclear weapons | 707-5064 | Technology | 707-7040 | |
| Oil industries | 707-7040 | Telecommunications | 707-5804 | |
| | 707-7232 | | 707-7800 | |
| | 707-7800 | Textiles | 707-7577 | |
| Railways | 707-7800 | Timber | 707-7232 | |
| Science | 707-7040 | | 707-6006 | |
| Securities regulations | 707-6006 | Transportation | 707-7581 | |
| Semiconductor industry | 707-7073 | Uranium enrichment | 707-7076 | |

## Office of Technology Assessment

The Office of Technology Assessment (OTA) provides extensive analyses of emerging industries that are based on new technologies. It also reports on changes in established industries occasioned by the introduction of new processing technology. Call for a list of current studies or talk with those experts who conduct the studies.

| Industry | Specialist | Telephone (202) |
|---|---|---|
| Agribusiness | Patricia Durana | 228-6516 |
| Agricultural technology | Mike Phillips | 228-6521 |
| AIDS research | Maria Hewitt | 228-6590 |
| Arms control | Thomas Karas | 228-6430 |
| Aviation research | Kevin Dopart | 228-6937 |

| | | |
|---|---|---|
| Biotechnology | Kevin O'Connor | 228-6692 |
| Competitiveness | Wendell Fletcher | 228-6352 |
| Computer software | Joan Winston | 228-6760 |
| Defense industries | Jack Nunn | 228-6446 |
| Energy | Sam Baldwin | 228-6274 |
| | Peter Blair | 228-6260 |
| | Joy Dunkerley | 228-6267 |
| | Steven Plotkin | 228-6275 |
| Health care | Denise Dougherty | 228-6590 |
| | Elaine Power | 228-6590 |
| Information technology | James Curlin | 228-6787 |
| Insurance | Denise Dougherty | 228-6590 |
| Magnetically levitated vehicles | Kevin Dopart | 228-6937 |
| Mass transit | vacant | |
| Materials, advanced | Gregory Eyring | 228-6270 |
| Medical waste | Rosina Bierbaum | 228-6845 |
| Medicare | Elaine Power | 228-6590 |
| Miniaturization | Sunil Paul | 228-6790 |
| Neuroscience | Laura Lee Hall | 228-6696 |
| Nuclear waste | Peter Johnson | 228-6862 |
| Osteoporosis research | Katie Maslow | 228-6590 |
| Pharmaceutical labeling | Bob McDonough | 228-6590 |
| Pharmaceutical research | Judith Wagner | 228-6590 |
| Terrorism | Anthony Fainberg | 228-6429 |

### Congressional Committees

Many congressional committees conduct hearings on matters relating to U.S. industries. Executives of key companies in the industries as well as other industry experts testify or submit information for the committees' consideration. The information and insights provided to these committees can be very useful to job hunters. To learn which committees have studied your target industry, consult the *CIS/Index,* available in most libraries. It describes information contained in congressional hearings, reports, executive documents, and special publications.

### Your Congressional Representative and Senators

You are likely to find that all the offices mentioned above are cooperative. If they are not, enlist the help of the staff of your senators or member in the House of Representatives. You can start with the member's staff in either the state office, or in Washington. The Washington staff is usually more savvy about the kind of research that is done by the offices described above. Reach these staffers through the Capital Hill switchboard, 202-224-3121, or use one of the following directories. They will be in your library, or you can order them, for a fee, from the publishers:

*Congressional Directory* (GPO)—The official guide to the Congress and the departments of the government, including congressional committees and contact information.

*Congressional Staff Directory* (Staff Directories)—Easier to use and more comprehensive than the *Congressional Directory,* this publication lists representatives, staffs of members of Congress, committees, subcommittees, and independent agencies. Because it is expensive, you will want to use it in your local library.

*Almanac of the Unelected* (Almanac of the Unelected)—This book provides profiles of key congressional staffers and committee workers—the unelected officials, as distinguished from the elected ones. These people know how and where to find information on Capitol Hill.

# CHAPTER 9

# READING UP
# ON INDUSTRIES

If you are willing to do some reading, you can get a good start on industry research through published articles and reports. We have described the best of these below. Some of these reports can be found in large public or university libraries.

## GOVERNMENT REPORTS

The government devotes substantial resources to studying industries, both domestic and foreign. The resulting reports and studies can be excellent resources for the job hunter, and most are available to you. If the documents you want are not in your library, you can buy them or consult them in a U.S. government depository library. In some cases, the documents are inexpensive, costing only a few dollars each. In other cases they are more costly. Usually, they are well worth the price, given the wealth of information you will obtain. Most can be purchased from the Superintendent of Documents. The U.S. government depository libraries, numbering about fourteen hundred and located throughout the United States, house all the documents listed below. You can get a free list of these libraries by contacting the Superintendent of Documents. Your public library or university library may be a repository for government documents or will be able to refer you to the closest library that is.

## The Best and Quickest Industry Overview

◇ *U.S. Industrial Outlook* (U.S. Department of Commerce)—Written by industry analysts, the *U.S. Industrial Outlook* is an inexpensive way to get an overview of more than 350 U.S. industries. It includes a three- to four-page description of the industry as a whole, its major players, and its long-term prospects.

◇ *Career Guide to Industries*—A companion to the *Occupation Outlook Handbook,* this publication provides career information from an industry perspective, and supplies up-to-date information on forty industries. GPO S/N 029-001-03127-1. Bulletin 2403.

## Industry Statistics

◇ *Survey of Current Business* (Bureau of Economic Analysis)—A monthly journal that contains analyses of U.S. economic activity, including earnings by industry and region.

◇ *Business Statistics* (Bureau of Economic Analysis, U.S. Department of Commerce)—This biennial publication provides data on business and economic conditions in the United States and includes information on construction, energy, finance, forest products, manufacturing, transportation, and wholesale and retail trade. This series is a supplement to *Survey of Current Business.*

◇ *Business Conditions Digest* (Bureau of Economic Analysis)—A monthly publication containing tables and charts for more than three hundred indicators that help evaluate economic and industry conditions.

◇ *Productivity Measures for Selected Industries* (Bureau of Labor Statistics)—Provides data on employment and productivity for 130 industries; annual.

## Individual Industries

◇ The International Trade Administration (ITA) produces dozens of publications analyzing trends and forecasts, each focusing on a particular industry. For example: "A Competitive Assessment of the U.S. Digital Central Office Switch Industry"; "A Competitive Assessment of the U.S. Ethylene Industry"; "A Competitive Assessment of the U.S. Fiber Optics Industry"; and "High Technology Industries: The Robotics Industry."

*ITA Periodic Reports* (International Trade Administration)—Periodic reports on dozens of industries, including the U.S. steel industry, auto industry, and nonrubber footwear.

*Current Industrial Reports* (Bureau of the Census)—These reports present timely data on the production, inventories, and orders of approximately five thousand products and ninety industries, including: aerospace, apparel, chemicals, food, and textile mill products.

*Industry Wage Surveys* (Bureau of Labor Statistics)—Describe salary levels with the backdrop of industry conditions for dozens of industries, banking, hospitals, millwork, and meat products, for example.

## Reports on Industries by Region

*Statistical Abstract of the United States* (Bureau of the Census)—This annual publication, available in most libraries, provides data on dozens of industries, as well as regional demographics. It is also available from the Government Printing Office or most larger book stores.

*County Business Patterns* (Bureau of the Census)—Provides data on employment, unemployment and personal income by industry/sector and state; fifty-three volumes.

*Annual Survey of Manufactures* (Bureau of the Census)—Reports on 452 manufacturing industries in every state. Includes the number of establishments, employment, payrolls, hours worked, value added by manufacturing, quantity and value of products shipped and materials consumed, and capital expenditures. The Bureau also publishes detailed surveys for the construction, mineral, retail trade, service, transportation and wholesale trade industries.

### Other Government Reports

◇ *Monthly Catalog of U.S. Government Publications* (Superintendent of
◇ Documents)—Lists many U.S. government publications, including ones
◇ that focus on industries. The monthly catalog is very large, so review it
◇ at a large public or university library or one of the government deposi-
◇ tory libraries.

## INDUSTRY SURVEYS

Another good source of industry information are various reputable industry surveys that are regularly updated and can be found in most large public or university
libraries. These surveys are useful for quick, basic research into industries and as a
starting point for more ambitious investigations.

They were of critical importance to Ted, who lost his job as comptroller in a textile
company as the result of a corporate takeover and needed to find a job fast. He
soon had job offers from three companies: an electronics firm, a beverage company, and a multi-industry conglomerate. He made a quick trip to the library and
read about each company's industries in *Value Line Investment Survey*. The beverage industry got the highest marks for growth, so he decided to cast his lot with
that company. Although it is a good idea to do additional research, sometimes you
have to make quick decisions.

◇ *Moody's Industry Review* (Moody's Investors Service)—This publication,
◇ available in many libraries, gives useful lists of leading companies in 139
◇ industries ranked according to twelve financial categories such as
◇ revenue, net income, and price-earnings ratio.

◇ *Predicasts Basebook* (Predicasts)—A comprehensive loose-leaf
◇ publication of industry statistics, including production, consumption,
◇ exports/imports, wholesale price, plant and equipment expenditures,
◇ and wage rates; arranged by SIC code.

- *Predicasts Forecasts* (Predicasts)—This publication gives short- and long-range forecast statistics for individual industries and products, arranged by SIC code; annual with quarterly updates.

- *Standard & Poor's Industry Surveys* (Standard & Poor's)—This source provides basic data on thirty-three industries, with financial comparisons of the leading companies in each industry. For each industry there is an annual analysis and triennial updates; available in many libraries.

- *Value Line Investment Survey* (Value Line)—Reports on ninety-five industries; available in many libraries.

- *Wall Street Transcript* (Wall Street Transcript)—This weekly publication contains security analysts' discussions on industries as well as financial and investment news about many companies.

## BUSINESS PERIODICALS

Business magazines and large newspapers profile a wide variety of industries and report on industry trends and news. Some devote entire editions to a single industry; others have special editions in which industries are compared and contrasted. Some feature industries in considerable detail. The most important business publications for your industry research are likely to be:

| Magazines | Newspapers |
|---|---|
| *Barron's* | *New York Times* |
| *Business Week* | *Wall Street Journal* |
| *Dun's Business Month* | *Financial Times* |
| *Forbes* | Newspapers in regions |
| *Fortune* | where the industry |
| *Industry Week* | is prominent |
| *Institutional Investor* | |

Among these, be sure to look for special editions devoted to surveys of industry. *Forbes* magazine (Forbes) has an "Annual Report on American Industry" in which the profitability and growth are tabulated for public companies in thirty-one industries, and industry averages computed. This is an excellent and inexpensive way to get an overview of dozens of industries. The magazine is available in many libraries.

Similarly *Business Week* magazine (McGraw Hill) annually publishes "Industry Outlook," which is an overview of about twenty-five industries that is considered by experts to be an excellent source of information. This magazine, too, is available in many libraries.

## Indexes

The most efficient way to find the publications that deal with your target industry is to consult the numerous indexes to periodicals. You are likely to find one or more indexes that we have listed available in your library. If you do not, ask which of the business periodicals mentioned above are available. Then scan the table of contents of each issue for the past year or two. This is a hit-or-miss way to find information on a particular industry that you have targeted, but it is a good way to discover up-and-coming industries and to identify industries that are in trouble.

Many other business magazines have special issues—such as lists of top companies, industry retrospectives and forecasts, or buyers' guides that list and describe industry suppliers—that can be very useful to job hunters. To learn about such special issues, use one of the following indexes. These indexes are old, but the special issues they identify continue to be produced, most on an annual basis.

◇ *Guide to Special Issues and Indexes of Periodicals* (Special Libraries
◇ Association)
◇
◇ *Special Issues Index: Specialized Contents of Business, Industrial, and*
◇ *Consumer Journals* (Greenwood Press)
◇
◇ *Guide to Industry Special Issues* (Harper & Row)—Although this is no
◇ longer in print, a copy may still be available in your library.

Other indexes may guide you to articles about your target industries that have been published in newspapers or magazines.

◇ *Business Periodicals Index* (H. W. Wilson)—This index is excellent for
◇ locating articles on companies, products, and business topics that have
◇ appeared in the 345 most influential business journals; available in most
◇ libraries.

*Predicasts F&S Index United States* (Predicasts)—This is a continually updated index of articles about U.S. companies and industries that appear in more than 750 financial publications, business-oriented newspapers, trade magazines, and special reports.

*Public Affairs Information Service Bulletin* (Public Affairs Information Service)—An index to selected private industry and government publications, covering the subject areas of economic and social conditions, public administration, and international relations; also available online on DIALOG.

*New York Times Index* (New York Times)—An index of articles that have been published in the *New York Times*. This is an extensive index: the *Times* has published articles on almost any industry that you can imagine; available in most libraries.

*Wall Street Journal Index* (Dow Jones)—*The Wall Street Journal* is full of feature articles and news about companies, products, and industries. It has its own index, published monthly, with annual accumulations; available in most libraries and online on Dow Jones News/Retrieval and NEXIS.

Your library may have some of these indexes on a computer database as well as in print. Most libraries charge for searching their on-line databases, so be sure to ask what the fee will be before you request a search. There also may be indexes created for regional or local publications at the library. Some larger public and university libraries also have National Newspapers Indexes on CD-ROM for free public searching. In addition, there are hundreds of on-line databases that focus on particular industries. Ask the librarian which databases may be appropriate to your needs.

## INDUSTRY REPORTS

Several commercial organizations study industries in depth and provide detailed reports. The reports have big price tags but you may be able to look at them, or their highlights, free of charge. To identify the reports that interest you, ask the librarian at the industry's trade association for recommendations or use *FINDEX* (see below) in your library. Once you have identified the report title, ask your library if it has a copy or can obtain one through interlibrary loan. You can also contact the author who may be willing to discuss the report's highlights or send you a free summary.

◈ *FINDEX: The Worldwide Directory of Market Research Reports, Studies,*
◈ *and Surveys* (National Standards Association)—Provides abstracts and
◈ price information for about twelve thousand industry and market
◈ research studies, reports, and surveys on marketing plans and strategies;
◈ also available online on DIALOG.

# DIRECTORIES

Many other publications provide excellent data on industries. Check these directories to pinpoint the publications relevant to your target industry:

◈ *Business Rankings Annual* (Gale Research)—Index to many published
◈ lists and rankings of companies and business-related organizations
◈ appearing in directories and business journals. This is also an excellent
◈ source for finding major competitors in particular industries; available
◈ in most libraries.

◈ *Encyclopedia of Business Information Services* (Gale Research)—This is
◈ an excellent survey of information sources for individual industries;
◈ available in most libraries.

◈ *Business Information Sources* (University of California Press)—This
◈ is a basic bibliography that describes all sorts of business information
◈ sources including those for domestic statistics and economic trends;
◈ two chapters, Industry Statistics and Basic U.S. Statistical Sources, are
◈ important compilations of industry information sources; available in
◈ most libraries.

◈ *Directories in Print* (Gale Research)—Lists approximately fourteen thou-
◈ sand business and industrial directories of all kinds, professional and
◈ scientific rosters, and other lists and guides; use for identifying directo-
◈ ries dealing with a target industry; available in most libraries.

*Statistical Reference Index* (Congressional Information Service)—
 An extensive guide to private statistical sources.

 *Statistics Sources* (Gale Research)—Provides general sources of statistics
on industries.

# PART IV

# COMPANIES AND EMPLOYERS

)•(( )•(( )•(( )•(( )•((

Financially successful organizations, in general, make the best employers. Consequently, financial performance should be a major criterion in your selection of an employer. Once you identify a prospective employer, immediately learn all you can about its current and historical sales and profits.

An employer's fortunes can change dramatically in a year or two, so you need to examine its performance trends. For example, if a company has a great year, preceded by five disastrous ones, you should proceed cautiously, examining the reasons for the sudden success, before signing on with the company. Likewise, when a giant such as IBM, after showing years of handsome growth and profits, lays off thousands of employees, you should be sensitive not only to their impressive record, but also the winds of change.

Depending upon the ownership and structure of your prospective employer, you may easily find detailed, exhaustive financial data, or you may have to piece together fragments of information to assemble a financial picture. There are, for our purposes, five types of employers you may want to research, the first four being for-profit.

*Public Companies.* Companies that sell their stock to the public provide detailed financial statements and narratives about financial performances to stockholders and anyone else who requests the information.

*Private companies.* Companies that do not sell their stock to the public usually release no comprehensive financial statements, unless they are in a regulated industry.

*Divisions or subsidiaries of companies.* Financial information about businesses that are owned by parent companies is usually buried within the parents' financial statements.

*Foreign companies.* Companies that have their headquarters outside the United States provide varying amounts of financial information, depending on the requirements of their countries of domicile and their activities in the United States.

*Not-for profit organizations.* If the organization is located in the United States, its tax returns, with full financial reporting, are released to any citizen through the regional Internal Revenue office. A Freedom of Information Act (FOIA) letter may be required. (The Freedom of Information Act allows individuals to gain access to certain types of information contained in the files of the federal government. To obtain such information, you must make your request, in writing and citing the act. In most cases you should try other methods, such as calling or writing, before sending a Freedom of Information Act letter. The government's response to FOIA requests is seldom speedy.)

# CHAPTER 10

# SHORTCUTS TO
# SUCCESSFUL COMPANIES

)•( )•( )•(

All the leads in this book notwithstanding, there are some people who are in a rush, who are too impatient or simply cannot allocate the time to follow them exhaustively. This chapter points you directly to a handful of companies that have been identified as outstanding by some notable experts. The criterion is financial prosperity. Although not every financially successful company is a first-rate employer, there is evidence that successful companies, as a rule, provide the best opportunities for employees. Companies offering the highest salaries, greatest promotion opportunities, the best work environments, and the best benefit packages are usually among the most prosperous. For example, the companies listed in the respected book *The 100 Best Companies to Work for in America* outperformed most industry norms for the past decade. Some were more than twice as profitable as the average company in their industry and, as a group, their mean stock price grew at nearly three times the rate of the Standard and Poor's 500. Because the fortunes of companies can change, it is smart to do even a little research on the company you plan to work for, including those in the lists that follow.

# THE MOST PROFITABLE COMPANIES

We have compiled our own list of overall winners, which is a composite of the companies consistently placed in the top ten in the lists, compiled by *Forbes, Fortune,* and *Business Week* magazines, of the most profitable U. S. companies. You can write or call their corporate headquarters for employment information.

Amoco Corporation
200 E. Randolph Drive
Chicago, IL 60601
312-856-6111

AT&T
538 Madison Avenue
New York, NY 10022
212-754-0020

Chevron Corporation
225 Bush Street
San Francisco, CA 94104
415-894-7770

E. I. du Pont de Nemours & Co.
1007 Market Street
Wilmington, DE 19898
302-774-1000

Exxon Corporation
225 E. John W. Carpenter Freeway
Irving, TX 75062
214-444-1000

General Electric Company
3135 Easton Turnpike
Fairfield, CT 06431
203-373-2211

IBM (International Business Machines
   Corporation)
Old Orchard Road
Armonk, NY 10504
914-765-1900

Merck & Company, Inc.
P.O. Box 2000
Rahway, NJ 07065
201-594-4000

Mobil Corporation
3225 Gallows Road
Fairfax, VA 22037
703-846-3000

Philip Morris Companies, Inc.
120 Park Avenue
New York, NY 10017
212-880-5000

## Industry Rankings

To identify leading employers in any industry, you can use library sources or interview industry experts.

Ask the periodicals librarian for the annual listings of top companies that are prepared by major business magazines. The following publications rank companies, within industry groups, by several factors, including sales, profits and assets.

*Forbes* magazine, 500 Annual Directory—Published each May, this directory provides lists of the top 500 U.S. companies ranked by sales, assets, market value, jobs and productivity, and profits. The lists are also ranked by industry.

*Forbes* magazine, Annual Report on American Industry—Published each January, this is a report in which the profitability and growth for public companies in thirty-one industries are compared and industry averages computed.

*Fortune* magazine, The Fortune 500—Published annually in April, this special issue lists the largest industrial corporations in the United States. The companies are ranked by sales (not by profitability) and are ranked within industries. The issue, as well as the other *Fortune* issues, has excellent articles profiling individual companies and industry segments.

*Business Week* magazine Top 1000—Not to be outdone, *Business Week* publishes a ranked list of one thousand companies, based on market value. The lists are also arranged by industry, with a brief financial profile of each.

Other publications available in your library can give you additional information.

*Business Ranking's Annual* (Gale Research)—Index to many published lists and rankings of companies and business-related organizations appearing in directories and business journals. This is an excellent source for ascertaining the major competitors in particular industries.

*Dun's Business Rankings* (Dun & Bradstreet Information Services)—This directory ranks over twenty-five thousand U.S. companies according to sales and number of employees. Four rankings are given: by state, by 151 industrial categories, derived from SIC code classifications (See page 91 for an explanation), by size of public businesses, and by size of private businesses. Data for each company usually include the address, telephone number, sales (in dollars and by rank), total employees (by number and rank), employees at entry location, the primary SIC number assigned to the company, and stock ticker symbol. In the front of the directory you will find an index of all the businesses listed.

*Moody's Industry Review* (Moody's Investors Service)—This service gives useful ranked lists of leading companies in 139 industries according to twelve financial categories such as revenue, net income, and price-earning ratios.

*Ward's Business Directory of U.S. Private and Public Companies* (Gale Research)—This is the most comprehensive source for ranked lists, by sales size, of the largest U.S. corporations, arranged by twenty-one manufacturing and thirty-seven nonmanufacturing SIC categories.

If you prefer getting your information by telephone, call some of the industry experts described below. It is a good idea to check several sources and compare your findings.

### Trade Associations

Trade association executives, research managers, and librarians can direct you to the leading companies in the industry. Although they may not provide detailed financial information, they will usually provide names of top-ranked companies and tell you which companies have moved up, and down, in the rankings during the past few years. The *Encyclopedia of Associations* can help you find the appropriate association.

At the very least, associations can refer you to other sources that can help you, as Hal discovered. Hal wanted to work in a reputable organization that develops housing for the elderly, but he didn't know where to begin looking. The National

Institute of Senior Housing gave him a list of the best experts in the senior housing field. These experts, whom he interviewed by telephone, gave him names of the best and most profitable companies in the field. They also told him which companies to avoid. With a narrowed list, Hal was able to focus his job search.

)⊩( )⊩(( ()⊩(( )⊩( )⊩(( )⊩( )⊩(( )⊩(( )⊩(( )⊩(( )⊩( )⊩(( )⊩( )⊩(( )⊩(( )⊩( ()⊩(( )⊩( )⊩(( )⊩( )⊩(( ()⊩(( )⊩( )⊩(( )⊩(

### Trade Press

Reporters who work for journals and newsletters specializing in an industry can tell you which companies are the leaders, and which are growing or declining. Just call the publication and ask for an editor or reporter. Use the sources outlined on pages 106-107 to find the trade publications for your target industry.

### Securities Analysts

Most securities analysts specialize in particular industries and monitor both the stock prices and general performance of companies in those industries over a long period of time. They are in a perfect position to identify companies that consistently perform well and companies on an upswing. Use *Nelson's Directory of Investment Research* to locate analysts for your target industry.

## THE REGIONAL STARS

To target employers in a specific region of the country, scan listings of the top companies that are published by the major business magazines. From their addresses, you can quickly spot those that are top performers anywhere in the country.

Regional business information sources can provide more information. Responsible for promoting businesses in the state, the State Economic Development Offices can tell you about leading companies in any city or country. Find this office in any state by contacting the state government operator in the state capital. Look for a regional group, or a regional chapter of a national trade group. You can find many regional associations listed in the *Encyclopedia of Associations*. The State Economic Development Offices, described above, can also identify these trade groups. Being business-development organizations, local chambers of commerce or boards of trade are good sources of information on companies, plants, or other employers in a community. Find the number through local directory assistance.

# CHAPTER 11

# WHO'S WHO

)•(( )•(( )•((

The first step to researching a company as a prospective employer is to identify it. This sounds easy enough, but, in this merger-maniacal, global era, it may take some detective work to ferret out the real identities. The small, family-operated company you want to work for may actually be a subsidiary of a large conglomerate; the all-American company that is recruiting you may actually be owned by the Japanese, the British, or the Germans. If you do not know much about who owns whom in corporate America, you are not alone. It is usually not difficult to unravel the mysteries of business ownership, but it is very important to do so. A company's merit as an employer may be substantially increased by a healthy vibrant parent or decreased by a parent with too many unprofitable businesses in its portfolio.

)•(( )•(( )•(( )•(( )•(( )•(( )•(( )•(( )•(( )•(( )•(( )•(( )•(( )•(( )•(( )•(( )•(( )•(( )•(( )•(( )•(( )•((

Sid learned this lesson the easy way—with a little research into the corporate relationship of his prospective employer, a software company in Orange, California. He had read in the local business press that the company was thriving, so he felt optimistic about growth opportunities there. Just to be sure, Sid decided to do a bit of research into the company's ownership by calling the local business-press reporter and several employees of the company. Sid learned that the business was owned by a large conglomerate with a rocky financial history, and that corporate management systematically siphoned off the profits of its Orange, California, software business, redirecting them to other cash-hungry businesses within the corporation. As a result of his research, just a few hours on the telephone, Sid decided to target another software business. Its profits, although a bit less, were kept in the company to stimulate growth and new business.

)•(( )•(( )•(( )•(( )•(( )•(( )•(( )•(( )•(( )•(( )•(( )•(( )•(( )•(( )•(( )•(( )•(( )•(( )•(( )•(( )•((

It is important to know about a company's ownership before you begin to research it, because the type of ownership suggests your research strategy. Companies owned by public stockholders are called *public companies* and, because they look to the public for investment, are regulated by the government. Companies that sell stock in a single state (intrastate) are regulated by that state's securities office (see the list on page 130). Those that sell stock to investors in more than one state (interstate) are regulated by the U.S. Securities and Exchange Commission (SEC). These regulators can provide detailed information about the finances and management of public companies. Because information is so readily available on public companies through the securities regulators, you will see much more coverage of them in company directories, the press, and elsewhere than you will about companies that do not seek investors from the general public.

Companies that do not sell stock to the public are called *private companies* or *privately held* companies. Most small companies are privately held, but so are some corporate giants. Private companies are more difficult to research than public companies are because they do not file information with securities regulators.

If the employer you are targeting is a subsidiary, division, or plant of a public company, you will have to hunt a bit harder for information. The securities regulators are interested in the performance of the company as a whole, rather than of the components, and do not require companies to file much information about individual businesses. There are, however, many other sources of information beyond the securities regulators.

# PUBLIC OR PRIVATE?

The best way to learn whether your target employer is a public corporation or is privately owned is to call the company and ask for the public information office. This office can tell you quickly if the company is private or public and, if public, whether stock offerings are limited to the state. If the company is not forthcoming with the information, there are other sources. Your stock broker or any securities analyst can quickly identify which companies are public or private. The *Wall Street Journal*, the *New York Times, Barron's National Business*, or *Financial Weekly* carry price listings of publicly traded stocks. The *Directory of Companies Required to File Reports with the SEC* (GPO) identifies companies that sell stocks to investors in more than one state, and would be useful if you are checking on several companies. Some city newspapers list companies that sell stocks exclusively in the state.

# OWNED BY ANOTHER COMPANY?

To learn whether your target is a division or subsidiary of another company, call the employer's switchboard or public information office directly. Most will explain how they fit into their parent company's structure. Or go to the library to look at a copy of one or more of the directories listed below, each of which identifies many, but not all, divisions and subsidiaries of companies.

*America's Corporate Families: Billion Dollar Directory* (volume 1); *America's Corporate Families and International Affiliates* (volume 2) (Dun & Bradstreet Information Services)—Volume 1 lists approximately ninety-two hundred parent companies, and provides identification information on forty-five thousand divisions and subsidiaries. Volume 2 lists identification information for more than seventeen hundred U.S. parent companies and thirteen thousand Canadian and foreign sub-sidiaries. More than twenty-five hundred Canadian parent companies and their six thousand subsidiaries also are covered.

*Directory of Corporate Affiliations* (Reed Reference)—The new edition of this reference to "who owns whom" in the United States is in two sets: a two-volume edition for public companies and a one-volume edition for private companies. The directory of public companies consists of information on nearly four thousand parent companies and forty-three thousand subsidiaries, divisions, and affiliates. The directory of private companies provides information on the Forbes 400 list, the one thousand largest private companies in the world, and the top hundred companies in major urban markets.

*Directory of Corporate Affiliations/International* (Reed Reference)—A compilation of information on more than thirty-six thousand of the most influential companies in the world; addresses, telephone numbers, and information about key personnel and finances are provided.

If your library will do database searches free of charge, try:[1]

Dun's Market Identifiers (Dun & Bradstreet Information Services)—This on-line database is a directory of over two million public and private U.S. companies with ten or more employees, or companies with at least $1 million in sales. Lists addresses, products, and sales executives for each, as well as information on corporate organization and subsidiaries. (Vendor—DIALOG)

Business Information Report (Dun & Bradstreet Information Services)—Dun & Bradstreet's database of more than nine million U.S. companies, covering nearly every report and service published by the firm, including company histories, financial profiles, payment habits, performance trends, industry comparisons, credit recommendations, government activities, and corporate family trees. (Vendor—Dun's Marketing Service)

## FOREIGN-OWNED OR AMERICAN?

U.S. companies all over the country are being bought by foreign interests. The company that was as American as apple pie yesterday may be Japanese or French today. You need to know whether a potential employer is domestic or foreign in order to know how to research it effectively. To learn your target company's nationality, contact the company's switchboard and ask or go to the library and check one of two directories:

---

[1]A list of database readers appears in appendix III.

*Directory of Foreign Manufacturers in the U.S.* (Georgia State University Business Press)—Provides the names and addresses of forty-eight hundred foreign-owned U.S. companies engaged in manufacturing, mining, and petroleum.

*Principal International Businesses* (Dun & Bradstreet Information Services)—Provides identifying information on more than fifty thousand leading companies in 143 countries.

## FOR PROFIT OR NOT FOR PROFIT?

If you want to work for a private foundation, an educational institution, a charitable organization or the like, chances are it is a not-for-profit organization. This means that it has tax-exempt status and is regulated by the Internal Revenue Service. You can determine if your prospective employer is a not-for-profit organization by making a telephone call to the FOIA Reading Room, Internal Revenue Service, Department of the Treasury, 202-822-6200.

# CHAPTER 12

# FINANCIAL INFORMATION ABOUT PUBLIC COMPANIES

)•(( )•(( )•((

I f the employer you are targeting is a public company—a company that sells stock to the public—you are in luck. Public companies are easy to research because they are required to report an enormous amount of financial information to government securities regulators. Even foreign companies that sell stock in the United States are regulated by the Securities and Exchange Commission (SEC).

## INTERSTATE PUBLIC COMPANIES

Financial information about interstate public companies is especially easy to obtain. Because these companies are regulated by the SEC, they disclose detailed financial records and information on their performance to both the SEC and their shareholders. Usually they are willing to provide this same information to anyone who asks. Because information about public companies is so readily available, you will be able to find much information about them in company directories, the press, and elsewhere.

Your first step is to contact the company's public-information or stockholder-relations office. Ask for a free copy of the company's annual report for the most recent year and for previous years—five years back if they have them. Read the financial section carefully. Have sales and profits been increasing or decreasing? Do not let the facts become clouded by the optimistic predictions or by a good performance in a single area of the company.

## The Securities and Exchange Commission

For more detailed information, you can tap the employer's filings at the SEC. To obtain filings, contact the document rooms of the SEC, listed below, or Disclosure, Inc., a for-profit firm specializing in SEC documents, at 800-945-3647. Ask for a copy of the company's annual report to stockholders and a 10-K filing, for domestic companies, or a 20-F filing, for foreign companies. Also find out the costs involved for retrieval of the documents. If one of the SEC offices is close by, you may prefer to go there to review the reports, which you can do free of charge. You may even find the reports you need in a large library.

)⟩⟨( )⟩⟨( )⟩⟨( )⟩⟨( )⟩⟨( )⟩⟨( )⟩⟨( )⟩⟨( )⟩⟨( )⟩⟨( )⟩⟨( )⟩⟨( )⟩⟨( )⟩⟨( )⟩⟨( )⟩⟨( )⟩⟨( )⟩⟨( )⟩⟨(

Securities and Exchange Commission
450 5th Street NW
Washington, DC 20549
202-272-3100

### SEC Regional Offices

*Region 1* (New York, New Jersey)
7 World Trade Center, Suite 1300
New York, NY 10048
212-748-8000

*Region 2* (Connecticut, Maine,
   Massachusetts, New Hampshire,
   Rhode Island, Vermont)
73 Tremont Street, Suite 600
Boston, MA 02108
617-424-5900

*Region 3* (Alabama, Georgia, Florida,
   Louisiana [southwestern portion only],
   Mississippi, North Carolina,
   South Carolina, Tennessee,
   Virgin Islands,
   Puerto Rico)
3475 Lenox Road NE, Suite 100
Atlanta, GA 30326
404-842-7600

*Region 4* (Illinois, Indiana, Iowa, Kentucky, Michigan, Minnesota, Missouri, Ohio, Wisconsin)
Northwestern Atrium Center
500 W. Madison Street, #1400
Chicago, IL 60604
312-353-7390

*Region 5* (Arkansas, Kansas, Louisiana [except southwestern portion], Oklahoma, Texas)
801 Cherry Street, 19th Floor
Fort Worth, TX 76102
817-334-3821

*Region 6* (Colorado, Kansas, New Mexico, North Dakota, South Dakota, Utah, Wyoming)
1801 California Street, Suite 4800
Denver, CO 80202
303-391-6800

*Region 7* (Arizona, California, Hawaii, Nevada, Guam)
5670 Wilshire Boulevard, 11th Floor
Los Angeles, CA 90036
213-965-3998

*Region 8* (Alaska, Idaho, Montana, Oregon, Washington)
915 2d Avenue, Room 3040
Seattle, WA 98174
206-442-7990

*Region 9* (Delaware, District of Columbia, Maryland, Pennsylvania, Virginia, West Virginia)
601 Walnut Street, Room 1005E
Philadelphia, PA 19106
215-597-3100

*Vendor Specializing in SEC Documents*
Disclosure, Inc.
5161 River Road
Bethesda, MD 20816
800-945-3647 or 301-951-1350

## Library Sources

Most larger public libraries provide numerous reference sources, many of which analyze the health and stability of companies in addition to providing financial information.

)·(( )·(( )·(( )·(( )·(( )·(( )·(( )·(( )·(( )·(( )·(( )·(( )·(( )·(( )·(( )·(( )·(( )·(( )·(( )·((

Sandra used a publication called *Value Line Investment Survey* to learn some little-known facts about a major pharmaceutical company with an impressive financial history. She learned from the *Survey* that the company's biggest selling anti-ulcer drug would soon face a threat of increased competition when the FDA approved a new drug to compete with it. Sandra's discovery led her to contact some stock analysts to learn how the increased competition in this market would affect the company's future. She also made a note of her findings so that she could raise the question during her employment interview with the company.

Ask the business librarian at your public or university library for assistance with these sources. Remember, you only need to check one or two sources. We have listed many so you are assured of finding at least one in your library.

### *Publications and Microfiche*

Should you wish to own any of the publications, check with the publishers for price information. We would encourage you to use them in your public, university, or company library, as they are quite expensive.

*Moody's Industrial Manual* (Moody's Investors Service)—Most libraries have *Moody's Industrial Manual*, which covers industrial companies and provides detailed information on finances, capital structure, and businesses. It discusses the company's history, financial health, products, and future plans, in addition to listing subsidiaries and the officers and directors, available online on DIALOG.

Other more specialized titles from Moody's include:

*Moody's Bank and Finance Manual*

*Moody's International Manual*

*Moody's Municipal & Government Manual*

*Moody's OTC Industrial Manual*

*Moody's Public Utility Manual*

*Moody's Transportation Manual*

*Moody's OTC Unlisted Manual*

*Market Guide* (Market Service)—Similar in format to *Standard & Poor's Stock Reports*, this is a loose-leaf service containing two pages of objective research on smaller or more obscure OTC companies (those with stocks traded over the counter). It includes, for each company, short statements on business, results of operations, recent developments, officers, a balance sheet, income statements statistics, and dividends. Each company's report is revised quarterly; a selection of reports is mailed weekly.

*Standard Corporation Descriptions* (Standard & Poor's)—A financial service similar in coverage to Moody's publications, described above, except that it offers information on finance, public utilities, and transportation companies in addition to industrial companies together in one series of loose-leaf volumes. Data on each company are completely revised annually. The latest developments are reported daily in *Standard & Poor's Corporation Records*. Corporate presidents' messages to stockholders are occasionally included; also available online on DIALOG.

*Standard & Poor's Stock Reports* (Standard & Poor's)—This is a multivolume, loose-leaf service consisting of basic financial data for a large number of public companies. The two-page reports are full of useful data. Included are ten-year income, balance-sheet, and per-share data. You will also find a business summary, news of important new developments, current outlook, dividends, capitalizations, and names of officers and directors. Three separate loose-leaf services are offered for the American, New York, and over-the-counter exchanges:

*Standard ASE Stock Reports*

*Standard NYSE Stock Reports*

*Standard OTC Stock Reports*

*Value Line Investment Survey* (Value Line)—A comprehensive advisory service, Value Line continuously analyzes and reports on seventeen hundred companies in ninety-nine industries. It is arranged in three parts, with most of the data given in its thirteen sections of Ratings and Reports. These are one-page analyses of each company, arranged by industry, and full of data essential to studying the company's financial position, including eighteen-year financial statistics, five-year quarterly sales, dividends paid, financial strength, price stability, earnings predictability, safety and timeliness ratings, a brief description of the business, new developments, and outlook. Also included are stock price charts.

*Wall Street Transcript* (Wall Street Transcript)—A weekly compilation of financial and other information drawn from brokerage house reports on companies, security analysts' discussions on industries and companies, company officials' speeches to financial analysts' groups, data from annual reports, and other financial news; also available online on NEXIS.

## Databases

Your public library may have access to electronic databases that make information on public companies easily and quickly retrievable. Remember, however, that database searches usually have a fee attached, and often the fee is substantial. Ask for estimates of charges before you make a request. If you are on a tight budget, you may want to stick with the library's printed resources, which are free of charge. Better still, ask the librarian if there are CD-ROM products available. They offer the advantage of databases without the cost.

At the end of each database description you will find, in parentheses, names of the vendors that provide access to the databases. If your librarian is not familiar with a particular database, he or she may be able to help you locate another library that has access to it. In this case, the vendors names will be important. Vendors' addresses and telephone numbers are listed in appendix III.

Disclosure SEC Database (Disclosure)—Contains financial and textual information extracted from the full text of documents that public companies file with the Securities and Exchange Commission (SEC). Covers more than ten thousand companies that trade securities on the New York and American stock exchanges, the over-the-counter and NASDAQ markets. Companies profiled must have at least $5 million in assets, five hundred shareholders, and have filed a 10-K or 20-F form in the past eighteen months. Includes full text of management discussion and president's letter from the annual report to shareholders. Company records from management investment companies, mutual funds, real estate limited partnerships, and oil or gas drilling finds are not included. (Vendors—DIALOG, BRS, CompuServe)

Investest (Thomson Financial Networks)—Provides the full text of financial and market-research reports and analysis on over eight thousand domestic and foreign firms, including six thousand of the largest publicly traded U.S. and Canadian corporations, one thousand smaller, high-growth OTC companies, and two thousand publicly traded foreign firms. Includes sales and earnings forecasts, market share projections, and research and development expenditures. (Vendors—CompuServe, Data-Star, DIALOG, Dow Jones News/Retrieval, Mead Data Central, NEXIS)

Moody's Corporate News—U.S. (Moody's Investor's Service)—Includes financial information on thirteen thousand public U. S. companies. For each company, it provides information on financial statements, annual reports, earnings statements, balance sheets, bankruptcy financing, mergers and acquisitions, joint ventures, new products, new branches, stock and bond listings, and changes in ratings. Corresponds to weekly news reports of Moody's *Bank and Finance Manual, Industrial Manual, OTC Investment Manual, Public Utilities Manual,* and *Transportation Manual.* (Vendor—DIALOG)

Moody's Corporate Profiles (Moody's Investors Service)—Contains an abbreviated business description and detailed financial information on approximately five thousand public U.S. companies, including fifteen hundred of the most actively traded OTC companies. For each company, it provides interim earnings and dividends, financial record for five years, SIC codes, and a five year statistical record. (Vendor—DIALOG)

PTS Annual Reports Abstracts (Predicasts)—Contains both textual and numeric abstracts from annual reports and statements filed with the U.S. Securities and Exchange Commission by over four thousand public companies in the manufacturing and service industries. Provides three categories of records: textual, financial, and corporate establishment. It is indexed by products, services, and financial size. (Vendors—Data-Star, DIALOG)

Standard & Poor's Corporate Descriptions (Standard & Poor's)—Provides financial and complete corporate background information on approximately ninety-five hundred public U.S. corporations. Includes all income and balance-sheet figures, and stock and bond data. In conjunction with Standard & Poor's News database, corresponds to the publication *Standard & Poor's Corporation Records.* (Vendor—DIALOG)

Standard & Poor's News (Standard & Poor's)—Contains full text of financial news items covering twelve thousand public U.S. companies. Coverage includes corporate background, mergers and acquisitions, contract awards, and management changes. Corresponds to *Standard & Poor's Corporation Records.* (Vendor—DIALOG)

# INTRASTATE PUBLIC COMPANIES

Some public companies sell stocks only within a single state. They are not listed with the SEC or mentioned in the daily stock reports, and most brokers will not know about them. You are not likely to find financial information about them in directories and databases mentioned previously. To learn if your prospective employer sells securities exclusively within one state, ask the employer's public information officer or call the securities office in the state where the employer is incorporated. State securities offices regulate intrastate securities sales, and can provide a wealth of financial information about the companies that fall within their jurisdiction.

### State Securities Offices

**Alabama**
Alabama Securities Commission
770 Washington Street, Suite 570
Montgomery, AL 36130
205-242-2984

**Alaska**
Division of Banking and Securities
and Corporations
Department of Commerce and
Economic Development
P.O. Box 110807
Juneau, AK 99811-0807
907-465-2521

**Arizona**
Securities Division of Arizona
    Corporation Commission
1200 W. Washington Avenue, Suite 201
Phoenix, AZ 85007
602-542-4242

**Arkansas**
Securities Department
201 E. Markham Street, Suite 300
Little Rock, AR 72201
501-324-9260

**California**
Franchise and Securities Information
Department of Corporations
1115 11th Street
Sacramento, CA 95814
916-445-7205

**Colorado**
Division of Securities
1580 Lincoln, Suite 420
Denver, CO  80203
303-894-2320

**Connecticut**
Department of Banking
44 Capital Avenue
Hartford, CT  06106
203-566-4560

**Delaware**
Department of Justice
Office of the Securities Commissioner
State Office Building, 8th Floor
820 North French Street
Wilmington, DE 19801
302-577-2515

**District of Columbia**
Office of Securities
    Public Service Commission
450 5th Street, NW, Suite 821
Washington, DC 20001
202-626-5105

**Florida**
Office of the Comptroller
    Division of Securities
The Capitol Building, L. L. 22
Tallahassee, FL 32399-0350
904-488-9805

**Georgia**
Secretary of State
    Business Services and Regulation
West Tower, Suite 315
2 M. L. King Jr. Drive, SE
Atlanta, GA 30334
404-656-2894

**Hawaii**
Commissioner of Securities
    Business Registration Division
Department of Commerce and
    Consumer Affairs
P.O. Box 40
Honolulu, HI 96810
808-586-2727

**Idaho**
Department of Finance
    Securities Bureau
State House Mail
700 W. State Street
Boise, ID 83720
208-334-3684

**Illinois**
Secretary of State
  Securities Department
900 S. Spring Street
Springfield, IL 62704
217-782-2256

**Indiana**
Secretary of State
Securities Division
302 W. Washington Street, Room E-111
Indianapolis, IN 46204
317-232-6681

**Iowa**
Securities Bureau
Lucas State Office Building, 2d Floor
Des Moines, IA  50319
515-281-4441

**Kansas**
Securities Commission
618 S. Kansas Avenue, 2d Floor
Topeka, KS 66603-3804
913-296-3307

**Kentucky**
Division of Securities State of Kentucky
477 Versailles Road
Frankfort, KY 40601
502-564-2180

**Louisiana**
State of Louisiana Commissioner
  of Securities
1100 Poydras Street, Suite 2250
New Orleans, LA  70163
504-568-5515

**Maine**
Securities Division Bureau of Banking
Department of Professional
  and Financial Regulation
State House, Station 121
Augusta, ME 04333
207-582-8760

**Maryland**
Division of Securities
200 St. Paul Place, 20th Floor
Baltimore, MD 21202-2020
410-576-6362

**Massachusetts**
Secretary of State Securities Division
1 Ashburton Place, Room 1701
Boston, MA 02108
617-727-7190

**Michigan**
Department of Commerce
  Corporation and Securities Bureau
  Securities Division
P.O. Box 30222
6546 Mercantile Way
Lansing, MI 48909
517-334-6200

**Minnesota**
Department of Commerce
  Securities Division
133 E. 7th Street
St. Paul, MN 55101
612-296-4026

**Mississippi**
Secretary of State Securities Division
P.O. Box 136
Jackson, MS 39205
601-359-6371

**Missouri**
Secretary of State
  Commissioner of Securities
600 W. Main Street
Jefferson City, MO 65101
314-751-4136

**Montana**
State Auditor's Office
  Securities Department
P.O. Box 4009
Helena, MT 59604-4009
406-444-2040

**Nebraska**
Bureau of Securities
  Department of Banking and Finance
P.O. Box 95006
Lincoln, NE 68509
402-471-2171

**Nevada**
Office of Secretary of State
  Securities Division
1771 E. Flamingo Road, Suite 212B
Las Vegas, NV 89158
702-486-6440

**New Hampshire**
Department of State
  Bureau of Securities Regulation
State House, Room 400
Concord, NH 03301-4989
603-271-1463

**New Jersey**
New Jersey Bureau of Securities
2 Gateway Center
Newark, NJ 07102
201-648-2040

**New Mexico**
Securities Division
725 St. Michaels Drive
Santa Fe, NM 87501
505-827-7140

**New York**
New York State Department of Law
  State Attorney General
  Bureau of Investor Protection
  and Securities
120 Broadway
New York, NY 10271
212-341-2000

**North Carolina**
Secretary of State
Securities Division
Legislative Office Building
300 N. Salisbury Street, Suite 404
Raleigh, NC 27603
919-733-3924

**North Dakota**
Secretary of State
  Securities Department
600 East Boulevard, 5th Floor
Bismarck, ND 58505
701-224-2910

**Ohio**
Division of Securities
77 S. High Street, 22nd Floor
Columbus, OH 43266-0548
614-466-3001

**Oklahoma**
Securities Commission
P.O. Box 53595
Oklahoma City, OK 73152
405-521-2451

**Oregon**
Department of Insurance and Finance
    Securities Section
21 Labor and Industries Building
Salem, OR 97310
503-378-4387

**Pennsylvania**
Securities Commission
Eastgate Office Building, 2nd Floor
1010 N. 7th Street
Harrisburg, PA 17102
717-787-8061

**Rhode Island**
Banking, Insurance and Securities
Administration
    Department of Business Regulation
    Securities Division
233 Richmond Street, Suite 232
Providence, RI 02903-4232
401-277-3048

**South Carolina**
Securities Division
Edgar Brown Building, Suite 501
1205 Pendleton Street
Columbia, SC 29201
803-734-1087

**South Dakota**
Securities Division
910 E. Sioux Street
Pierre, SD 57501
605-773-4823

**Tennessee**
Department of Commerce and Insurance
    Securities Division
Volunteer Plaza, Suite 680
500 James Robertson Parkway
Nashville, TN 37243
615-741-2947

**Texas**
State Securities Board
P.O. Box 13167
Austin, TX 78711-3167
512-474-2233

**Utah**
Securities Division
P.O. Box 45808
Salt Lake City, UT 84145
801-530-6600

**Vermont**
Securities Division
    Department of Banking and Insurance
89 Main Street
Montpelier, VT 05609
802-828-3301

**Virginia**
Division of Securities and Retail
Franchising
P.O. Box 1197
Richmond, VA 23209
804-371-9784

**Washington**
Securities Division
    Department of Licensing
P.O. Box 8001
Olympia, WA 98507-8001
206-753-6928

**West Virginia**
State Auditor's Office,
Securities Division
State Capital Building, Room W-118
Charleston, WV 25305
304-348-2257

**Wisconsin**
Office of the Commissioner of Securities
111 W. Wilson
P.O. Box 1768
Madison, WI 53701
608-266-3431

**Wyoming**
Secretary of State,
Securities Division
State Capital, Room 109
Cheyenne, WY 82002-0020
307-777-7370

# CHAPTER 13

# FINANCIAL INFORMATION ABOUT OTHER COMPANIES

⟫•⟨ ⟩•⟨⟨ ⟩•⟨

Researching public companies is usually a snap. Other companies can be a bit more challenging and require greater resourcefulness. In this chapter, we will show you which information sources to use for researching private companies, divisions and subsidiaries of corporations, foreign firms that do not sell stock in the United States, and not-for-profit organizations.

## PRIVATE COMPANIES

Private companies make up the majority of employers and provide the preponderance of new jobs created each year. Many small companies are privately held, but it does not follow that a private company is necessarily a small company. Large and outstanding companies, such as Mars, the creator of a candy empire, Milliken, the textile giant, and Cargill, the huge grain merchant, are privately held.

Because researching the finances of private companies is usually more difficult and time consuming than investigating public companies is, it is important to have realistic expectations. Do not look for perfect information, and be resourceful in your approach. For example, if you cannot find profit and sales information published in any form, get estimates and evaluations by interviewing people who understand the company. Often you will need to use several types of sources before you find sufficient data.

The following sources are considered among the best for researching private company finances.

*The company.* The employer is the best source of financial information. Try calling and asking your questions directly. In large companies, try the public information office or the corporate library. In small companies, start with the marketing department or the CEO's office. They may not be willing to provide concrete sales or profit data, but will likely give you some information about the company's overall financial health and trends. It pays to call—you may save yourself a lot of digging by asking the company first.

*Local newspapers and business publications.* The business editor of the local newspaper or business journal may be familiar with the company. To identify the local publications, contact the chamber of commerce or public library where the company is located. (While you have these sources on the phone, ask them what they know about the company.) You can also use the *Standard Periodical Directory* or other directories in your library to find newspapers in a particular city.

*Trade and industry journals.* Refer to the indexes mentioned on pages 151-152 for articles that have been written about your target organization in trade journals. Some may contain financial information.

*State offices.* Some state offices require that a company doing business in the state provide financial information. In addition, you may find people in these offices who are intimately familiar with your company. To locate the office mentioned below, contact the state government operator in the state capital.

Corporation Commission—Most states require companies doing business in the state to file annual reports; some states require a complete balance sheet.

Banking regulators—If the company is a state-chartered bank, chances are the state banking offices will have detailed financial information.

Health regulators—These offices regulate hospitals, nursing homes, and related facilities. Often you can obtain financial reports on such organizations.

Insurance regulators—These offices have copies of insurance companies' financial reports, as well as sample policies, legal documents, articles of incorporation, and policy rate classifications.

Although published sources and on-line databases do contain information on privately held companies, it is not wise to rely on them completely. The coverage is spotty and financial data are often estimated and may be unreliable. If you choose to use library sources, be sure to corroborate what you learn by talking to people who understand the company. The following directories and databases may have financial information about private companies.

## Publications

*Directory of Corporate Affiliations—U.S. Private* (Reed Reference)— This book provides business and financial data on more than eight thousand privately held companies (those with $10 million or more in annual revenues), their subsidiaries, divisions, and affiliates.

*Million Dollar Directory* series (Dun & Bradstreet Marketing Services)— Volumes 1 to 3 provide brief information about U.S. companies, including address, telephone number, names of officers and directors, line of business, SIC code, approximate sales, number of employees, stock exchange abbreviation, stock ticker symbol, and division names and functions. Volume 4 contains indexes of companies by location and volume 5, by SIC code; also available on-line on DIALOG.

*Standard and Poor's Register of Corporations, Directors, and Executives* (Standard and Poor's)—Volume 1 of this directory lists about fifty-five thousand corporations with address, telephone number, products or services provided, SIC code, annual sales, and number of employees; also available on-line on DIALOG.

State industrial directories—These are important sources for private companies. Normally, they will include an estimate for the sales of the companies in the state, and some have additional information. You can learn what directories exist for the company's state by checking with the library nearest the company, or by calling the state librarian. (Call the state operator in the state capital, and ask for the reference/information number of the state library.)

## Databases

Dun's Financial Records Plus (Dun & Bradstreet Information Sevices)— Provides detailed financial data and key business ratios for more than seven hundred thousand public and private companies and their subsidiaries and divisions. (Vendor—DIALOG)

Dun's Electronic Business Directory (Dun and Bradstreet Information Services)—Directory of 8.5 million public and private U.S. companies, providing company name, address, phone numbers, size range by number of employees, and type of business. (Vendor—DIALOG)

Standard & Poor's Register—Corporate (Standard & Poor's)—Provides information on fifty-three thousand companies, both public and private, with annual sales of at least $1 million or with fifty or more employees. For each company includes name, address, telephone number, business description, SIC code, annual sales, and number of employees. Corresponds to the publication, *Standard & Poor's Register of Corporations,* volume 1. (Vendor—DIALOG)

American Business Directory (American Business Information)— Contains industry-specific information on ten million public and private companies in the United States and includes the name of the company, the name(s) of the owner(s), location, telephone number, number of employees, details of manufacturing, and sales figures; formerly **TRINET Company Database**. (Vendor—DIALOG)

# DIVISIONS AND SUBSIDIARIES

If your target is actually a division or subsidiary of another company—perhaps a giant conglomerate—you will need to research both entities. You want to satisfy yourself that both division and parent company are healthy. Researching subsidiaries, divisions, and plants of companies requires you to work a bit harder to ferret out financial information than if you were researching a public corporation. Even if your prospective employer is owned by a public company, there is likely to be little financial information revealed in the parent's securities filings. The securities regulators are interested in the performance of the company as a whole, rather than those of the individual business components. Consequently, they require companies to file little or no information about individual businesses.

The methods for researching divisions, subsidiaries, and even individual plants are similar to those for researching private companies. Refer to the sources mentioned on pages 136-139.

# FOREIGN FIRMS

Foreign firms that sell stock in the United States must file financial information with the Securities and Exchange Commission. Researching other foreign firms requires different techniques—and a bit more effort—than those used to learn about U.S. corporations. The sources listed below will give you the financial information needed to evaluate an employer with headquarters outside the United States.

*The company's U.S. offices.* Most major foreign companies have an office or manufacturing facility in the United States. If you do not know the locations in the United States of the employer you have targeted, use one of the directories described below to find telephone numbers. Otherwise you might assume that a European company has an office in New York City, or that an Asian company has an office in San Francisco or Los Angeles. Try directory assistance in those cities. Once you have reached the company's office, ask for an annual report and any other information available. If no printed information is available, simply discuss your questions with a representative of the company.

*Securities analysts.* Many financial analysts in the United States monitor both U.S. and foreign companies. Find the analysts who monitor your target employer in *Nelson's Directory of Investment Research.*

*Foreign embassies in the United States.* Embassies are good sources of information about their country's companies. Most possess specialized directories that provide some information. When you contact the embassy, ask for the economic officer. These individuals can tell you how to obtain additional information on companies headquarters in their country, and may have personal insights into the company you are researching. To find the country's embassy, contact directory assistance in Washington, D.C. 202-555-1212.

*International Trade Administration (ITA).* As part of the U.S. Department of Commerce, this agency is responsible for monitoring foreign industries. ITA analysts may not be able to give you specific information about your target employer, but can likely refer you to sources that can. They are assigned to product or industry areas, so you will need to know the type of product your target employer imports into the United States. If you do not know what the company is importing, either ask the company itself, or the embassy's economic officer. Once you know the type of product, you can telephone one of the four major industry groups at ITA:

> Basic industries (including automotive, machinery, chemical, energy, environment, infrastructure): 202-482-5023
>
> Service industries and finance: 202-482-5261
>
> Technology and aerospace industries: 202-482-1872
>
> Textiles, apparel, and consumer goods industries: 202-482-3737

*Foreign annual reports.* You may find annual reports on some foreign firms at your local library. Otherwise, try contacting Global Research or Disclosure, Inc. Both companies charge a fee for any information provided, so be sure to ask about cost.

# Publications

*Moody's International Manual* (Moody's Investor Services)—This manual covers over seven thousand companies in ninety countries, and includes financial data.

*Principal International Businesses* (Dun & Bradstreet Information Services)—In addition to being useful in identifying foreign companies, this directory also lists sales and number of employees.

# Databases

Databases with information about foreign firms are growing in numbers. We have listed only those that are most likely to be available in your public or university library. If you have access to a large corporate library, ask the librarian for recommendations about other databases. All databases can be expensive to use, and the information you get may be disappointing. Ask your public or corporate librarian for estimates of charges.

International Dun's Market Identifiers (Dun & Bradstreet Information Services)—Provides directory listings, sales volume and corporate data on two hundred thousand private and public companies in 133 countries. (Vendor—DIALOG)

ICC British Company Financial Datasheets (ICC Information Group)—Provides directory, commercial, and financial reports and ratios on one hundred sixty thousand public and private companies operating in the United Kingdom. (Vendor—DIALOG)

Japan Economic Newswire Plus (Kyodo News International)—Contains the full text of items of important business news from Japan and the Pacific Rim. This database may include financial information on selected companies. (Vendor—DIALOG)

Moody's Corporate News—International (Moody's Investor Service)—Provides financial information on thirty-nine hundred public companies in over 100 countries. For each company, it includes financial statements, earnings statements, balance sheets, bankruptcy financing, mergers and acquisitions, and other information. (Vendor—DIALOG)

Hoppenstedt Directory of German Companies (Hoppenstedt Wirtschafsdatenbank)—This database covers forty-nine thousand German companies with sales exceeding DM 2 million or a minimum of twenty employees. (Vendor—DIALOG)

ICC British Company Directory (ICC Information Group)—This file contains a record for each company included on the Index of Companies maintained by the official Companies Registration Offices in the United Kingdom. (Vendor—DIALOG)

Extel International Financial Cards (Extel Financial)—This database covers companies worldwide and allows cross-country comparison and analysis of companies, industries, and financial markets. About five thousand are U.K. companies and the remainder are from North America, Europe, Australia and the Pacific Rim. (Vendor—DIALOG)

# NOT-FOR-PROFIT ORGANIZATIONS

All tax exempt organizations regulated by the IRS must file annual tax returns with the agency. Unlike those of for-profit companies, the tax returns of not-for-profits are available to the public. The filings provide information about the organization's total assets and liabilities and net worth. Tax-exempt organizations may be private foundations, professional associations, hospital service organizations, nonprofit business leagues, credit unions, charities, educational institutions, and religious groups. Generally, IRS records are kept in the regional offices. To learn how to reach the regional office for your prospective employer, call the FOIA (Freedom of Information Act) Reading Room, Internal Revenue Service, Department of the Treasury, 202-622-6200.

## CHAPTER 14

# LOOKING BEYOND
# THE FINANCIAL STATEMENTS

)•(( )•(( )•((

Financial performance is usually the most important indicator of a company's success, but you should look beyond the financial statements and research other factors that contribute to a company's prosperity and growth: the employer's reputation, its competitiveness, the management's aptitude, and whether it is investing in the future. You should also be aware of events within, and outside, the company, that may affect its future prosperity.

In conducting your research, it is important to recognize that successful companies can take many forms—they can be small or large, liberal or conservative, global or regional. There is no single formula for a successful company, or a great employer. Keep an open mind as you evaluate your prospective employers, looking for signs of strength and weaknesses.

## REPUTATION

Reputation, for a company, is built on, among other things, good products or services, advanced production processes, responsible management, and fair labor practices. Increasingly, social concerns, such as the company's environmental record, contribute to—or detract from—its reputation.

Does your prospective employer enjoy a good reputation among customers, industry peers, and the public? This is important to you as an employee. It is unlikely that you will work for the same company for your entire career—probably you will move around within the industry. You will be far more marketable if you have performed successfully in a well-respected company. In addition, it is nice to feel proud of your employer rather than apologetic about its reputation. You can easily learn about the reputation of your target employer by interviewing representatives of other companies in the industry, stock analysts, and trade-press reporters. If you are targeting a company that is regional, talk with local business people, the chamber of commerce, the board of trade, and the local newspaper reporter who covers the company. Also check *Fortune* magazine for an article entitled America's Most Admired Corporations (usually in the January issue) that gives an excellent overview of the best-liked large companies in the United States.

## Competitiveness

In today's market, companies have to be highly competitive to survive. Increasingly, as trade barriers are removed and major markets move from socialism to capitalism, competitiveness requires a global outlook.

Is your prospective employer an aggressive competitor? The best way to gauge this is to compare the company's sales and earnings with the industry average. Sales and earnings growth, although important, do not necessarily constitute competitiveness. A company can have strong sales and profits, but still be losing market share to competitors. This decline in market position will have a long-term, if not short-term, effect on employees. You will want to ensure that your prospective employers are aggressive about market-share growth; in other words, their growth rate should, ideally, exceed the growth rate of the industry as a whole. Use the sources listed in chapters 12 and 13 to determine the sales growth of companies, and the sources listed in part III to learn industry averages.

Other measures of competitiveness are the ability to anticipate and stimulate market needs in the United States and abroad, and to reduce production and distribution costs. Stock analysts and trade-association executives can give you a feeling for the market innovativeness and production efficiency of large companies.

## Management Aptitude

Good management is important to a company's success. Without solid management, a company finds it hard to sustain growth and market share. But management aptitude is hard to measure. The answers to the following questions will help you measure your target employer's management strengths.

**Is there a high turnover in upper or lower management?**
Changes can be positive, but excessive changes can indicate confusion about goals and direction.

**Are key executive strong in experience and performance?**
Ascertaining this requires some examination of management's backgrounds.

**How long have executives been on the job, and how has the company performed during their tenure?**

**If managers are newly installed, what was their record and reputation in other companies?**

The sources that provide information about management styles include:

*Employer.* Many companies' public-information offices willingly provide dossiers on their key managers to anyone who asks.

*Company's annual report to stockholders.* For public companies, annual reports provide good information about who's who in company management. For management's strategic direction, read the letter to the shareholders that is in the front of the annual report. Look at several years of annual reports to discover the turnover of top management.

*Securities and Exchange Commission (SEC) documents.* If your target employer is a public company, you should check its 10-K filing with the SEC. The 10-K form provides background information on top executives in the company.

*Reference Book of Corporate Managements* (Dun & Bradstreet Information Services)—This directory lists basic biographical information on principal corporate officers and directors.

Standard and Poor's Register—*Biographical* (Standard and Poor's)— This database includes biographies of business executives and directors of publicly and privately held corporations. Includes personal, professional and educational information on seventy-two thousand executives of companies that have annual sales of at least $1 million.

*There are several* Who's Who *directories that may be useful to your research, including:* Who's Who in America, Who's Who in American Law, *and* Who's Who in Finance and Industry. Most of these are published by Reed Reference. Hundred of other *Who's Who* directories specific to certain industries and professions may be located by calling the appropriate professional and industry associations.

*Business press.* Use the indexes described on pages 151-152 to find articles written by the management of the company. These articles often contain insights into the managers' priorities and plans for the company.

*Local sources.* Hometown sources such as the newspaper reporter or chamber of commerce head are likely to have valuable insights about individual managers.

*Labor unions.* Unions make a practice of knowing about key executives and managers in both the companies they represent and those they hope to organize.

## Investing in the Future

It is important to determine whether your target employer is investing in future prosperity. For example, does the company invest in research and development, marketing research, and strategic planning? Is the company automating production and processes? Is it investing in modern, efficient communications and computer systems? These factors contribute much more to future success than plush offices and corporate jets do. It is short-sighted to go to work for a company that is not adequately investing in its future.

Some companies not only fail to invest in the future, they actually borrow from it in order to appear more prosperous today. Companies may cut back long-term development programs or sell off assets in order to increase current profits. A good example is Eastern Airlines' sale of its profitable shuttle to Donald Trump, which improved Eastern's immediate financial picture, but hurt the long-run performance of the company. If you look at your prospective employer's performance over several years, you should be able to identify companies that have gained false profits through heroic measures.

)•(( )•(( )•(( )•(( )•(( )•(( )•(( )•(( )•(( )•(( )•(( )•(( )•(( )•(( )•(( )•(( )•(( )•(( )•(( )•(( )•(( )•((

There are some simple ways to gauge an employer's propensity toward building a successful future, as Sam discovered when he was offered a management job at a very successful family-owned publishing firm. During his final interview, he was given a tour of the facilities. He noticed that the accounting department had dozens of employees bent over ledgers; there were no computers in sight. The interviewer was proud of the fact that the company chose to use manual systems for financial and marketing analysis rather than "replace people with machines." Sam decided not to take the job, believing that the company was not looking ahead.

)•(( )•(( )•(( )•(( )•(( )•(( )•(( )•(( )•(( )•(( )•(( )•(( )•(( )•(( )•(( )•(( )•(( )•(( )•(( )•(( )•(( )•((

To determine whether your prospective employer is investing in its future, review its annual report to stockholders and articles in the local and trade press for references to expansions, automation, employee retraining programs, and other indications that the company is "on the move." Securities analysts and trade-association personnel can also provide useful insights on a company's investment in its future.

## Current Events

Your research should include a scan of current events and conditions that may affect future performance. Look for evidence of plant closings, employee layoffs, and other indications of decline. Conversely, look for optimistic, encouraging news about plant openings, hiring programs, and the like. Mergers and acquisitions may be good or bad for the employee.

⟫⟨⟩⟨⟩⟨⟩⟨⟩⟨⟩⟨⟩⟨⟩⟨⟩⟨⟩⟨⟩⟨⟩⟨⟩⟨⟩⟨⟩⟨⟩⟨⟩⟨⟩⟨⟩⟨⟩⟨⟩⟨⟩⟨⟩⟨⟩⟨⟩⟨⟩⟨⟩⟨⟩⟨⟩⟨

As you monitor company-related events, also keep your eyes and ears open to events that can lead you to specific jobs. Melanie landed her dream job simply by carefully monitoring news about the handful of universities in her state that she considered desirable employers. After applying unsuccessfully at each university, she made a project of finding a niche for herself in one of the institutions. One day she read in the newspaper that one of the universities had a substantial new endowment that was earmarked for computer purchases and training. Taking advantage of her experience in the field, Melanie contacted the university development office and talked her way into the job of administrator for the new endowment fund.

⟫⟨⟩⟨⟩⟨⟩⟨⟩⟨⟩⟨⟩⟨⟩⟨⟩⟨⟩⟨⟩⟨⟩⟨⟩⟨⟩⟨⟩⟨⟩⟨⟩⟨⟩⟨⟩⟨⟩⟨⟩⟨⟩⟨⟩⟨⟩⟨⟩⟨⟩⟨⟩⟨⟩⟨⟩⟨

## SOURCES OF INFORMATION

Because any information you learn is quickly dated, focus on the most current information—and the best projections—available. The best sources for timely insights are likely to be:

*The Employer.* Ask your target employer's public-information office for copies of press releases and any internal publications, such as newsletters and memos to stockholders. Request copies for the past year or two, and ask to be put on the employer's mailing list for future issues. Scan these for information about significant new developments in the company and its local business environment. Remember, however, that company publications may emphasize events favorable to the company. To get a balanced picture, also consult more objective sources.

*Local Sources.* Good sources of up-to-date information on your target employer are local press reporters, politicians, and business leaders. You can locate these individuals through the local chamber of commerce or the mayor's office.

*Stock Analysts.* When a company is a large enough player in the market-place, even if it is not public, stock analysts will take notice of important trends in, and surrounding, the company.

*Association Executives.* News travels fast in an industry; trade-association executives are excellent sources for information about significant events affecting companies in their industry.

*Trade and Business Press.* Talk directly to the editors of the leading trade press in the employer's industry. In addition to reporting current news, journalists try to scoop one another, predicting the future of companies and industries. Use the indexes described on pages 151-152 to find articles about the company, and call the authors of those articles for more information.

A variety of published sources and databases can also provide you with insights into your prospective employer's future. For example, employers' press releases, which alert you to their trends and plans, are tracked by these on-line databases:

BusinessWire (BusinessWire)—This database contains the full text of press releases and news stories from companies, public and investor relations firms, business organizations and associations, government agencies, colleges and universities, trade associations, and legal and investment firms. (Vendor—DIALOG)

PR Newswire (PR Newswire)—Contains the full texts of press releases from more than twenty thousand companies, government agencies, and other news sources. (Vendor—DIALOG, NewsNet, NEXIS)

PTS New Product Announcements-Plus (Predicasts)—Offers the full texts of corporate news releases and selected PR Newswire records announcing new products and technologies, with a special emphasis on high technology and emerging industries. (Vendor—DIALOG)

For information about a company's merger and acquisition activities, consult these sources.

M & A Filings (Charles E. Simon)—This database provides detailed abstracts of original and amended merger and acquisition documents released by the Securities and Exchange Commission. It identifies the target company, the SIC code, purchase, percentage and number of shares held, approximate deal values, and abstracts of key points. (Vendor—DIALOG)

*Acquisition Mart* (Business Publications)—This is a periodical listing middle-market mergers and acquisition opportunities; between forty and sixty new candidates are profiled each month.

*The Mergers Yearbook* (SDC Publishing)—This publication lists mergers and joint ventures announced during the preceding year.

Both the local and business press track strategic events that affect employers. Local newspaper articles will keep you posted on local developments, such as plant expansions and closings, employee hirings and layoffs, and major contracts. Trade journals are likely to report on significant new technology developments in the product or manufacturing process, as well as on government regulations and economic conditions that may affect the industry and its companies.

## Using Indexes

Check your library for indexes to published articles. These indexes may be available in printed or on-line versions. The indexes will direct you to articles that refer to your prospective employer. You can then read the articles in the printed version of the periodicals. A faster way is to search the text of articles on line. Remember that this can be expensive. If your library has databases on CD-ROM products, you may be able to have the benefits of electronic searching without the costs.

Use the indexes listed below to identify recent articles about your target company. Most libraries have access to at least one good business periodicals index. These indexes will refer you to specific journals and magazines. You will then need to find those periodicals and read the articles. If your library does not subscribe to the periodicals you need, try calling the publishers of the journals, asking for a free copy of the articles you have identified. Most will oblige. To locate the publishers of the journals, use *Magazines for Libraries* (Reed Reference), which includes magazines and research journals.

*Business Index* (Information Access)—Not as comprehensive as some indexes, this one is nevertheless worth checking because it includes important articles from *The Wall Street Journal, Barron's,* and more than eight hundred other periodicals.

*Business Periodicals Index* (H. W. Wilson)—This index is excellent for locating articles on companies, products, and business topics that have appeared in the 345 most influential business journals; also available online on Wilsonline.

*Predicasts F&S Index United States* (Predicasts)—This is a continually updated index of articles about U.S. companies and industries that appear in more than 750 financial publications, business-oriented news-papers, trade magazines and special reports; also available online on BRS, Data-Star, and DIALOG.

*Wall Street Journal Index* (Dow Jones)—*The Wall Street Journal* often contains news about companies, products and industries. It has its own index, published monthly, with annual accumulations; also available online from Dow Jones News/Retrieval, and NEXIS.

## Using Databases and CD-ROMs

Databases and CD-ROMs provide an efficient way of tracking events that affect your prospective employers. Some give you access to information that may be difficult or impossible to find in published form. The following databases give you direct access to all types of articles about your target employer. Many of these articles can be retrieved in their entirety—the full text—from the library's termi-nal. Although most libraries charge a substantial fee for searching databases, these can save you considerable time tracking down articles and photocopying them. Your library may also have CD-ROMs that contain extensive information about employers. If so, you will save time and money, as CD-ROM use is generally free of charge. Large university and public libraries are your best bets for information on CD-ROMs.

ABI/Inform (UMI/Data Courier)—Contains summaries of business articles from more than eight-hundred business and management publi-cations. Includes specific product, company, and industry information.

Some libraries have ABI/Inform available for public searching on CD-ROM. (Vendors—BRS, Data-Star, DIALOG)

AP News (Associated Press)—Contains the full text of each day's national, international, financial, and sports news as compiled by the worldwide news-gathering sources of the Associated Press. (Vendors—DIALOG, DataTimes, NEXIS, NewsNet)

Business Dateline (UMI/Data Courier)—Contains thousands of articles on regional business trends and activities, as well as features on local U.S. and Canadian companies, products, and executives. (Vendors—DIALOG, NEXIS)

BusinessWire (BusinessWire)—Full text of press releases and news stories from public and investor relations firms, business organizations and associations, government agencies, colleges and universities, trade associations, and legal investment firms; topics covered include finance, business, science, labor, education, and entertainment. (Vendor—DIALOG)

Magazine Index; Magazine ASAP (Information Access)—Magazine Index contains citations to articles in more than four hundred U.S. and Canadian magazines, covering current affairs, business, consumer information, science and technology, economics, and arts and entertainment. Magazine ASAP contains the full text, indexed, to articles from over eighty magazines covered in Magazine Index. Some libraries have similar magazine indexes on CD-ROM, available for free searching. (Vendors—Data-Star, DIALOG, Mead Data Central)

McGraw-Hill Publications Online (McGraw-Hill)—Complete texts of all articles from eighteen major McGraw-Hill business and trade magazines and newsletters that cover general business and specific industries such as defense, aerospace, chemical processing, electronics, and construction. Provides information on new products, government regulations, technological developments, and business and industry tracking. (Vendors—DIALOG, NEXIS)

National Newspaper Index (Information Access)—Extensive indexes of the contents of the *Christian Science Monitor, New York Times,* and *Wall*

*Street Journal;* to national and international stories in the *Washington Post* and *Los Angeles Times;* articles from PR Newswire. Many large libraries have the National Newspaper Index on CD-ROM for free public searching. (Vendor—DIALOG)

Newsearch (Information Access)—Daily index to news articles about business, specific companies, current affairs, law, government regulation, and congressional action relating to business. Includes information on local and private companies. (Vendor—DIALOG)

NewsNet Business and Industry Newsletters (NewsNet)—Contains the full texts of seven hundred business newsletters and wire services covering thirty-four industries and professions. (Vendor—NewsNet)

Newspaper Abstracts (UMI-Data Courier)—Indexes and abstracts for over twenty regional, national, and international newspapers, including the *Atlanta Constitution, Boston Globe, Chicago Tribune, Christian Science Monitor,* and *Wall Street Journal.* (Vendor—DIALOG)

Newswire ASAP (Information Access)—Complete text and indexing of several newswire transmissions. Current and retrospective information on companies, industries, economics and finance. (Vendor—DIALOG)

NEXIS (Mead Data Central)—Several files are on NEXIS, including the full text and abstracts of news, business, government, financial, trade, and technology publications, as well as of six hundred trade publications covering advertising campaigns, new products, executive changes, market research, mergers, and acquisitions. (Vendor—Mead Data Central)

PTS F&S Indexes (Predicasts)—Provides concise one- and two-line article abstracts from more than five thousand business, trade, government, and industry publications; covers both U.S. and foreign companies and industries; contains information on acquisitions and mergers, new products, and technologies; includes company profiles and forecasts by securities firms and company officers. (Vendor—DIALOG)

PTS PROMT (Predicasts)—Contains abstracts of business and trade literature covering the worldwide business and industrial environment with an emphasis on products, companies, and markets. Covers international marketing policies and developments, licensing, taxation and regulation, new products, new technologies, and foreign trade. (Vendor—DIALOG)

Trade and Industry Index; Trade and Industry ASAP (Information Access)—Trade and Industry Index lists business-related articles from more than one thousand trade and business periodicals, magazines, journals, and newspapers, as well as news releases from PR Newswire. Trade and Industry ASAP includes the full texts and indexing to articles for over eighty journals covered in Trade and Industry Index. (Vendor— DIALOG)

Wall Street Transcript (Wall Street Transcript)—Contains the full text of *Wall Street Transcript,* a verbatim report of roundtable discussions between corporate officers and industry analysts; also includes *Corporate Critics Confidential,* a report from confidential sources on industries and companies, as well as interviews with CEOs; provides exclusive company and industry information and broker's reports. (Vendor—DataTimes)

Washington Post Electronic Edition (Washington Post)—Provides the full text of the final edition of the *Washington Post* for all stories the *Post* has copyrighted. (Vendors—DIALOG, DataTimes, NEXIS)

Dozens of databases follow particular industries, from aerospace to pharmaceuticals. For extensive listings refer to *How to Find Information about Companies, Part I* (Washington Researchers) or *Gale Directory of Databases* (Gale Research).

## CHAPTER 15

# THE VALUE OF YOUR CONTRIBUTION

)•(( )•(( )•((

Whatever your field of expertise or specialty, it will provide more clout, prestige, and career advancement in some organizations than in others. In both the short run and the long run, it pays to work where your job or profession is highly valued—where you are a VIP.

)•(( )•(( )•(( )•(( )•(( )•(( )•(( )•(( )•(( )•(( )•(( )•(( )•(( )•(( )•(( )•(( )•(( )•(( )•(( )•(( )•(( )•(( )•((

Beverly, the manager of competitive analysis for a large industrial manufacturing company, learned the hard way what it means to have an undervalued job. Because her employer's commitment to competitive analysis was erratic, her budget and staff were the first to be cut whenever a new project had to be funded. Also, there was a chain effect that had a direct impact on her advancement in the company: Her job was not valued, so she had little prestige; because she had little prestige, she was unable to advance her career, either by building her own department or by advancing into other areas of the company.

When Beverly finally changed jobs, she selected a company that had been strongly committed to competitive analysis for more than a decade. There was evidence that the budget for the function increased each year, and that the competitive analysts advanced in the company. She was willing to give up her management po-sition in a company that promised no career growth for an analyst's position in a company that valued her skills.

)•( )•(( )•(( )•( )•(( )•( )•(( )•( )•(( )•( )•(( )•( )•(( )•( )•(( )•( )•(( )•( )•(( )•( )•(( )•( )•(( )•( )•(( )•( )•(( )•( )•((

# ASKING THE RIGHT QUESTIONS

Determining how much value an individual employer would place on your profes-sional contribution requires some resourcefulness and imagination. You will have a good idea, however, if you find answers to these questions:

**Is your profession or skill important to the organization's success and image of itself?**
For example, inventive companies such as Dupont and Apple value creative, inventor types. Such companies are likely to provide more support for R&D professionals than would be found at some competing companies.

**How does the employer rate, compared to others in the same business, as far as pay, advancement, and job mobility for people in your profession or special field?**

**Does the employer offer any specialized training programs for your profession? Does it continue training to update skills?**

**For how many years has the position (or type of position) you're targeting existed in the organization?**
A new position that is not well defined may not offer clear levels of advancement or compensation. For an aggressive person, this type of position may, however, offer flexibility.

**What happened to the previous people in the position?**
If they were promoted, that's a good sign. If they made a lateral move to another department or left the company, you may want to find out if this has been a pattern.

**What manager does the person in the position report to, and to whom does the manager report? Are these influential people?**

The line of reporting usually indicates the importance of the position. If the line of reporting is ill defined, or if the reporting is to a junior-level manager, the position may be out of the loop of professional advancement, or may be a likely target for obliteration by an austerity program.

### Does the supervisor or department head control the hiring, firing, and salary levels, including raises and bonuses?

If your immediate boss does not have the power to give you a raise, you may need to question the importance of your profession or department within the company.

### How will your profession be treated in light of changes in the organization?

If you are a retail marketing expert in an organization that decides to concentrate on the industrial market, your retail marketing expertise may be devalued. If the company discontinues a product line, and you happen to be an engineer in that area, you may be out of a job, or at least lose status. Try to avoid these problems by examining the company's trends and priorities and deciding how you fit in.

Among the sources you can tap to learn more about how your profession is valued are professional associations, labor unions, and the local press.

*Professional Associations.* People who work for professional associations keep abreast of their members' treatment by employers. There may be a formalized system of monitoring, or information may be transferred by word of mouth. Contact the association, and request a frank conversation about employers, off the record. Ask to speak with the executive director of the association. He or she is most likely to know the most details about the member companies. Ask for a brief rundown on the best and worst employers, and ask for an explanation of the choice.

You should also obtain a copy of the association's membership directory. From the directory you can learn names and contact information for hundreds or thousands of individuals in the profession. Listings in these directories often include the member's company affiliation. You can target particular companies, or contact individuals from several companies for their opinions.

*Unions.* For the jobs that they represent, unions can provide excellent information about individual employers. On a national level, they can identify those employers that provide the best wages and benefits, and those that have the largest numbers of employee grievances. On a regional or local level, they can be frank about the employers in the area. Even if your target employer is not unionized, the union may have gathered information about it in the hope of organizing the employees.

*Local Papers.* Newspaper editors are likely to know how local employers treat the various trades. They also have a good feel for the general employment atmosphere in the company. They are less likely to know how the various white-collar professions fare in the company, but may have useful insights.

The best way to learn how specific employers may value your occupation is to talk with people who work in similar positions in the organization. You may have identified employees in your profession from interviews with professional associations or through directories or local sources. If you do not know of someone to call, contact the organization's personnel department to request the names of several employees in your field. You can preface your request by saying something like, "I'm interested in learning more about how your organization uses people in engineering; specifically, what kinds of jobs engineers hold. Can you assist me or arrange for me to speak with an engineer in your organization?" Most personnel departments will comply. Once you get your source on the phone, what do you say? Your approach should be consistent with your personal style; the interview guidelines beginning on page 12 will help you. Remember always to be honest about who you are and why you are calling. To save money, check to see if the company has a toll-free 800 line by calling toll-free directory assistance at 1-800-555-1212.

When you talk to the personnel department, you should also ask for any printed material that the company prepares for future job applicants. Although the material will be written with a bias—to show the company to best advantage as an employer—you can get clues about the company's personality.

If you are reluctant to call, try writing a letter. Letters are, however, usually less successful than the more personal approach. A telephone call seems less formal than a letter, and it encourages an informal, spontaneous response. People are apt to be most honest—especially about their employer—when they are chatting "off the record" than when they are responding to a written request. Use the telephone if you possibly can.

When you are interviewing an employee in your occupation or profession, questions similar to the following will help you discover what you need to know about the employer's attitude toward your field:

How did you get this job? What qualifications were necessary?

Does the company promote from within? How are upper-management positions filled? What are the qualifications of those individuals? How often have you been promoted?

What qualifications, training, or degrees would help you advance?

What satisfactions do you get from your position? What is the best— and worst—thing about working for XYZ company?

How are the salaries, benefits, work environment, coworkers?

Do you have any advice for me? What else do you think I should know if I hope to work for your company?

Do not feel as if you are intruding by contacting these individuals. Most people feel flattered by the interest taken in them and their profession. In fact, you may have trouble getting off the phone once people begin talking about themselves!

If you are looking at a particular line of business within a company—for example, a product line or a division—you should focus on the way in which the management of that business values your profession—and how the corporation as a whole values that particular business. For this information, too, professional associations, labor unions, and the local papers should be helpful.

## Publications

You may want to augment your research by looking at the following publications. Each discusses employment within particular companies.

Levering, Robert, and Milton Maskowitz, *The One Hundred Best Companies to Work for in America* (Signet)—Extremely well researched, this book identifies the one hundred most popular employers in the country and tells what it is like to work for them. Each company was evaluated in terms of pay, benefits, job security, opportunities for promotion, and ambiance. The information is dated, but still useful as a baseline.

*Peterson's Engineering, Science & Computer Jobs 1993* (Peterson's Guides)—This annually updated book lists opportunities and job openings in hundreds of companies for engineering, science and computer-related fields. For each company, there is information concerning background and operations, employment opportunities, application information, and benefits, salaries and training data. There is also an excellent table providing an overview of the types of engineering and science disciplines sought by employers in 1993.

*Job Seeker's Guide to Private and Public Companies* (Gale Research)—Four volumes, each covering a geographic area. The listings, for more than fifteen thousand companies, include names, addresses, telephone numbers, a description of the business, number of employees, benefits offered, and the name of a person to be contacted about jobs.

Nadler, Burton Jay, *Liberal Arts Jobs: Where They Are and How to Get Them* (Peterson's Guides)—A listing of companies in the fifteen most promising fields for liberal arts majors; company names, qualifications required, and job titles and functions.

*Federal Career Opportunities* (Federal Research Service)—A biweekly list of current vacancies in the federal government in the United States and abroad; permanent, part-time, and temporary positions are arranged by occupation and by federal agency.

*Dun's Employment Opportunities Directory/The Career Guide* (Dun & Bradstreet Information Services)—An annual listing five thousand companies planning to hire individuals within the next year. Has a geographic and discipline index; includes benefits offered by each company.

# CHAPTER 16

# COMPATIBILITY

)•(( )•(( )•((

Most organizations have personal traits just like individuals do. These traits relate to the general way an employer conducts itself and the way it interacts with its employees and its community. Your personal happiness in a company may depend upon a compatibility of personalities—yours with your employer's. Furthermore, your professional progress may depend on how well you can fit into an employer's corporate culture.

)•(( )•(( )•(( )•(( )•(( )•(( )•(( )•(( )•(( )•(( )•(( )•(( )•(( )•(( )•(( )•(( )•(( )•(( )•(( )•(( )•((

Pamela discovered the importance of a good personality fit when she was hired as the marketing director for a medium-sized publisher. She had gained her experience with companies strongly committed to marketing and, having proven her skills in supporting roles, she was eager to direct an aggressive marketing program. In fact, she had enough confidence in her abilities that she negotiated a compensation plan based largely on performance bonuses. Unfortunately, Pamela failed to research the corporate culture of her new employer before accepting the job. The company, a wholly owned subsidiary of a newspaper syndicate, had a strong editorial commitment, but a weak record in marketing. Pamela found that the editorial managers called all the shots, even when their decisions had disastrous results for marketing and revenues. She found herself with substantial responsibility but no authority—and little or no chance to earn the bonuses that she had expected.

Should she try to convince the company to see things her way, or should she bail out? Unless there is a management upheaval, changing corporate culture is often like moving mountains. Pamela decided to cut her losses and find a new job. She found a smaller publisher in the same area whose management loved her aggressive views on marketing. The personality of the company suited Pamela's style and both parties benefited by the match.

)•( )•(( )•(( )•(( )•( )•( )•(( )•( )•( )•(( )•( )•( )•(( )•( )•( )•(( )•( )•( )•(( )•( )•( )•(( )•( )•( )•(( )•( )•( )•(( )•(

Pamela's experience is not unusual. You probably know people who are unhappy with the general style of their employers. Perhaps you feel that way about your own employer. Because, all other things being equal, you will make the best progress in a work environment that is compatible with your own personal style, think about the factors that are important to you and size up those factors within prospective employers. Watch for clues to corporate style throughout your job-hunting process—from initial exploration to final job interview. Sometimes everything looks right about a company until you get down to serious negotiations.

)•( )•(( )•(( )•(( )•( )•( )•(( )•( )•( )•(( )•( )•( )•(( )•( )•( )•(( )•( )•( )•(( )•( )•( )•(( )•( )•( )•(( )•( )•( )•(( )•(

Melissa was ready to accept a job with a company that had been courting her for several months. In the final interview, she asked the personnel officer about paying for the licensing exams that the company required. She learned that the company does not pay for exams—even those they require—despite the fact that most firms do so. Melissa decided that penny pinching at the expense of employees reflected a company culture that was unacceptable to her, so she turned down the job.

)•( )•(( )•(( )•(( )•( )•( )•(( )•( )•( )•(( )•( )•( )•(( )•( )•( )•(( )•( )•( )•(( )•( )•( )•(( )•( )•( )•(( )•( )•( )•(( )•(

If you are very short of time and want a quick method of evaluating companies, you will find some invaluable quick-reference lists on pages 166-167. They identify selected companies that rank high in the quality of the work environment, pay, benefits, job security, and upward mobility. If you do not happen to be working for a company on that list, you will need to do a little research. Chapters 17 and 18 show you how to evaluate employers on the four aspects of style that are likely to be most important to the job hunter: the employee benefits, the quality of the employment environment, the organization's culture, and its social conscience and contribution to society. Each chapter also includes the sources of information you need for researching any of the employers you have targeted.

If you have been in the job market for many years, you likely know what work environment characteristics are important to you. You know whether you value a corner office more than flexible work hours, or rank good company reputation or child-care assistance. You can skim through chapters 17 and 18 and pinpoint the specific characteristics you need to research. If you are looking for your first career position, you may still be trying to sort out your priorities. In this event, you should carefully review these chapters. They will help you think through what is important to you in an employer, as well as tell you how to conduct your research.

## SHORTCUTS TO FINDING CONGENIAL COMPANIES

What characterizes a great place to work? Although we each have our own particular preferences, there are certain characteristics that most of us want in our workplace, according to experts who have studied hundreds of workplaces and asked the opinions of hundreds of employees about what they value in their work environments. In their book *The 100 Best Companies to Work for in America* (Signet, 1985, 1993), Robert Levering and Milton Moskowitz give meaty, qualitative assessments of the 100 best U.S. business employers. With the permission of the authors, highlights of their research are provided. You can use the following lists of "company bests" for quickly spotting some of the stars. Better yet, buy a copy of the revised, 1993 edition, and read, in detail, about the strengths and weaknesses of all one hundred companies. Even if you end up working for none of the companies listed, the book gives you standards for evaluating any company.

In compiling candidates for the revised edition, Levering and Moskowitz had more than four hundred nominations. Only fifty-five of the original one hundred best are still on their list nine years later. They found some improvements in the workplace. There was more employee participation, a change as result of layoffs, more sensitivity to work and family issues, more sharing of the wealth through profit sharing, gain-sharing programs, and employee stock ownership, more fun, and more trust between management and employees, a result of the existence of training employee committees and an absence of time clocks.

Remember that many of the companies mentioned are highly diversified conglomerates, and their corporate culture may not extend to all their subsidiaries and facilities. Look, not only at the culture of the company, but also at the particular segment of the company that you are targeting. According to Levering and Moskowitz, in addition to offering good pay and benefits, the ideal employer would:

- Make people feel that they are part of a team or, in some cases, a family

- Encourage open communication, informing its people of new developments and encouraging them to offer suggestions and complaints

- Promote from within; let its own people bid for jobs before hiring outsiders

- Stress quality, enabling people to feel pride in the products or services they are providing

- Allow its employees to share in the profits, through profit sharing or stock ownership or both

- Reduce the distinctions of rank between top management and those in entry-level jobs; put everyone on a first-name basis; bar executive dining rooms and exclusive perks for high-level people

- Devote attention and resources to creating as pleasant a workplace environment as possible; hire good architects

- Try not to lay off people without first making an effort to place them in other jobs either within the company or elsewhere

- Be especially considerate of conflicts between work and family needs and of health-care needs

• Care enough about the health of its employees to provide physical fitness centers and regular exercise and medical programs

• Expand the skills of its people through training programs and reimbursement of tuition for outside courses

### The Ten Best Companies to Work for in the United States

Beth Israel Hospital, Boston
Donnelly
Fel-Pro
Publix Super Markets
Southwest Airlines

Delta Air Lines
Federal Express
Hallmark Cards
Rosenbluth International
USAA

### The Ten Offering the Best Pay and Benefits

Leo Burnett
Goldman Sachs
Hewlett-Packard
Merck
Syntex

Fel-Pro
Hallmark Cards
IBM
Proctor & Gamble
Xerox

### The Seventeen Offering the Best Job Security

Acipco
Donnelly
Federal Express
Hallmark Cards
Hewitt Associates
Lincoln Electric
Physio-control
Southwest Airlines
Worthington Industries

Alagasco
Erie Insurance
H B Fuller
Haworth
SC Johnson Wax
Northwestern Mutual Life
Rosenbluth International
USAA

### The Ten Offering the Best Opportunities

Dayton Hudson

Motorola

J. C. Penney

Rosenbluth International

USAA

Microsoft

Nordstrom

Publix Super Markets

Southwest Airlines

Wal-Mart

### The Nine Offering the Most Beautiful Corporate Headquarters

Cummins Engine

Erie Insurance

Los Angeles Dodgers

Northwestern Mutual Life

Weyerhaeuser

John Deere

SC Johnson Wax

Merck

Reader's Digest

Much of what you value in a workplace is likely to be included in the characteristics defined by Levering and Moskowitz. There may, however, be additional criteria that are important to you. Also, you may be committed to a region of the country where the companies listed above are not located. For these reasons, you need to be able to research the personality, style, and behavior of any company.

# CHAPTER 17

# EMPLOYEE BENEFITS AND THE COMPANY CULTURE

)•(  )•(( )•(( )•((

Employee benefits and the company culture are both factors that make working for a company more or less rewarding, depending on the company. Employee benefits are considered compensation over and above the wage for the job. The amount varies with the company, but they all have a specific monetary value. The company culture is less tangible. Essentially it is made up of the atmosphere in the workplace and prevailing attitudes and expectations. These may be fairly abstract notions, but their effects on day-to-day working conditions are not negligible.

## EMPLOYEE BENEFITS

If employee benefits are an essential criterion in your choice of an employer, it pays to shop around and to investigate the benefits offered. You will find that some companies offer packages worth about one-third of the employees' salaries, whereas other companies' benefits are negligible. Companies with progressive views toward benefits are offering a choice—a cafeteria approach. Being able to select your benefits automatically increases their value to you.

While some benefits provide financial rewards, others improve the quality of life. Health clubs and country-club memberships are prime examples, as are pro grams that extend benefits not just to marriage partners but also to unmarried "do mestic partners." Flextime enables people to adjust their work hours to their personal preferences and family obligations. Telecommuting allows employees to work away from the office, delivering their output by modem and fax. According to *Newsweek* magazine, although many companies have been slow to respond to the needs of working parents, there are examples of creative family assistance, such as Johnson & Johnson's "sick bay" for ailing children and Stride Rite's on-site day care facility, where children and the elderly can be cared for and benefit from intergenerational interaction.

)·(( )·(( )·(( )·(( )·(( )·(( )·(( )·(( )·(( )·(( )·(( )·(( )·(( )·(( )·(( )·(( )·(( )·(( )·(( )·((

All benefits should be carefully evaluated. They are not always as valuable as they first appear, and for some so-called benefits, you may even pay a price. Ben, a University of Maryland student, hoped to find employment with a local company that would provide good training in computer systems. In reading one company's annual report, he found an entire section devoted to the employee training program. He applied to the company and was hired. As a condition for employment, he signed a promissory note agreeing to pay back the cost of the company training program if he resigned before completing twenty-four months of employment.

Ben was disappointed with the quality of the training he received. When he resigned after eighteen months, the company sued him to recover $9,000 in training costs. The same company has brought similar suits against thirty former employees, who contended that the training benefits were substantially overvalued.

)·(( )·(( )·(( )·(( )·(( )·(( )·(( )·(( )·(( )·(( )·(( )·(( )·(( )·(( )·(( )·(( )·(( )·(( )·(( )·((

On a more positive note, training programs offered by companies such as IBM, Xerox, and K-Mart have provided employees with valuable skills and made them attractive prospects for other companies looking for well-trained personnel.

In this chapter, we list some benefits that you should look for—benefits that many companies provide to their employees. To help you gauge the benefits of your prospective employers, we also include information about the prevalence of each type of benefit in corporate America. For example, if an employer does not provide paternity leave, it is no different from 74 percent of companies; if it provides no health care benefits at all, it is in a minority of 17 percent. These and the following statistics are taken from a survey of medium and large firms released by the Bureau of Labor Statistics in Washington in 1991.

*Family Benefits.* Eight percent of the workers in the survey were eligible for employer-subsidized child-care benefits. These benefits included reimbursement for child-care expenses, as well as facilities provided by the employer. Unpaid maternity leave was available under plans covering 37 percent of the employees and unpaid paternity leave under plans for 26 percent of the employees. Formal flexible work schedules were available to 9 percent of workers.

*Defined Benefit Pension Plans.* Defined benefit pension plans, which specify a formula for determining an employee's annuity, covered 59 percent of full-time workers in 1990. The purchasing power of a fixed monthly pension benefit can be eroded in periods of even moderate inflation. To compensate for this, some pension plans provide an occasional ad hoc benefit increase; relatively few provide automatic cost-of-living adjustments.

*Defined Contribution Plans.* The most common defined contribution plans were savings and thrift (covering 29 percent of full-time workers), profit-sharing (16 percent), money-purchase pension (5 percent), and employee stock ownership plans (3 percent). Overall, 48 percent of the workers were covered by one or more of these plans.

*Health Care Benefits and Life Insurance.* Eighty-three percent of full-time employees were provided medical care benefits (such as hospitalization, care by physicians, X-ray and laboratory work) wholly or partially financed by the employer; 60 percent had dental coverage. Medical coverage was fully provided by the employer for 50 percent of participants, while family coverage was fully paid for 33 percent of participants. When employee contributions for medical care were required, they averaged $27 per month for individual coverage and $97 per month for family coverage. Ninety-four percent of employees received life-insurance benefits. The cost of this coverage was paid entirely by the employer for 80 percent of the respondents.

*Paid Leave.* Leave with pay is available to employees in a variety of forms—from daily rest breaks to annual vacations of several weeks. Most types of paid leave were available to a majority of the employees in the survey. The number of paid holidays averaged 10.2 per year; vacation leave, which commonly increased with length of service, averaged 9.3 days after one year of service, 16.5 days after ten years, and 20.4 days after twenty years. Paid rest time averaged twenty-six minutes a day; funeral leave, 3.3 days per occurrence; military leave, 14.8 days a year; and paid time-off for jury duty was usually provided as needed.

*Disability Income Benefits.* Income protection against short-term disabilities was available to 86 percent of the workers, through sick leave, sickness and accident insurance, or both. Long-term disability insurance, which provides income to employees during lengthy periods of disability, covered 45 percent of the employees.

*Flexible Benefits and Reimbursement Accounts.* Flexible benefits plans allow workers to choose from a menu of benefits offered, while reimbursement accounts provide funds from which workers could pay for expenses not covered by the regular benefits package. Forty-six percent of the workers were eligible for one or both of these arrangements.

Remember that benefits have real value. If few benefits are offered, then you should look for a higher salary or other advantages to compensate. It is perfectly acceptable to inquire about a company's benefit package during a job interview. Even if you are not at the interview stage, most companies will give you some information about benefits. Contact the personnel office for assistance, or talk with anyone you know at the company. If you do not have contacts, you can use the professional association directories listed on page 191 to identify a person who works for your target employer. It also pays to request company literature that is designed specifically for prospective employees. This material usually gives some indication of benefits.

# EMPLOYMENT ENVIRONMENT

By the term *employment environment* we mean the way in which the employer treats his employees. An organization's culture is defined by the way it makes decisions, the relationship between management and other employees, the way its employees interact, the accepted dress and demeanor, and the management style.

Many factors contribute to employment environment—some will be more important to you than others. For most job seekers, some important questions to ask about employment environment are:

Does the employer promote from within?

Is there a commitment to preserving job security?

Are benefits extended to all employees or do they favor the top executives?

Does the employer provide ownership opportunities for its employees?

Does the employer provide incentive bonuses based on performance?

Does the employer give recognition based on performance?

Does the employer offer flexibility in work hours?

Can employees voice their concerns without fear of retribution?

Do all employees have acceptable amenities (cafeteria, washroom, gym, and so on)?

Is the working environment safe and comfortable?

Is the working environment pleasant and attractive?

Does the employer provide continuous training for employees?

Is tuition reimbursement for outside training programs available?

Are employees encouraged to show initiative in the workplace?

You have to decide which factors are most important to you and then determine how important they are to your prospective employers. If an employer disregards areas that are important to you, either look for a position elsewhere, or make sure that you are offered compensating incentives, such as salary and benefits.

Merely reading extensively about an employer in business periodicals or the home-town newspaper, will enable you to learn a great deal about the type of work environment that exists in the organization. Your most direct route to information about quality of work life is, however, the employer itself.

If you are already interviewing for a position, it is appropriate to ask your interviewer the questions listed above. If you are not interviewing for a position, you can contact the personnel department, and ask to speak to an employee in a position similar to one that you would hope to have. If your request is declined, discuss your questions with a representative of the personnel department. You can also use the professional association membership directories mentioned on page 191 to find individuals who work for your target employer.

If you are unable to discuss your questions with an employee, try these sources.

*Contact the chamber of commerce,* and talk with a representative who may be familiar with the employer.

*Discuss your questions with the local union representative.*

*Call the local paper and talk to the business editor,* who may have gained useful insights into the quality of the workplace while researching a story about the employer.

*Talk to a securities analyst who monitors the employer.* To find analysts use *Nelson's Directory of Investment Research* (Nelson Publications).

## COMPANY CULTURE

The following guidelines should steer you into an organization with a culture that is suitable for you.

- If you consider yourself an innovator, seek an employer that encourages innovation rather than conformity.

- If you like to have a voice in decision making, join an organization with participative management, not one that provides little access from one level of management to another.

• If you like predictability in your job, join an established organization with established job descriptions, not one that is undergoing rapid changes.

• If you work best in the wee hours of the morning, look for an employer that watches the quality of your performance rather than the time clock.

• If you resist traditional business dress, hook up with an employer that does not expect you to wear a coat and tie or dress-for-success pumps.

To learn about the culture of any corporation, operation, or organization, find out what the employer's representatives and others have to say about it. This will give you the insider's view as well as more objective opinions. Most organizations portray themselves as congenial environments where hard work and persistence result in increased responsibility, esteem, and higher income. Just try to "read between the lines" of the employer's statements in order to understand the operative culture.

*Recruitment brochure.* A good starting point is the employer's recruitment brochures, which you can probably find in a university career-counseling office. Or, you can contact the personnel department and ask for any literature that has been prepared for prospective employees.

*Annual reports to stockholders.* You should also obtain the company's annual report from the public-relations or stockholder-relations office. You do not have to be a stockholder to qualify for a free copy. Think about the corporate image being presented in the report—is it stodgy and predictable or innovative and progressive? Are employees featured in the report? How do they look—their dress, sex, race, general demeanor? What is being emphasized by the pictures and graphics? Read the chief executive officer's message (usually on the first page of the annual report), which describes the overall philosophy of the organization.

*Company employees.* To get the most balanced view of the employer's culture, interview employees with different perspectives. Try to talk with employees in a variety of departments and at different levels—white collar, blue collar, pink collar—of the organization. Also use the suggestions on page 10 to find appropriate subjects. Also talk with the target's college recruiters and interview the personnel department staff.

*On-site observation.* If possible, visit the organization. One glimpse of a working environment can reveal more about an organization's culture than dozens of phone calls. Most not-for-profit organizations will welcome your visit. Some companies give public tours, and many more will give a private tour to a prospective employee. When you are touring, observe the working environment:

> Are senior managers segregated from the rest of the office, or is there an open-plan environment?

> Are people generally open and friendly, or is there an air of suspicion or resentment? Would you want to work with the people you see?

> Do people seem genuinely enthusiastic about the organization?

> Do employees dress with conformity? Would you be comfortable with similar attire?

> Is the work area comfortable? Would you like to work there?

Although it is important to learn what the organization says about itself in its public statements as well as what its employees say about it, you will not want to stop there. Also learn what outside observers have to say about the employer's culture. You can use the same information sources on pages 3-11 to learn more about the organization's culture.

# CHAPTER 18

# A SOCIAL CONSCIENCE

)•(( )•( )•(( )•((

For some job hunters, the social conscience of their employer is extremely important. You may be unwilling to work for a company—even an extremely successful company that treats its employees very well—if it has a record of irresponsible environmental pollution or if it sells products that it knows to be dangerous to consumers. If you are interested in making a better world as well as making money for yourself or your employer's stockholders, you will have to pick your employer carefully.

)•(( )•( )•( )•(( )•(( )•( )•(( )•( )•(( )•( )•(( )•( )•(( )•( )•(( )•( )•(( )•( )•(( )•( )•(( )•( )•(( )•( )•(( )•(( )•((

Elsa, an MBA student nearing graduation, was looking forward to moving from her low-paying job with a public-interest group to a fast-track position in international finance. After several interviews with large companies, she felt discouraged. The companies seemed to have only one objective—to make the most money possible—and she found that distasteful. Elsa decided that she preferred to work for human rather than commercial causes. She recognized that she was unsuited to international finance and redirected her job search to government and nonprofit organizations with an international scope. She was willing to accept a lower salary in order to work for what she perceived to be the public good.

)•(( )•( )•(( )•( )•(( )•( )•(( )•( )•(( )•( )•(( )•( )•(( )•( )•(( )•( )•(( )•( )•(( )•( )•(( )•( )•(( )•( )•(( )•( )•(( )•( )•(( )•( )•((

The single best reference for assessing the social responsibility records of companies is *Shopping for a Better World* (Council on Economic Priorities), a compilation in a chart-style format, of companies rated in a variety of areas, among them, charitable contributions, community and family outreach, environmental responsibility, employee safety, and equal employment opportunity. The companies mentioned below are cited by the Council on Economic Priorities for their excellent performance. Also provided are the sources that will help you learn more about your target employer's record in each category of social responsibility.

# CHARITABLE CONTRIBUTIONS

Companies with an excellent record for charitable donations are:

Avon

Ben & Jerry's Homemade Ice Cream

Colgate-Palmolive

General Mills

Newman's Own

Quaker Oats

Tom's of Maine

You can learn about any company's philanthropic gifts from the public-relations office because most companies are proud of their contributions to charities. There may be a list of charities already prepared. If not, ask for the person in charge of charitable giving.

Useful publications would include:

*Corporate 500: The Directory of Corporate Philanthropy* (Gale Research)—Gives descriptive details of the philanthropy, whether through direct-giving programs or foundation grants, of six hundred companies. Three-year comparisons are provided so that a company's trends in giving can be determined.

*The Foundation Directory* (The Foundation Center)—Lists 7,521 foundations with assets over $1 million or that gave $100,000 or more in the latest year; includes independent and company-sponsored foundations.

*Shopping for a Better World* (Council on Economic Priorities). See above.

The following companies are considered to have made significant contributions to positive community action.

| | |
|---|---|
| Anheuser-Busch | Eastman Kodak |
| Chevron | Newman's Own |
| Clorox | Campbell Soup |
| Dow Chemical | Hershey Food |

Information about community programs sponsored by a company may come from various sources. The public relations department, because some companies make substantial contributions to programs in their immediate area and the public-relations department should be able to tell you about programs they have sponsored. Local charitable groups, such as the United Way office or other major charities in the area, will be able to tell you how the company has reacted to their requests, and what local charities the company supports. Local corporate giving may have been covered by the press. Call the local paper and ask for the business editor.

## ENVIRONMENTAL AWARENESS

Increasing numbers of companies are developing environmental awareness in terms of their products and manufacturing processes. These companies are considered to have exceptionally responsible environmental policies:

| | |
|---|---|
| The Body Shop | Johnson & Johnson |
| Celestial Seasonings | S.C. Johnson |
| Church & Dwight | Kellogg |
| Clorox | Marcal Paper Mills |

The environmental record of many other companies is mentioned in *Shopping for a better World,* referred to earlier. You might also check Cohn, Susan, *Green at Work* (Island Press), a directory of business careers with an environmental focus and the names of more than two hundred companies that have environmental policies and programs or offer environmental products or services. Other sources of information about the company's environmental record might include regional offices of the Environmental Protection Agency and local environmental groups.

# Regional Environmental Protection Agency Offices

The purpose of the Environmental Protection Agency (EPA) is to control pollution in the air and water, caused by solid waste, pesticides, radiation, and toxic substances. The job hunter can learn about the company's record of compliance—or its violations—by talking to the individual who inspects the facility. Contact the regional EPA office in the jurisdiction of your target company.

)I·(( )·(( )·(( )·(( )·(( )·(( )·(( )·(( )·(( )·(( )·(( )·(( )·(( )·(( )·(( )·(( )·(( )·(( )·(( )·(( )·(( )·(( )·(( )·(( )·(( )·(( )·(( )·(( )·(( )·(( )·((

*Region I* (Maine, Vermont,
    New Hampshire, Massachusetts,
    Connecticut, Rhode Island)
John F. Kennedy Federal Building
One Congress Street
Boston, MA 02203
617-565-2713

*Region II* (New York, New Jersey,
    Puerto Rico, Virgin Islands)
26 Federal Plaza
New York, NY 10278
212-264-2515

*Region III* (Pennsylvania, West Virginia,
    Virginia, Delaware,
    District of Columbia)
841 Chestnut Building
Philadelphia, PA 19107
215-597-9370

*Region IV* (Florida, Georgia,
    Mississippi, Alabama, Tennessee,
    Kentucky, North Carolina,
    South Carolina)
345 Courtland Street, NE
Atlanta, GA 30365
404-347-3004

*Region V* (Minnesota, Wisconsin,
    Michigan, Indiana, Illinois, Ohio)
77 W. Jackson Boulevard
Chicago, IL 60604
312-353-2072

*Region VI* (New Mexico, Texas,
    Oklahoma, Arkansas, Louisiana)
1445 Ross Avenue, Suite 1200
Dallas TX 75202
214-655-6444

*Region VII* (Nebraska, Kansas,
    Missouri, Iowa)
726 Minnesota Avenue
Kansas City, KS 66101
913-551-7000

*Region VIII* (Montana, North Dakota,
    South Dakota, Wyoming, Utah,
    Colorado)
999 18th Street, Suite 500
Denver, CO 80202
303-293-1692

*Region IX* (California, Nevada, Arizona, Hawaii, American Samoa, Guam)
75 Hawthorn Street
San Francisco, CA 94105
415-744-1020

*Region X* (Alaska, Washington, Oregon, Idaho)
1200 6th Avenue
Seattle, WA 98101
206-553-4973

## Local Environmental Groups

Local watchdog groups monitor environmental violations of companies in their area. To learn of the local group nearest your company, check with the national organizations listed below, or contact the local chamber of commerce or newspaper.

)•(( )•(( )•(( )•(( )•(( )•(( )•(( )•(( )•(( )•(( )•(( )•(( )•(( )•(( )•(( )•(( )•(( )•(( )•(( )•(( )•(( )•(( )•(( )•((

**Greenpeace, U.S.A**
1436 U Street
Washington DC 20009
202-462-1177

**Point Foundation**
(publishes *Whole Earth Review*)
27 Gate Five Road
Sausalito, CA 94965
415-332-1716

**Sierra Club**
730 Polk Street
San Francisco, CA 94109
415-776-2211

**U.S. Environment and Resources Council**
1584 Keswick Place
Annapolis, MD 21401
410-721-1399

**Wilderness Watch**
P.O. Box 782
Sturgeon Bay, WI 54235
414-743-1238

**World Environment Center**
419 Park Avenue, Suite 1800
New York, NY 10016
212-683-4700

# OCCUPATIONAL SAFETY

There are some excellent sources for information about occupational safety.

## National Safety Council

*Work Injury & Illness Rating* (National Safety Council) is a booklet in which hundreds of companies are cited for having the best safety record in individual industries. A few of many companies mentioned frequently for their good safety record are Kraft, Dupont, 3M Companies, Texas Industries, M&M/Mars, Johnson & Johnson, and John Deere.

## Occupational Health and Safety Administration

The Occupational Health and Safety Administration (OSHA) is responsible for monitoring safety violations in the workplace. You can learn about violations of your target company by contacting the appropriate regional office. It is better to interview the inspector responsible for monitoring the company, rather than request expensive and voluminous records.

)•(( )•( )•(( )•(( )•(( )•(( )•(( )•(( )•(( )•(( )•(( )•(( )•(( )•(( )•(( )•(( )•(( )•(( )•(( )•(( )•(( )•(( )•(( )•(( )•(( )•(( )•(( )•(( )•(( )•(( )•((

### Regional OSHA Offices

*Region I* (Maine, Vermont,
    New Hampshire, Massachusetts,
    Connecticut, Rhode Island)
133 Portland Street, 1st Floor
Boston, MA 02114
617-565-7164

*Region II* (New York, New Jersey,
    Puerto Rico)
201 Varick Street, Room 670
New York, NY 10014
212-337-2325

*Region III* (Pennsylvania, West Virginia,
    Virginia, Delaware, District of
    Columbia, Maryland)
3535 Market Street, Suite 2100
Philadelphia, PA 19104
215-596-1201

*Region IV* (Florida, Georgia, Mississippi,
    Alabama, Tennessee, Kentucky,
    North Carolina, South Carolina)
1375 Peachtree Street, Suite 587
Atlanta, GA 30367
404-347-3573

*Region V* (Minnesota, Wisconsin,
    Michigan, Indiana, Illinois, Ohio)
230 S. Dearborn Street
Chicago, IL 60604
312-353-2220

*Region VI* (New Mexico, Texas, Oklahoma,
    Arkansas, Louisiana)
525 Griffin Street, Room 602
Dallas, TX 75202
214-767-4731

*Region VII* (Nebraska, Kansas, Missouri, Iowa)
911 Walnut Avenue, Room 406
Kansas City, MO 64106
816-374-5861

*Region VIII* (Montana, North Dakota, South Dakota, Wyoming, Utah, Colorado)
1961 Stout Street
Denver, CO 80204
303-844-3061

*Region IX* (California, Nevada, Arizona, Hawaii)
71 Stevenson Street, Room 415
San Francisco, CA 94105
415-744-6670

*Region X* (Alaska, Washington, Oregon, Idaho)
111 3rd Avenue, Suite 715
Seattle, WA 98101
206-553-5930

## Local Health Departments

County and town health departments also monitor the safety of the workplace. You can find the appropriate department by contacting the mayor's office. Ask which local agencies are responsible for gathering information on violations of safety regulations.

## Local Union Offices

Unions keep a close watch over the safety records of companies whose employees they represent, and also of the companies they have unsuccessfully unionized. You can ask the switchboard or personnel department of your target employer for the name of its unions, and then call them directly to ask what they know about company employee safety policies and practices. Unions are also listed in *Encyclopedia of Associations*. A few of the unions you should know about are listed below.

)⊣( )⊣( )⊣( )⊣( )⊣( )⊣( )⊣( )⊣( )⊣( )⊣( )⊣( )⊣( )⊣( )⊣( )⊣( )⊣( )⊣( )⊣( )⊣( )⊣( )⊣( )⊣(

AFL-CIO
815 16th Street NW
Washington, DC 20006
202-637-5000

Association of Theatrical Press Agents and Managers
165 W. 46th Street
New York, NY 10036
212-719-3666

Communication Workers of America
501 Third Street NW
Washington, CD 20001
202-434-1100

Federation of Nurses and Health Professionals
555 New Jersey Avenue, NW
Washington, DC 20001
202-879-4491

International Union of Allied Novelty and
    Production Workers (Toys)
25 Roslyn Road
Mineola, NY 11501
212-889-1212

The Newspaper Guild
8611 2nd Avenue
Silver Spring, MD 20912
301-585-2990

United Auto Workers
8000 E. Jefferson
Detroit, MI 48214
313-926-5000

United Rubber, Cork, Linoleum and
    Plastic Workers of America
570 White Pond Drive
Akron, OH 44320
216-869-0320

United Steelworkers of America
5 Gateway Center
Pittsburgh, PA 15222
412-562-2400

United Textile Workers of America
P.O. Box 749
Voorhees, NJ 08043
609-772-9699

Utility Workers Union of America
815 16th Street, NW, Suite 605
Washington, DC 20006
202-347-8105

## Local Newspapers

Major industrial accidents, or a poor record of occupational safety, may be reported in the local press. Check with the business editors. To identify the newspaper, call the area library or chamber of commerce, or consult *Editor and Publisher Yearbook,* which is available in most libraries.

# EQUAL EMPLOYMENT OPPORTUNITIES

The following companies are considered to have excellent records for promoting women and minorities, or for other equal opportunity issues:

BE & K
Ben & Jerry's Homemade Ice Cream
Beth Israel Hospital, Boston
Federal Express
Fel-Pro
First Federal Bank of California

IBM
Inland Steel
Los Angeles Dodgers
Mary Kay Cosmetics
Morrison & Foerster
Nordstrom

| | |
|---|---|
| Patagonia | Polaroid |
| Pitney Bowes | Xerox |

There are three principal sources about the treatment of women and minorities in any organization.

### Equal Employment Opportunity Commission

The purpose of the Equal Employment Opportunity Commission is to eliminate discrimination based on race, color, religion, sex, national origin, or age in all terms and conditions of employment. Complaints regarding employers are filed with the commission's field offices. To find the field office with jurisdiction over your company, contact the Commission at 1801 L Street, NW, Washington, DC 20507, 202-663-4637.

### State and Local Equal Opportunity Offices

Most states and some localities have an employment office that receives similar complaints against employers. To find the correct office, contact the county government telephone operator in the county seat or the state government operator in the capital city.

### Local Newspapers

Local newspapers may publish exposés on the treatment of women, minorities, and other employees in local companies. Contact the business editor.

## OTHER ISSUES

Other issues may be important to you.

Does the company use live animals for testing its products?

Does the business produce or promote habit-forming substances?

Does the organization support political causes with which you disagree?

There is a public-interest group that follows almost any social or public interest issue that concerns you. If you use your imagination as you search the key-word index in the *Encyclopedia of Associations,* you are certain to locate one or more organizations that can provide information about your prospective employer's record.

# PART V

# GEOGRAPHY AND THE QUALITY OF LIFE

□□□□□□

Your decision about employment must go hand in hand with your preferences about where you want to live. If you do not find good career opportunities in an area where you would enjoy living, you will have to make some decisions about where and how to compromise.

□□□□□□□□□□□□□□□□□□□□□□□□□□□□□□□□□□

If you are currently unemployed, a job may take precedence, as it did for Granger. A recent Ph.D. graduate from a Boston university, Granger very much wanted to stay in Boston to teach. After four months of unsuccessful searching, he was ready to "follow the jobs." At the end of 1991, when much of the United States was experiencing stagnant or negative job growth, the Bureau of Labor Statistics reported job growth in educational occupations in both Nebraska and Oregon, states in which Granger had some interest. After a few weeks of interviewing, he located a job with a college in Oregon. Increasing numbers of job seekers may find themselves fleeing the faltering Northeast for the greener fields of the Southwest, the mountain states, or the Deep South.

If you are comfortably employed, you may choose to compromise job opportunity to live where you prefer. Kathy and Gretchen were friends and co-workers in a university counseling office in Washington, D.C. Both were looking for career advancement and began their job search at the same time. Kathy was ultimately offered an excellent position at a university in western Ohio. The salary and opportunities for growth were terrific, but the small town's atmosphere was not her cup of tea. After carefully assessing her priorities, Kathy decided to accept the job, putting her career above her life-style.

Gretchen's job offer came from New York City. Although she was offered double her current salary, she declined the position. She decided she was not ready to trade the relatively comfortable commuting, quality housing, and relaxing life-style available in Washington for New York's career and cultural advantages.

◻◻◻◻◻◻◻◻◻◻◻◻◻◻◻◻◻◻◻◻◻◻◻◻◻◻◻◻◻

Whatever your priorities, it is important to assess how the region where you want to live and work will affect your life-style. For example:

- The cost of living is much lower in some parts of the country than it is in others.

- Some areas' public schools offer excellent education programs, whereas the decline of other public school systems almost mandates expensive private education for tots to teens.

- The value of homes appreciates rapidly in some regions and stagnates in others.

- Various communities offer different amenities—spectator sports, cultural events, natural beauty, parks, recreational programs, and so on.

If you're already committed to a particular region, because of its superb job opportunities, family ties, or other reasons, you can bypass this section. If you are not set on living in a particular city or region of the country, you will want to choose your home base after careful research and reflection. The following chapters give you the tools you need to select the best locations for your particular interests and needs and compare the assets and liabilities of *any* areas that interest you.

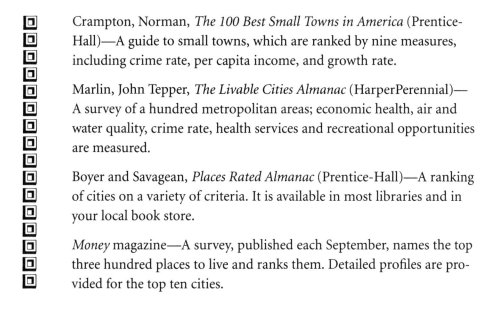

# THE BEST PLACES

Although everyone has personal preferences about desirable places to live, four publications have taken a survey approach to determining the so-called best places and provide a quick overview of communities considered to be desirable.

Crampton, Norman, *The 100 Best Small Towns in America* (Prentice-Hall)—A guide to small towns, which are ranked by nine measures, including crime rate, per capita income, and growth rate.

Marlin, John Tepper, *The Livable Cities Almanac* (HarperPerennial)— A survey of a hundred metropolitan areas; economic health, air and water quality, crime rate, health services and recreational opportunities are measured.

Boyer and Savagean, *Places Rated Almanac* (Prentice-Hall)—A ranking of cities on a variety of criteria. It is available in most libraries and in your local book store.

*Money* magazine—A survey, published each September, names the top three hundred places to live and ranks them. Detailed profiles are provided for the top ten cities.

## CHAPTER 19

# A GEOGRAPHIC FOCUS
# FOR OCCUPATIONS

□□□

It is important to understand that many occupations cluster around specific industries and in particular regions of the country—advertising executives in New York, wine makers in northern California, oceanographers near the coasts, mining engineers in the mountains. In fact, a job with dismal prospects in one part of the country, or even in the country as a whole, may have excellent prospects in a particular region. For example, lobbying and government contract consulting, which thrive in Washington, D.C. and state capitals, can hardly be found outside capital cities.

If you are already committed to living in a particular part of the country, go directly to page 194 to find the best career opportunities in that area. If you are flexible about job location, and want to make the most of your career by selecting the location that provides the best opportunities, this chapter tells you how. You will also learn how to target industries that promise opportunities for your occupation.

You can use many of the statistical sources described in chapter 4 to determine which geographical areas and industries are most promising for particular professions. For example, the *Occupational Outlook Handbook* reports that millwrights, on the average, earn about 18 percent more in wages in Indianapolis than in Pittsburgh, and that maintenance machinists in San Francisco earn nearly 60 percent more than their counterparts in Greenville, South Carolina. *Employment and Earnings* provides labor statistics on two hundred local areas. U.S. Labor Department wage surveys also provide information about regional differences in pay levels. You can also use the *Area Wage Surveys* for data on regional differences in pay.

In order to get more precise, reliable information, you also need to contact sources that specialize in your profession. The sources described below will provide, or guide you to, information about not only national, but also regional- and industry-level statistics and projections.

## PROFESSIONAL ASSOCIATIONS

If yours is a white-collar occupation, one of your best sources for information about nationwide career opportunities is the appropriate professional association. For almost any occupation you can imagine there is an international or national organization of its members. These organizations exist not only for doctors and lawyers, but also for dental hygienists, market researchers, book indexers, chemical marketers, and hundreds of other professions. The purpose of these associations is to guide and support the interests of their members. They collect massive amounts of data, including information on where the jobs are, regional salaries, and starting salaries.

Some of this information is collected through surveys of the members. Other data are gathered from government and private sources. Remember that, behind all the statistics produced by the association, there are people who are experts in your target profession. The most efficient way to research your profession is to interview those experts directly.

- *Finding the experts.* When you contact the association, ask to speak with the association's director, the journal editor, or someone on the research staff. If the association has a library, you may also want to interview the librarian. Keep in mind that individuals who have had actual experience in the profession are likely to be more helpful than someone whose job with the association is strictly administrative.

- *Asking the experts.* In your interviews, try to get insights into the dynamics and changes of the particular profession, as well as the best industries and geographic areas in which to work. Ask about the areas where there are the highest concentrations of people in the profession, where the salaries are highest, and where job mobility and advancement are greatest. Ask where, as a member of the occupation, you are likely to prosper, and where there might be special opportunities. For example, for physicians, the best income opportunities usually are in the cities, but many small communities are prepared to offer tremendous financial incentives to doctors, including subsidies, offices, homes, and more.

• *Consulting the publications.* Most professional associations also publish reports and journals devoted in whole or part to the profession. They can be found in a large library or ordered through the association. If you prefer to research published materials before interviewing experts, these journals are a good starting point. They provide basic information as well as insights that you can build on in later interviews.

For example, *Internal Auditor,* the journal of the Institute of Internal Auditors, surveys the members annually to learn about trends in the job market. A recent survey revealed that internal auditors with an accounting background employed by large organizations in large cities earn approximately 25 percent more in salary than do internal auditors employed by small organizations in small cities. It also revealed that industries such as public transit/transportation, entertainment, agriculture, distribution, and communications accounted for the largest turnover of internal auditors, while internal auditors employed by the government showed the least turnover.

Likewise, the National Society of Professional Engineers (703-684-2800) ranks pay for metropolitan areas. In the *NPSE 1993 Income and Salary Survey,* for example, Washington, D.C. had dropped from sixth to tenth place among the highest paying metropolitan areas for engineers. The median income of $66,000 still ranked above the national median of $60,000 and had risen $1,700 in one year. Petroleum engineers, with a median income of $72,000 earned the most; agricultural engineers came in at the bottom of the scale with a median income of $55,000.

• *Interviewing the members.* Ask your contacts at the professional association for referrals to those of the association's members who have expertise in particular aspects of the profession that interest you and are in the location that you are targeting.

• *Finding the associations.* Two directories, available in most libraries, provide the best description of most professional associations in the United States.

*Encyclopedia of Associations* (Gale Research)—This is a directory of thousands of national trade and professional associations. It includes some state and local associations as well. The index is organized alphabetically by the main words in the organizations' titles. Do not be surprised if you find several associations that appear to cover your profession. Look at the descriptive entry of each to determine which you wish to contact. You will find information about the association's size, location, publications, activities, and more.

*National Trade and Professional Associations in the United States* (Columbia Books)—This directory also describes national offices of trade and professional associations and labor unions. Because it is less expensive and more compact than the *Encyclopedia of Associations,* it is preferred by some libraries. It will serve your purpose, because it includes all the major associations.

## SPECIAL-INTEREST ASSOCIATIONS

Some special-interest associations provide career information. For example, the Foundation Center publishes a career guide, *Careers for Dreamers and Doers: A Guide to Management Careers in the Voluntary Sector.*

Even more helpful are the opinions of professionals at these associations. When Fred approached the World Future Society for insights on trends in management and business, he learned that logistics management would be an expanding field. He created his own MBA curriculum in logistics management, and was amply rewarded. Before he was halfway through his degree program, employers were calling the university's career service office, asking for MBAs with logistics management expertise. There is now an established track of logistics management at his university.

## Unions

For information about blue-collar occupations, labor unions are among your best resources. In order to represent their members efficiently, unions must closely monitor the outlook for each occupation they represent. Many unions build databases to track the movements, benefits, salaries, and opportunities of their members. In addition, unions are especially adept at spotting technological innovations that could affect their members' jobs. Because local union groups share resources with their counterparts nationwide, they are keenly aware of wage levels and benefits in different areas of the country. Start out by contacting the union at its national headquarters in order to get the widest snapshot of the occupation. If you are targeting a particular geographic area, ask the national union representative for the name and telephone number of the local union shop. Then talk with a local representative about the opportunities—and problems—in that area.

To learn which union represents your occupation, consult the *Encyclopedia of Associations* or the *National Trade and Professional Associations in the United States.* Listed on page 182 are some of the largest unions, including the AFL-CIO.

# PLACEMENT ORGANIZATIONS

Many professional placement organizations have information about the best locations to practice certain professions. For example, Robert Half International Inc. regularly conducts salary surveys in the accounting, finance, banking, and information services fields. Their 1993 survey reveals that professionals in those fields in Florida earn an average of 10 percent less than the national average, and that, in Alaska, wages exceed the national average by 10 percent. To find a placement organization in your field, consult one of these associations:

▣▣▣▣▣▣▣▣▣▣▣▣▣▣▣▣▣▣▣▣▣▣▣▣▣▣▣▣▣▣

Association of Outplacement
Consulting Firms
364 Parsippany Road
Parsippany, NJ 07054
201-887-6667

Association of Executive
Search Consultants
230 Park Avenue, Suite 1549
New York, NY 10169
212-949-9556

**National Association of Personnel Services**
3133 Mount Vernon Avenue
Alexandria, VA 22305
703-684-0180

If you contact private employment service for information, it is likely that they will want to place you in a job. Remember to use these services intelligently. They provide a valuable service, but because most make their commission from the employer upon your initial placement, some firms care more about placing you quickly than optimizing your opportunities. Use the techniques in this book to research and evaluate the industry, the employer, and the job before you take the plunge.

# CHAPTER 20

# TARGETING
# A PARTICULAR PLACE

□ □ □

I f, because of family responsibilities or preferred life-style, you are committed to a particular geographic area, a little research can help you determine either which occupations are most promising in that area (if you can be flexible about a career) or how your occupation is faring (if you are committed to a career).

□□□□□□□□□□□□□□□□□□□□□□□□□□□□□□

If you are committed to a particular area, you may have to be more flexible about the work you do. Ginger was a training specialist with a Fortune 500 company in Pittsburgh until her husband was offered partial ownership in a thriving company in a small Montana town. Both Ginger and her husband thought the experience would be good for them and their children, and decided to make the move. Ginger investigated the opportunities for corporate training managers within commuting distance of their new community and found them to be very limited. Committed to their new location, she decided to look for a new career to which she could transfer her experience. She began by finding out which careers were prospering in the local area. Because of high unemployment in the community, the employment counseling field was booming. Within a few weeks, Ginger found a position in employment counseling and retraining.

State and local government agencies and private organizations monitor the employment situation in their jurisdictions. To learn about the outlook for your career, or others, you should start with the sources within your chosen region. For example, if you know you want to live somewhere in Minnesota, the state-level organizations will be very helpful. If you are absolutely committed to Minneapolis, the city-level sources should provide the information you need.

# STATE-LEVEL JOB RESEARCH

Whether you want to learn about opportunities for your occupation in a given state, or discover the fastest growing occupations within the state, these are the organizations and publications to consult:

## State Employment Security Agencies

If you are looking for information about the growth of your occupation within a particular state, you should contact the State Employment Security Agency. Most of these state agencies develop employment projections for area occupations, detailing hiring and job-growth prospects for specific occupations. You can usually subscribe to a free agency newsletter that describes the trends. The newsletters also have tips on job-training programs and other employment news.

▣▣▣▣▣▣▣▣▣▣▣▣▣▣▣▣▣▣▣▣▣▣▣▣▣▣▣▣

**Alabama**
Director, Labor Market Information
Department of Industrial Relations
649 Monroe Street, Room 422
Montgomery, AL 36130
205-242-8855; Fax: 205-242-2543

**Alaska**
Chief, Research and Analysis
Department of Labor
P.O. Box 25501
Juneau, AK 99802-5501
907-465-6022; Fax: 907-465-2101

**Arizona**
Research Administrator,
Department of Economic Security
1789 West Jefferson
P.O. Box 6123, Site Code 733A
Phoenix, AZ 85005
602-542-3871; Fax: 602-542-6474

**Arkansas**
State and Labor Market Information
Employment Security Division
P.O. Box 2981
Little Rock, AR 72203
501-682-1543; Fax: 501-682-3713

**California**
Chief, Employment Data &
    Research Division
Employment Development Department
P.O. Box 942880, MIC 57
Sacramento, CA 94280-0001
916-262-2176; Fax: 916-262-2490

**Colorado**
Director, Labor Market Information
393 S. Harlan, 2d Floor
Lakewood, CO 80226
303-937-4947; Fax: 303-937-4945

**Connecticut**
Director, Research and Information
Employment Security Division
Labor Department
200 Folly Brook Boulevard
Wethersfield, CT 06109
203-566-2120; Fax: 203-566-1519

**Delaware**
Chief, Office of Occupational
    and Labor Market Information
Department of Labor
University Plaza, Building D
P.O. Box 9029
Newark, DE 19702-9029
302-368-6962; Fax: 302-368-6748

**District of Columbia**
Chief of Labor Market Information
Department of Employment Services
500 C Street NW, Room 201
Washington, DC 20001
202-639-1642; Fax: 202-639-1765

**Florida**
Chief, Bureau of
    Labor Market Information
Department of Labor &
    Employment Security
2012 Capitol Circle SE, Room 200
Hartman Building
Tallahassee, FL 32399-0674
904-488-1048; Fax: 904-488-2558

**Georgia**
Director, Labor Information System
Department of Labor
223 Courtland Street NE
Atlanta, GA 30303
404-656-3177; Fax: 404-651-9568

**Hawaii**
Chief, Research and Statistics Office
Department of Labor and
    Industrial Relations
830 Punchbowl Street, Room 304
Honolulu, HI 96813
808-586-8999; Fax: 808-586-9022

**Idaho**
Chief, Research and Analysis
Department of Employment
317 Main Street
Boise, ID 83735
208-334-6169; Fax: 208-334-6300

**Illinois**
Director, Economic Information
    and Analysis
Department of Employment Security
401 S. State Street, 2 South
Chicago, IL 60605
312-793-2316; Fax: 312-793-6245

**Indiana**
Director, Labor Market Information
Department of Employment
    & Training Services
10 N. Senate Avenue
Indianapolis, IN 46204
317-232-8456; Fax: 317-232-6950

**Iowa**
Supervisor, Audit and
    Analysis Department
    Department of Employment Services
1000 E. Grand Avenue
Des Moines, IA 50319
515-281-8181; Fax: 515-281-8195

**Kansas**
Chief, Labor Market Information Services
Department of Human Resources
401 Topeka Avenue
Topeka, KS 66603
913-296-5058; Fax: 913-296-0179

**Kentucky**
Manager, Labor Market Research
    and Analysis
Department for Employment Services
275 E. Main Street
Frankfort, KY 40621
502-564-7976; Fax: 502-564-7452

**Louisiana**
Director, Research and Statistics Division
Department of Employment and Training
P.O. Box 94094
Baton Rouge, LA 70804-9094
504-342-3141; Fax: 504-342-9193

**Maine**
Director, Division of Economic
    Analysis and Research
Department of Labor
Bureau of Employment Services
20 Union Street
August, ME 04330
207-289-2271; Fax: 207-289-2947

**Maryland**
Director, Office of Labor Market Analysis
    and Information
Department of Economic and
    Employment Development
1100 N. Eutaw Street, Room 601
Baltimore, MD 21201
410-333-5000; Fax: 410-333-7121

**Massachusetts**
Director of Research
Division of Employment Security
19 Staniford Street, 2d Floor
Boston, MA 02114
617-727-6868; Fax: 617-727-0315

**Michigan**
Director, Bureau of Research and Statistics
Employment Security Commission
7310 Woodward Avenue
Detroit, MI 48202
313-876-5505; Fax: 313-876-5587

**Minnesota**
Director, Research and Statistical Services
Department of Jobs and Training
390 N. Robert Street, 5th Floor
St. Paul, MN 55101
612-296-6546; Fax: 612-296-0994

**Mississippi**
Chief, Labor Market
    Information Department
Employment Security Commission
P.O. Box 1699
Jackson, MS 39215-1699
601-961-7424; Fax: 601-961-7405

**Missouri**
Chief, Research and Analysis
Division of Employment Security
P.O. Box 59
Jefferson City, MO 65104
314-751-3591; Fax: 314-751-5620

**Montana**
Chief, Research and Analysis
Department of Labor and Industry
P.O. Box 1728
Helena, MT 59624
406-444-2430; Fax: 406-444-2638

**Nebraska**
Research Administrator,
    Labor Market Information
Department of Labor
550 S. 16th Street
P.O. Box 94600
Lincoln, NE 68509
402-471-9964; Fax: 402-471-2318

**Nevada**
Chief, Employment Security Research
Employment Security Department
500 E. 3rd Street
Carson City, NV 89713
702-687-4550; Fax: 702-687-3424

**New Hampshire**
Director, Labor Market Information
Department of Employment Security
32 S. Main Street
Concord, NH 03301-4587
603-228-4123; Fax: 603-228-4172

**New Jersey**
Assistant Commissioner,
    Policy and Planning
Department of Labor
John Fitch Plaza, Room 607
Trenton, NJ 08625-0056
609-292-2643; Fax: 609-292-6692

**New Mexico**
Chief, Economic Research
    and Analysis Bureau
Department of Labor
401 Broadway Boulevard NE
P.O. Box 1928
Albuquerque, NM 87103
505-841-8645; Fax: 505-841-8421

**New York**
Director, Division of Research
    and Statistics
Department of Labor
State Campus, Building 12, Room 400
Albany, NY 12240-0020
518-457-6181; Fax: 518-457-0620

**North Carolina**
Director, Labor Market
    Information Division
Employment Security Commission
P.O. Box 25903
Raleigh, NC 27611
919-733-2936; Fax: 919-733-8662

**North Dakota**
Director, Research and Statistics
Job Service North Dakota
P.O. Box 1537
Bismarck, ND 58502
701-224-2868; Fax: 701-224-4000

**Ohio**
Labor Market Information Division
Bureau of Employment Services
145 S. Front Street
Columbus, OH 43215
614-752-9494; Fax: 614-752-9621

**Oklahoma**
Director, Research Division
Employment Security Commission
308 Will Rogers Memorial Office Building
Oklahoma City, OK 73105
405-557-7116; Fax: 405-557-7256

**Oregon**
Assistant Administrator,
   Research and Statistics
Oregon Employment Division
875 Union Street NE
Salem, OR 97311
503-378-3220; Fax: 503-373-7515

**Pennsylvania**
Director, Research and Statistics Division
Department of Labor and Industry
1216 Labor and Industry Building
Harrisburg, PA 17121
717-787-3265; Fax: 717-772-2168

**Puerto Rico**
Director, Research and Statistics Division
Department of Labor
   and Human Resources
505 Munoz Rivera Avenue, 20th Floor
Hato Rey, PR 00918
809-754-5385; Fax: 809-751-7934

**Rhode Island**
Administrator, Labor Market Information
   and Management Services
Department of Employment and Training
101 Friendship Street
Providence, RI 02903-3740
401-277-3730; Fax: 401-277-2731

**South Carolina**
Director, Labor Market Information
Employment Security Commission
P.O. Box 995
Columbia, SC 29202
803-737-2660; Fax: 803-737-2838

**South Dakota**
Director, Labor Information Center
Department of Labor
P.O. Box 4730
Aberdeen, SD 57402-4730
605-622-2314; Fax: 605-622-2322

**Tennessee**
Director, Research and Statistics Division
Department of Employment Security
500 James Robertson Parkway, 11th Floor
Nashville, TN 37245-1000
615-741-2284; Fax: 615-741-3203

**Texas**
Director, Economic Research and Analysis
Texas Employment Commission
15th and Congress Avenues, Room 208T
Austin, TX 78778
512-463-2616; Fax: 512-475-1241

**Utah**
Director, Labor Market
 Information and Research
Department of Employment Security
140 E. 300 South
P.O. Box 11249
Salt Lake City, UT 84147
801-536-7400; Fax: 801-536-7420

**Vermont**
Director, Policy and Information
Department of Employment and Training
5 Green Mountain Drive
P.O. Box 488
Montpelier, VT 05602
802-229-0311; Fax: 802-828-4022

**Virgin Islands**
Chief, Research and Analysis
Department of Labor
P.O. Box 3159
St. Thomas, VI 00801
809-776-3700; Fax: 809-774-5908

**Virginia**
Director, Economic Information
 Service Division
Virginia Employment Commission
P.O. Box 1358
Richmond, VA 23211
804-786-7496; Fax: 804-786-7844

**Washington**
Labor Market Information
Employment Security Department
212 Maple Park, Mail Stop KG-11
Olympia, WA 98504-5311
206-438-4804; Fax: 206-438-4846

**West Virginia**
Assistant Director,
 Labor and Economic Research
Department of Employment Programs
112 California Avenue
Charleston, WV 25305-0112
304-538-2660; Fax: 304-348-0301

**Wisconsin**
Director, Labor Market Information
 Bureau
Department of Industry, Labor and
 Human Relations
201 E. Washington Avenue, Room 221
P.O. Box 7944
Madison, WI 53707
608-266-5843; Fax: 608-267-0330

**Wyoming**
Manager, Research and Planning
Division of Administration
Department of Employment
P.O. Box 2760
Casper, WY 82602
307-265-6715; Fax: 307-265-6717

## State Occupational Information Coordinating Committees

To learn about the projected demand for your occupation and selected training programs in a particular state, contact the State Occupational Information Coordinating Committee (SOICC). These committees were mandated by the 1976 Education Act amendments to provide occupational and training information across the country. Many of these state committees operate computerized databases, called Occupational Information Systems (OIS), of labor-market and occupational information. The systems contain extensive state and local labor-market information, including current and projected demand for workers by occupation and information on the current supply of graduates of related training and educational programs. Many of the states' systems also contain information on working conditions, educational requirements, and wages and benefits of specific occupations as well as information about training programs and educational institutions offered by the state. Information developed from the data can help identify major changes and trends in local, state, and regional labor markets.

Many other states offer similar services. Individuals seeking career information are encouraged to write or visit the offices below. You may be referred to a local office that is more convenient to your location. Trained counselors are employed by these state agencies to help you analyze the data you obtain.

▣▣▣▣▣▣▣▣▣▣▣▣▣▣▣▣▣▣▣▣▣▣▣▣▣▣▣▣▣▣

**Alabama**
Alabama OICC
401 Adams Avenue
P.O. Box 5600
Montgomery, AL 36130
205-242-2990

**Alaska**
Alaska Department of Labor
Research and Analysis Section
P.O. Box 25501
Juneau, AK 99802
907-465-4518

**Arizona**
Arizona State OICC
P.O. Box 6123, Site Code 897J
1789 W. Jefferson Street,
1st Floor North
Phoenix, AZ 85005
602-547-6466

**Arkansas**
Arkansas OICC/Arkansas Employment
   Security Division
Employment and Training Services
P.O. Box 2981
Little Rock, AR 72203
501-682-3159

**California**
California OICC
1116 9th Street, Lower Level
P.O. Box 944222
Sacramento, CA 94244-2220
916-323-6544

**Colorado**
Colorado OICC
State Board Community College
1391 Speer Boulevard, Suite 600
Denver, CO 80204-2554
303-866-4488

**Connecticut**
Connecticut OICC
Connecticut Department of Education
25 Industrial Park Road
Middletown, CT 06457
203-638-4042

**Delaware**
Office of Occupational and
    Labor Market Information
Department of Labor
University Office Plaza
P.O. Box 9029
Newark, DE 19714-9029
302-368-6963

**District of Columbia**
District of Columbia OICC
Department of Employment Services
500 C Street NW, Room 215
Washington, DC 20001
202-639-1090

**Florida**
Bureau of Labor Market Information
Department of Labor and
    Employment Services
Suite 200, Hartman Building
2012 Capitol Circle SE
Tallahassee, FL 32399-0673
904-488-1048

**Georgia**
Georgia OICC
Department of Labor
148 International Boulevard
Sussex Place
Atlanta, GA 30303
404-656-9639

**Hawaii**
Hawaii State OICC
830 Punchbowl Street, Room 315
Honolulu, HI 96813
808-586-8750

**Idaho**
Idaho OICC
Len B. Jordan Building, Room 301
650 W. State Street
Boise, ID 83720
208-334-3705

**Illinois**
Illinois OICC
217 E. Monroe, Suite 203
Springfield, IL 62706
217-785-0789

### Indiana
Indiana OICC
309 W. Washington Street, Room 309
Indianapolis, IN 46204
317-232-8528

### Iowa
Iowa OICC
Iowa Department of Economic
    Development
200 E. Grand Avenue
Des Moines, IA 50309
515-242-4890

### Kansas
Kansas OICC
401 Topeka Avenue
Topeka, KS 66603
913-296-2387

### Kentucky
Kentucky OICC
500 Metro Street, Capital Plaza Tower,
    Room 305
Frankfort, KY 40621-0001
502-564-4258 or 5331

### Louisiana
Louisiana OICC
P.O. Box 94094
Baton Rouge, LA 70804
504-342-5149

### Maine
Maine OICC
State House Station No. 71
Augusta, ME 04333
207-624-6200

### Maryland
Maryland SOICC
State Department of
    Employment and Training
1100 N. Eutaw Street, Room 205
Baltimore, MD 21201
410-333-5478

### Massachusetts
Massachusetts OICC
Division of Employment Security
C.F. Hurley Building, 2d Floor
Government Center
Boston, MA 02114
617-727-6718

### Michigan
Michigan OICC
Victor Office Center, 3d Floor
201 N. Washington Square
Box 30015
Lansing, MI 48909
517-373-0363

### Minnesota
Minnesota OICC
Department of Jobs and Training
390 N. Robert Street
St. Paul, MN 55101
612-296-2072

### Mississippi
SOICC Office
301 W. Pearl Street
Jackson, MS 39203-3089
601-949-2002

**Missouri**
Missouri OICC
400 Dix Road
Jefferson City, MO 65101
314-751-3800

**Montana**
Montana OICC
1327 Lockey Street, 2d Floor
P.O. Box 1728
Helena, MT 59624
406-444-2741

**Nebraska**
Nebraska OICC
P.O. Box 94600
State House Station
Lincoln, NE 68509-4600
402-471-4845

**Nevada**
Nevada OICC
1923 N. Carson Street, Suite 211
Carson City, NV 89710
702-687-4577

**New Hampshire**
New Hampshire State OICC
64B Old Suncook Road
Concord, NH 03301
603-228-3349

**New Jersey**
New Jersey OICC
609 Labor and Industry Building, CN 056
Trenton, NJ 08625-0056
609-292-2682

**New Mexico**
New Mexico OICC
401 Broadway NE,
    Tiwa Building
P.O. Box 1928
Albuquerque, NM 87103
505-841-8455

**New York**
New York State OICC
Department of Labor Research
    and Statistics Division
State Campus, Building 12, Room 400
Albany, NY 12240
518-457-6182

**North Carolina**
North Carolina OICC
1311 St. Mary's Street, Suite 250
P.O. Box 27625
Raleigh, NC 27611
919-733-6700

**North Dakota**
North Dakota SOICC
1720 Burnt Boat Drive
P.O. Box 1537
Bismarck, ND 58502-1537
701-224-2733

**Ohio**
Ohio OICC
Division of Labor Market Information
Bureau of Employment Services
1160 Dublin Road, Building A
Columbus, OH 43215
614-752-6863

**Oklahoma**
Oklahoma OICC
Department of Voc/Tech Education
1500 W. 7th Avenue
Stillwater, OK 74074
405-743-5198

**Oregon**
Oregon OICC
875 Union Street NE
Salem, OR 97311
503-378-5490

**Pennsylvania**
Pennsylvania OICC
Department of Labor and Industry
1224 Labor and Industry Building
Harrisburg, PA 17120
717-787-8646 or 8647

**Puerto Rico**
Puerto Rico OICC
202 Del Cristo Street
P.O. Box 6212
San Juan, PR 00936-6212
809-723-7110

**Rhode Island**
Rhode Island OICC
22 Hayes Street, Room 133
Providence, RI 02908
401-272-0830

**South Carolina**
South Carolina OICC
1550 Gadsden Street
P.O. Box 995
Columbia, SC 29202
803-737-2733

**South Dakota**
South Dakota OICC
Department of Labor
420 S. Roosevelt Street
P.O. Box 4730
Aberdeen, SD 57402-4730
605-622-2314

**Tennessee**
Tennessee OICC
11th Floor Volunteer Plaza
500 James Robertson Parkway
Nashville, TN 37219
615-741-6451

**Texas**
Texas OICC
Employment Commission Building
3520 Executive Center Drive
Austin, TX 78778
512-502-3750

**Utah**
Utah OICC
Department of Employment Security
P.O. Box 11249
140 E. 300 South
Salt Lake City, UT 84147
801-536-7806 or 7861

**Vermont**
Vermont OICC
Green Mountain Drive
P.O. Box 488
Montpelier, VT 05601-0488
802-229-0311

**Virginia**
Virginia OICC
Employment Commission
703 E. Main Street
P.O. Box 1358
Richmond, VA 23211
804-786-7496

**Virgin Islands**
Virgin Islands OICC
P.O. Box 3359
St. Thomas, US VI 00801
809-776-3700

**Washington**
Washington OICC
P.O. Box 9046
Olympia, WA 98504-5311
206-438-4803

**West Virginia**
West Virginia OICC
One Dunbar Plaza, Suite E
Dunbar, WV 25064
304-293-5314

**Wisconsin**
The Wisconsin OIC Council
Division of E&T Policy
201 E. Washington Avenue
P.O. Box 7972
Madison, WI 53707
608-266-8012

**Wyoming**
Wyoming OICC
P.O. Box 2760
100 W. Midwest
Casper, WY 82602
307-265-7017

# LOCAL-LEVEL JOB RESEARCH

If you know precisely the city or county in which you want to work, or if you have narrowed your search to a few locations, you should focus on the information sources that know about your occupation's role in that particular job market. The best sources follow.

## Regional Wages

*Occupational Compensation Surveys* from the Bureau of Labor Statistics provide wage data on occupational categories common to a variety of industries in seventy Metropolitan Statistical Areas (MSAs). This is an excellent source for comparing average wages in different areas of the country as well as in three types of industry: manufacturing, nonmanufacturing, and transportation and utilities.

▣▣▣▣▣▣▣▣▣▣▣▣▣▣▣▣▣▣▣▣▣▣▣▣▣▣▣▣▣▣

When Bill, a systems analyst, decided to move to the Washington metropolitan area to be near his elderly mother, he wanted to make the best of his job opportunities and maximize his earnings. He checked the *Occupational Compensation Survey* for the Washington, D.C./Maryland/Virginia metropolitan area and discovered that computer systems analysts in manufacturing companies earn a mean of $812 per week, while those employed in transportation and utilities earn a mean of $710 per week. By spending a few minutes doing some basic research, he learned to target his job search on manufacturing companies. The difference in salary is more than $5,300 per year.

▣▣▣▣▣▣▣▣▣▣▣▣▣▣▣▣▣▣▣▣▣▣▣▣▣▣▣▣▣▣

You can order the wage surveys for individual metropolitan areas from the Government Printing Office, using the stock number provided with each. The surveys are between 25 and 130 pages long and cost between $1.75 and $6.50 each. Summaries of occupational earnings data for the sixty-one metropolitan areas surveyed during 1988 and comments on establishment practices and benefits for twenty-eight of those areas may be found in *Occupational Compensation Surveys: Selected Metropolitan Areas*, S/N 829-001-00000-4.

▣▣▣▣▣▣▣▣▣▣▣▣▣▣▣▣▣▣▣▣▣▣▣▣▣▣▣▣▣▣

U.S. Government Printing Office
Superintendent of Documents
Washington, DC 20402
202-512-2051

**Alabama**
Huntsville
829-001-00455-7

Mobile
829-001-00351-8

**Arizona**
Phoenix
829-001-00405-1

**Arkansas**
Little Rock, North Little Rock
829-001-00417-4

*see also* Tennessee, Memphis

**California**
Anaheim, Santa Ana
829-001-00441-7

Fresno
829-001-00362-3

Los Angeles, Long Beach
829-001-00453-1

Oakland
820-001-00392-5

Riverside, San Bernardino
829-001-00412-3

Sacramento
829-001-00407-7

San Diego
829-001-00438-7

San Francisco
829-001-00467-1

Visalia, Tulare, Porterville
829-001-00421-2

**Colorado**
Denver
829-001-00448-4

**Connecticut**
Danbury
829-001-00454-9

Hartford
829-001-00355-1

**New Britain**
820-001-00462-0

**Delaware**
Wilmington
829-001-00444-1

**Florida**
Bradenton
829-001-00282-1

Gainesville
829-001-00409-3

Miami, Hialeah
829-001-00440-9

Orlando
829-001-00372-1

Tampa, St. Petersburg, Clearwater
829-001-00442-5

**Georgia**
Atlanta
829-001-00403-4

Augusta; South Carolina
829-001-00406-9

**Idaho**
Boise City
829-001-00361-5

**Illinois**
Champaign, Urbana, Rantoul
829-001-00424-7

Chicago
829-001-00432-8

Decatur
829-001-00425-5

Joliet
829-001-00369-1

*see also* Iowa, Davenport; Missouri,
St. Louis

**Indiana**
Elkhart, Goshen
829-001-00451-4

Evansville; Kentucky
829-001-00461-1

Gary, Hammond
829-001-00458-1

**Indianapolis**
829-001-00423-9

Kokomo
829-001-00330-5

*see also* Kentucky, Louisville

**Iowa**
Davenport, Rock Island;
Moline, Illinois
829-001-00457-3

*see also* Nebraska, Omaha

**Kansas**
*see* Missouri, Kansas City

**Kentucky**
Louisville; Indiana
829-001-00443-3

*see also* Indiana, Evansville

**Louisiana**
New Orleans
829-001-00433-6

Shreveport
829-001-00375-5

**Maine**
Portland
829-001-00380-1

**Maryland**
Baltimore
829-001-00428-0

*see also* Delaware, Wilmington;
Washington, D.C.

**Massachusetts**
Lawrence, Haverhill; New Hampshire
829-001-00437-9

Worcester
829-001-00435-2

*see also* Rhode Island, Pawtucket

**Michigan**
Detroit
829-001-00449-2

*see also* Ohio, Toledo

**Minnesota**
St. Cloud
829-001-00464-6

**Mississippi**
Jackson
829-001-00456-5

*see also* Tennessee, Memphis

**Missouri**
Kansas City; Kansas
829-001-00419-1

St. Louis; Illinois
829-001-00463-8

**Montana**
Billings
829-001-00436-1

**Nebraska**
Omaha
829-001-00370-4

**New Hampshire**
*see* Massachusetts, Lawrence

**New Jersey**
Middlesex, Somerset, Hunterdon
829-001-00430-1

Monmouth, Ocean
829-001-00401-8

Newark
829-001-00460-3

Trenton
829-001-00429-8

*see also* Delaware, Wilmington;
Pennsylvania, Philadelphia

**New York**
Buffalo
829-001-00411-5

Nassau, Suffolk
829-001-00447-6

Poughkeepsie
829-001-00455-0

Rochester
829-001-00446-8

**North Carolina**
Charlotte, Gastonia, Rockhill;
South Carolina
829-001-00416-6

**Ohio**
Cincinnati, Ohio
829-001-00466-2

Cleveland
829-001-00418-2

Columbus
829-001-00313-5

Toledo; Michigan
829-001-00387-9

**Oregon**
Portland
829-001-00422-1

**Pennsylvania**
Philadelphia
829-001-00452-2

Pittsburgh
829-001-00059-0

Scranton, Wilkes-Barre
829-001-00143-1

York
829-001-00427-1

**Rhode Island**
Pawtucket, Woonsocket;
Attleboro, Massachusetts
829-001-00414-0

**South Carolina**
Charleston
829-001-00371-2

Florence
829-001-00329-1

*see also* Georgia, Augusta;
North Carolina, Charlotte

**Tennessee**
Memphis; Arkansas; Mississippi
829-001-00434-4

**Texas**
Abilene
829-001-00468-9

Austin
829-001-00354-2

Corpus Christi
829-001-00350-0

Dallas, Ft. Worth
829-001-00450-6

Houston
829-001-00470-1

Longview, Marshall
829-001-00287-2

San Angelo
829-001-00336-4

San Antonio
829-001-00402-4

**Utah**
Salt Lake City, Ogden
829-001-00469-7

**Virginia**
Richmond, Petersburg
820-001-00410-7

*see also* Washington, D.C.

**Washington**
Seattle
829-001-00381-0

**Washington, D.C., Maryland, Virginia**
829-001-00465-4

**Wisconsin**
Appleton, Oshkosh, Neenah
829-001-00310-1

Milwaukee
829-001-00404-2

## County Business Patterns

A series of publications, *County Business Patterns* (Bureau of Labor Statistics) presents employment and payroll statistics by county and by industry for most metropolitan areas, counties, and states. It is useful for identifying, by county, industries with expanding firms or increasing payrolls. You can find the publications in most larger public libraries and academic institutions or you can use one of the U.S. government depository libraries (see page 101).

## Local Libraries

A call to the public library in your targeted community may provide good insights into jobs available. Ask about local studies, newspaper articles, and other published materials. Also ask the reference librarian for his or her own opinions on local hiring activities for your occupation. Librarians are often willing to do some research among their resources and even look beyond library materials to find answers for clients. Also ask for suggestions of other local organizations and individuals to contact.

## Local Press

Subscribe to the local newspaper to get a current assessment of how particular jobs are faring in an area. Look through the "help wanted" advertisements to see the number as well as the types of positions that are open and the salaries that are offered. Are those salaries higher or lower than the industry average you learned about from sources in chapter 4? If most of the advertisements are for entry-level positions, you may be looking at an area where mid-level or higher positions are hard to come by.

▣▣▣▣▣▣▣▣▣▣▣▣▣▣▣▣▣▣▣▣▣▣▣▣▣▣▣▣▣▣

Contact the editors of the paper to ask about employment prospects in the area. Focus on those editors or editor who would know about employment trends in your field. For example, Mike, who is in product research and development, got good advice from both the business editor and the science editor. Dierdre, a buyer for retail clothing stores, found that the life-style editor was able to give her helpful information and insights.

▣▣▣▣▣▣▣▣▣▣▣▣▣▣▣▣▣▣▣▣▣▣▣▣▣▣▣▣▣▣

Scan city magazines and business news tabloids for data and analyses on the job market. The Washingtonian magazine, for example, recently highlighted the best employment opportunities in Washington, D.C., providing detailed job-growth data and useful analyses. Also watch for articles about companies or organizations that are expanding in the area. Are they the kinds of organizations that have jobs in your field?

You can learn which local papers and other media cover an area by contacting directory assistance, the local chamber of commerce, or the public library. Or, you can consult the Gale *Directory of Publications and Broadcast Media* (Gale Research) or the *Standard Periodical Directory* (Oxbridge Communications). You will find them in most libraries.

## Job Training Partnership Act Offices

Local employment service offices of the Job Training Partnership Act (JTPA) put together statistics and projections on local labor markets. You can find the office nearest you by contacting one of the state-level JTPA liaison officers listed below.

▣ ▣ ▣ ▣ ▣ ▣ ▣ ▣ ▣ ▣ ▣ ▣ ▣ ▣ ▣ ▣ ▣ ▣ ▣ ▣ ▣ ▣ ▣ ▣ ▣ ▣ ▣ ▣ ▣ ▣

**Alabama**
Rebecca Morris
Alabama Department of Economic
 & Community Affairs
401 Adams Avenue
P.O. Box 5690
Montgomery, AL 36103-5690
205-242-5100

**Alaska**
Tony Nakazawa
Alaska Department of Community
 & Regional Affairs
JTPA Office, Rural Development
333 W. 4th Avenue, Suite 220
Anchorage, AK 99501
907-269-4500

**Arizona**
Manuel F. Meijia
Assistant Director
Division of Employment and
 Rehabilitation Services
1789 W. Jefferson
Site Code 920z
Phoenix, AZ 85007
602-542-3957

**Arkansas**
Sharon Robinette
Office of Employment & Training Services
Employment Security Division
P.O. Box 2981
Little Rock, AR 72203
501-682-5227

**California**
Judy Kuhlman
Director
Employment Development Department
P.O. Box 826880
Sacramento, CA 94280-0001
916-654-7110

**Colorado**
Leslie S. Franklin
Executive Director
Governor's Job Training Office
720 S. Colorado Boulevard, Suite 550
Denver, CO 80222
303-758-5020

**Connecticut**
Eli Gussen
Department of Labor
200 Folly Brook Boulevard
Wethersfield, CT 06109
203-566-4290

**Delaware**
Louis A. Masci
Director
Division of Employment and Training
University Plaza, Stockton Building
P.O. Box 9499
Newark, DE 19714-9499
302-368-6810

**District of Columbia**
Maria Borrero
Director
Department of Employment Services
500 C Street NW
Washington, DC 20001
202-639-1530

**Florida**
Frank Scruggs
Secretary
Department of Labor
   and Employment Security
2012 Capitol Circle SE
Suite 303, Hartman Building
Tallahassee, FL 32399-2152
904-488-4398

**Georgia**
H. G. Weisman
Commissioner
Department of Labor
148 International Boulevard NE, Suite 650
Atlanta, GA 30303
404-656-7392

**Hawaii**
Robert Watada
Director
Department of Labor
   and Industrial Relations
830 Punchbowl Street, Room 320
Honolulu, HI 96813
808-586-9060

**Idaho**
Cheryl Brush
JTPA Liaison
Department of Employment
317 Maine Street
Boise, ID 83735-0001
208-334-6131

**Illinois**
Herbert D. Dennis
Manager, JTPA Programs Division
Department of Commerce
  and Community Affairs
620 E. Adams, 6th Floor
Springfield, IL 62701
217-785-6006

**Indiana**
Susan Gray
Executive Director
Department of Employment
  and Training Services
10 N. Senate Avenue, Room 325
Indianapolis, IN 46204
317-232-0196

**Iowa**
Jeff Nall
Administrator, Division of Job Training
Department of Economic Development
200 E. Grand Avenue
Des Moines, IA 50309
515-242-4779

**Kansas**
Glenn Fondoble
Kansas Department of Human Resources
332 E. 8th Street
P.O. Box 398
Hays, KS 67601
913-628-1014

**Kentucky**
Jill Day
Department for Employment Services
Division of Job Training
275 E. Main Street, 2-W
Frankfort, KY 40621
502-564-5360

**Louisiana**
Robert Fore
Assistant Secretary
Office of Labor
P.O. Box 94094
Baton Rouge, LA 70804
504-342-7693

**Maine**
Marylou Dyer
Bureau of Employment
  and Training Programs
Hospital Street
State House Station 55
Augusta, ME 04333
207-289-3377

**Maryland**
Gary Moore
Office of Employment and Training
Department of Economic and
  Employment Development
1100 N. Eutaw Street, Room 600
Baltimore, MD 21201
303-333-5718

**Massachusetts**
Nils L. Nordberg
Commissioner
Department of Employment and Training
Charles F. Hurley Building
Government Center
19 Staniford Street
Boston, MA 02114
617-727-6600

**Michigan**
Mr. Lowell W. Perry
Director
Department of Labor
Victor Center Building
201 N. Washington Square
Lansing, MI 48909
517-373-9600

**Minnesota**
Frank Schneider
Community-Based Services
690 American Center Building
150 E. Kellogg Boulevard
St. Paul MN 55101
612-296-8004

**Mississippi**
Gary Anderson
Department of Economic
    and Community Development
301 Pearl Street
Jackson, MS 39203-3089
601-949-2234

**Missouri**
Larry Earley
Director
Division of Job Development and Training
Department of Economic Development
221 Metro Drive
Jefferson City, MO 65109
314-751-7796

**Montana**
Sue Mohr
Employment Policy Division
P.O. Box 1728
Helena, MT 59624
406-444-1309

**Nebraska**
Edward Kosark
Job Training Program Division
550 S. 16th Street
P.O. Box 95004
Lincoln, NE 68509
402-471-2127

**Nevada**
Barbara Weinberg
Executive Director
State Job Training Office
Capitol Complex
400 W. King
Carson City, NV 89710
702-687-4310

**New Hampshire**
Ray O. Worden
Executive Director
Job Training Council
64 B Old Suncook Road
Concord, NH 03301
603-228-9500

**New Jersey**
Robert Guandagnino
Division of Employment and Training
CN055, Room 703
Trenton, NJ 08625
609-984-2344

**New Mexico**
Ronald Martinez
Department of Labor
Job Training Division
P.O. Box 4218
Santa Fe, NM 87502
505-827-6827

**New York**
Robert Gulotty
Job Service and Training
State Office Building 12
Albany, NY 12240
518-457-2612

**North Carolina**
Joel C. New
Director
Division of Employment and Training
Department of Economic
    and Community Development
111 Seaboard Avenue
Raleigh, NC 27604
919-733-6383

**North Dakota**
Michael V. Deisz
Executive Director
Job Service North Dakota
P.O. Box 1537
Bismarck, ND 58501
701-224-2836

**Ohio**
Evelyn Bissonnette
Director
JTP-Ohio Bureau of Employment Services
145 S. Front Street, 4th Floor
Columbus, OH 43216
614-466-3817

**Oklahoma**
Glen E. Robards, Jr.
Office of the Governor
Employment Security Commission
Will Rogers Memorial Office Building,
    Room 201
Oklahoma City, OK 73105
405-557-7200

**Oregon**
Camille Preus-Braly
JTPA Administration
Economic Development Department
775 Summer Street NE
Salem, OR 97310
503-373-1995

**Pennsylvania**
Thomas Foley
Department of Labor and Industry
1700 Executive Suite
7th and Forster Streets
Harrisburg, PA 17120
717-787-5279

**Puerto Rico**
Ileana Echegoyen
Administrator
Right to Employment Administration
G.P.O. Box 4452
San Juan, PR 00936
809-754-5690

**Rhode Island**
Richard Beneduce
JTP Office
Department of Employment and Training
101 Friendship Street
Providence, RI 02903
401-277-3930

**South Carolina**
J.M. Rutland
Employment Security Commission
1550 Gadsden Street
Columbia, SC 29202
803-737-2611

**South Dakota**
Lloyd Schipper
Department of Labor
Kneip Building
700 Governors Drive
Pierre, SD 57501-2291
605-773-5017

**Tennessee**
Emmett Edwards
Commissioner
Department of Labor
501 Union Building
Nashville, TN 37219
615-741-1031

**Texas**
Barbara Cigainero
Director
Work Force Development Division
Department of Commerce
P.O. Box 12728-Capitol Station
Austin, TX 78711-2728
512-320-9801

**Utah**
Greg Gardner
Director
Job Training for Economic Development
324 S. State Street, Suite 500
Salt Lake City, UT 84111
801-538-8750

**Vermont**
Robert Ware
Director
Office of Employment
    and Training Programs
P.O. Box 488
Montpelier, VT 05602
802-229-0311

**Virginia**
James E. Price
Executive Director
Governor's Employment
    and Training Department
The Commonwealth Building
4615 W. Broad Street, 3d Floor
Richmond, VA 23230
804-367-9803

**Washington**
Larry Malo
Employment Security Department/JTPA
212 Maple Park
Mail Stop KG-11
Olympia, WA 98504
206-753-5114

**West Virginia**
Andrew Richardson
Bureau of Employment Programs
Division of Employment Security
112 California Avenue
Charleston, WV 25304-0112
304-558-2630

**Wisconsin**
June Suhling
Administrator
Education and Training Policy
Labor, Human Relations, Industrial
P.O. Box 7903
Madison, WI 53707
608-266-2439

**Wyoming**
Matt Johnson
Job Training Programs
P.O. Box 2760
Casper, WY 82602
307-235-3601

## Local Boards of Trade

Many metropolitan areas have a board of trade. These organizations are devoted to increasing the business opportunities of their members and promoting the economic health of the area. Consequently, they are keenly aware of the local job market. Most boards of trade sponsor numerous get-togethers during the year. These meetings are excellent places to meet the movers and shakers of the community, and to rub elbows with representatives of local employers. Networking in this fashion can help you learn about job openings long before they come to the attention of other job seekers. You can find the local board of trade through directory assistance, the local librarian, or the business editor of the local paper.

## Chambers of Commerce

Another business advocacy group that can provide you with timely occupational intelligence is the local chamber of commerce. Often the chamber will have its own newsletter. Many chambers also provide their members and outside interested parties with a profile of local wage rates, organized by occupation or skill. Also try to interview staff and executives of the chamber's member companies (your prospective employers). If you are already in the area, attend the chamber's social and business functions, which will also allow you to meet area employers. If you are not in the area or cannot make a trip, you should still call or write the chamber. Tell them you are interested in job opportunities in a particular profession, and ask that they steer you to the chamber member or employee who would be knowledgeable in that field.

Locate the local chamber of commerce through directory assistance. State-level chambers are listed in appendix IV.

## Local Trade and Professional Associations

Local industry or professional associations are excellent resources both for evaluating employment opportunities in their region and for providing contacts in your chosen field. These associations may be independent groups or local chapters of national associations. To find the local associations for a particular industry or profession, contact the national associations listed in the *Encyclopedia of Associations* or consult the local chamber of commerce, the local yellow pages, or the public library.

To use these associations most effectively, explain your interest in a letter or telephone call. Ask for information and advice about positions in your field. Also ask for referrals to local individuals who might know about opportunities for your profession, and a membership directory. If you are in the area, arrange to attend association meetings so you can make direct contact with employers and your professional peers.

## Local Universities and Colleges

There are two sources at area colleges that may be contacted for assistance.

### Career Guidance Offices

Most colleges and universities maintain career guidance offices where students can learn about a variety of career opportunities. Most career guidance offices also invite employers—local as well as others—onto campus to meet with students. Often, alumni are invited to take advantage of these services, so if you are working in the area where you attended college, you have a valuable resource at your disposal. Even if you did not attend school in the area, you should ask about using the resources of the area career guidance offices. Major universities tend to have a more national focus than many colleges do, but both can be excellent sources for local occupational information.

### College Faculty

Faculty members usually keep current with career opportunities affiliated with their subject area. Also, they can tell you about emerging occupations you may not have considered. Call the college and ask for professors in your particular field of interest. You might want to inquire about their office hours, which may be brief, and plan to contact them during that time.

## Local Employment Agencies and Job-Counseling Services

Private and public employment agencies have good insights into the local occupational outlook, and may provide counseling services. In general, the services provided by government-sponsored employment agencies are free, so you may want to try there first. Start with the appropriate state-level office; the lists begin on pages 195 and 201.

Most private employment agencies are listed in the local yellow pages. You may be charged for counseling services, so ask up front what the cost will be. Also, talk to some former clients to determine the quality of assistance provided.

▣▣▣▣▣▣▣▣▣▣▣▣▣▣▣▣▣▣▣▣▣▣▣▣▣▣▣▣▣

In some areas there are highly specialized counseling services. For example, in Washington, D.C., Morton Leeds, Ph. D., is an expert on the federal job market. He conducts seminars through Marymount University. David Edwards teaches a class, Getting a Job on the Hill through First Class, a nonprofit adult education center in Washington, D.C. The Women's Center of Northern Virginia offers career workshops for women and their families throughout the metropolitan area. Look for the experts and specialized counseling centers in your area.

▣▣▣▣▣▣▣▣▣▣▣▣▣▣▣▣▣▣▣▣▣▣▣▣▣▣▣▣▣

## Job Clearinghouses

In many communities, there are specialized clearinghouses for various occupations and interests. For example, the December 1991 issue of the *Washingtonian* magazine in Washington, D.C. lists job clearinghouses for arts and education, associations and nonprofits, business and accounting, computers, government and politics, law, media and public relations, and miscellaneous occupations. Also look for job clearinghouses within hiring organizations, such as the Democratic Study Group Job Referral Service, which lists openings in congressional offices. Write c/o The House Placement Office, Room 219, House Annex II, 3rd and D Streets, SW,

Washington, DC 20515. To identify local and regional clearinghouses, try calling the local press, the library, and university career services offices.

Some clearinghouses are in the form of electronic bulletin boards. The federal government's Office of Personnel Management sponsors bulletin boards for federal jobs available in the Midwest and the Northeast. Both bulletin boards can accept transmissions up to 2400 baud. For jobs in the Midwest, call by modem, 213-226-4423 or 213-226-2095. For jobs in the Northeast call by modem, 201-645-3887. Other job-related bulletin boards can be found at the following numbers:

| | |
|---|---|
| 201-543-4485 | 708-690-9860 |
| 212-279-4875 | 602-527-8404 |
| 413-592-9208 | 301-763-4574 |
| 602-947-4286 | |

Remember, however, that many bulletin boards are short lived. Keep tuned to learn about new ones.

## Publications

The books listed below focus on the career opportunities within particular regions of the country.

▢ "Job Bank" publications (Bob Adams)—A series of books offering an in-depth look at employment opportunities in different areas of the United States. These books are available for under $15 in most bookstores.

▢ Beach, Janet, *How to Get a Job in the San Francisco Bay Area* (Contemporary Books)—This book includes profiles of companies and industries, hiring practices, names of professional organizations and clubs, and a list of the fastest growing companies in the area.

▢ Benjamin, Janice, and Barbara Block, *How to Be Happily Employed in Washington D.C.* (Random House)—A book that covers job trends in Washington and includes a survey of the federal government and its influence on the employment outlook in the region.

◻
◻
◻
◻

*The Insider's Guide* series (Surrey Books)—Twelve books, each with the title, *How To Get a Job in . . .* ; Portland/Seattle, Chicago, Houston, and Boston are examples. The books tell you how to use the local networks in each city and list employers and contact information.

Also look for local resources. *National Business Employment Weekly* (Dow Jones) is a compilation of Help Wanted advertisements from regional editions of the *Wall Street Journal. National Ad Search* (National Ad Search) casts a wider net: It is a weekly compilation of Help Wanted advertisements culled from seventy-five newspapers and also publishes the names and résumés of executives who are seeking employment. Your library may subscribe to it. Newspapers in large cities often have employment supplements. For example, the *Miami Herald* newspaper publishes a weekly newsstand bulletin, *Job Book*, providing a listing of classified ads for jobs currently available and some analysis, hiring patterns, salaries, and benefits in the area. The *Herald* also give useful job-hunting advice at the beginning of its Sunday classified employment section.

# CHAPTER 21

# THE QUALITY OF LIFE

□□□

W hat kind of living environment is best for you? You may be looking for a stable, safe place to raise your children or for a city with excitement and sparkle. You may choose the suburbs or the revitalized inner city. Your priorities may call for sunny weather, excellent public transportation, or weekly symphony concerts. If you have not decided what characteristics you value most in your living environment, sit down and make a list, or start with the life-style characteristics, described below, that most job hunters rate as important. Decide which are most important to you, and concentrate on your top priorities.

It is likely that you will find most of the information you need about a particular region from the sources mentioned in the first part of this chapter. For more substantive research, we supply additional sources. If you are trying to compare regions all over the country, use the sources starting on page 235, with a nationwide perspective. If you have decided on your state of residence, use the sources beginning on page 235. Once you identify several specific towns or cities, use the sources with a local perspective, starting on page 238. Those sources will provide information on the quality of life, among them, the arts and cultural events, climate, cost of living, crime, education, environmental quality, health care, recreation, sports and leisure, and transportation. Sources that provide information about history, demography, and employment are described as general.

## THE ARTS AND CULTURAL EVENTS

Arts and culture are important to many job hunters. The type and intensity of your interests become very important when choosing a place to life. For example, if your cultural appetites can be satisfied by an evening with Pavarotti on the tube or by an occasional student production at the local university, you will be much more flexible about location than will someone who feels incomplete without a weekly dose of world-class ballet or opera. To find out about cultural events and attractions in any particular area, check the local newspaper for a calendar of events or contact the tourist board or chamber of commerce. There may also be a local arts council that can tell you about cultural events. Ask directory assistance for the numbers.

The regional arts councils listed below can help you determine which communities make arts and culture a top priority.

**Arts Midwest**
(Illinois, Indiana, Iowa, Michigan,
    Minnesota, North Dakota, Ohio,
    Southern Dakota, Wisconsin)
Hennepin Center for the Arts
528 Hennepin Avenue, Suite 310
Minneapolis, MN 55403
612-341-0755

**Mid-America Arts Alliance**
(Arkansas, Kansas, Missouri, Nebraska,
    Oklahoma, Texas)
912 Baltimore Avenue, Suite 700
Kansas City, MO 64105
816-421-1388

**Mid Atlantic Arts Foundation**
(Delaware, District of Columbia,
    Maryland, New Jersey, New York,
    Pennsylvania, Virginia, Virgin Islands,
    West Virginia)
11 E. Chase Street, Suite 2-A
Baltimore, MD 21202
410-539-6659

**New England Foundation for the Arts**
(Connecticut, Maine, Massachusetts,
    New Hampshire, Rhode Island,
    Vermont)
678 Massachusetts Avenue
Cambridge, MA 02139
617-492-2914

**Southern Arts Federation**
(Alabama, Florida, Georgia, Kentucky,
    Louisiana, Mississippi, North Carolina,
    South Carolina, Tennessee)
181 14th Street, Suite 400
Atlanta, GA 30309
404-874-7244

**Western States Arts Federation**
(Alaska, Arizona, California, Colorado,
    Hawaii, Idaho, Montana, Nevada,
    New Mexico, Oregon, Utah,
    Washington, Wyoming)
236 Montezuma Avenue
Santa Fe, NM 87501
505-988-1166

If you need a national perspective, try:

**Arts for America, The National Assembly**
    **of Local Arts Agencies**
927 15th Street NW, 12th floor
Washington, DC 20005
202-371-2830

**National Assembly of State Arts Agencies**
1010 Vermont Avenue NW, Suite 920
Washington, DC 20005
202-347-6352

# CLIMATE

Weather can greatly affect the mood and productivity of certain individuals. You should think about what kind of weather gives you the biggest lift, then research the areas of the country that offer lots of it. If sunshine makes you feel your best and you enjoy the activities that sunny weather allows, you might want to aim for a state such as Arizona, which gets about eighty percent of the possible maximum sunshine annually. If cold weather gives you energy, and snow-mobiling is your passion, you will prefer a state such as New Hampshire, which has about 210 days of temperatures at or below thirty-two degrees Fahrenheit.

Local and state-level chambers of commerce normally have plentiful information about the area's climate. If you want information about several areas, you can also contact the National Climatic Data Center, which publishes reports on 280 U.S. localities, available for a small charge. To order, call or write to the National Climatic Date Center, National Federal Building, Ashville, NC 28801; 704-271-4871.

# COST OF LIVING

The cost of living is one of the most important criteria for job hunters who are deciding whether, and where, to relocate. The cost of living determines the size of your house and the type of neighborhood in which you can afford to live, and how often you can eat out or go to a movie, and how much you can save for your children's education or your own retirement. The variations in living costs in different parts of the country are shocking. The variances occur not just between small towns and large cities, but also among communities of similar sizes. For example, the average cost of an apartment in Denver is about half that in San Diego.

The following table can help you compare relative price levels for consumer goods and services in selected cities. All cities are compared to a national average which is indexed at 100; in other words, if the number is less than 100, the cost of living is less than the national average.

## TABLE 9: COST OF LIVING INDEX FOR SELECTED CITIES—1992

| City | All items | Groceries | Housing | Utilities | Transportation | Health care | Misc. goods & services |
|---|---|---|---|---|---|---|---|
| Albuquerque | 102.7 | 99.5 | 112.4 | 95.3 | 102.6 | 116.2 | 97.6 |
| Atlanta | 98.6 | 99.2 | 96.3 | 109.6 | 98.3 | 127.1 | 93.3 |
| Boston | 139.5 | 123.8 | 181.5 | 146.3 | 129.4 | 148.8 | 111.6 |
| Chicago | 112.9 | 97.7 | 130.5 | 124.3 | 116.2 | 106.6 | 101.6 |
| Denver | 105.4 | 103.3 | 112.6 | 90.2 | 107.0 | 124.0 | 101.2 |
| Houston | 97.8 | 102.0 | 91.7 | 101.8 | 109.9 | 111.1 | 94.6 |
| Los Angeles | 127.9 | 110.5 | 173.4 | 83.3 | 117.4 | 150.1 | 109.3 |
| Miami | 108.2 | 98.7 | 108.3 | 126.4 | 104.6 | 120.5 | 106.3 |
| New York | 208.7 | 144.8 | 359.3 | 149.2 | 133.9 | 199.2 | 150.0 |
| Phoenix | 99.5 | 101.1 | 92.8 | 89.2 | 114.7 | 110.8 | 101.0 |
| Salt Lake City | 96.8 | 99.7 | 86.0 | 89.4 | 104.0 | 99.6 | 103.7 |
| San Diego | 130.4 | 112.7 | 190.0 | 72.9 | 131.2 | 127.8 | 104.2 |
| Seattle | 117.0 | 118.1 | 147.0 | 61.8 | 108.7 | 125.8 | 107.9 |
| St. Louis | 93.9 | 100.5 | 95.2 | 105.8 | 101.5 | 99.8 | 90.2 |
| Tucson | 102.8 | 97.9 | 97.7 | 99.9 | 105.5 | 111.1 | 107.4 |

SOURCE: *Cost of Living Index*, American Chamber of Commerce Research Association, 1993.

An extremely detailed record of the cost of living is prepared by the American Chamber of Commerce Research Association. This *Cost of Living Index* looks at hundreds of urban and rural communities and provides figures for the relative costs of groceries, housing, utilities, transportation, and health care, in addition to a composite index. It breaks each cost category into further detail, for example, contrasting the cost of twenty-two separate food items from T-bone steak to fresh peas. This survey is available in many large libraries and can often be found at local chambers of commerce. Cost-of-living data can also be obtained from *Places Rated Almanac* (Prentice-Hall) by Richard Boyer and David Pavageau. It may be found in most libraries and at your bookstore. In addition, *USA Today* regularly publishes comparative living data from across the country.

## SAFETY AND CRIME RATES

Crime rates vary widely from city to city. The best way to learn about the crime rate of a particular locality would be to check with local law-enforcement agencies. Call the city government operator and ask to speak with the chief of police or the sheriff's office. One office or the other should be able to give you crime reports of specific neighborhoods.

A handy chart, compiled by the U.S. Department of Justice, reveals the areas in the United States where crime is most likely to occur. It appears in the *Report to the Nation on Crime and Justice*, which may be ordered from the National Criminal Justice Reference Service, 1600 Research Boulevard, Box 6000, Rockville, MD 20850; 800-851-3420 or 301-251-5500. *Places Rated Almanac* also ranks cities by crime statistics. The publication is available in most libraries and at your bookstore.

## EDUCATION

Did you know that Alaska spends more per pupil on public education than any other state? Close behind are New York, New Jersey, and Wyoming. If you are raising a family, or plan to, the quality of public education—from preschool to postgraduate—should be a primary consideration in choosing a place to live and work. If public schools are poor, you could end up spending thousands of dollars each year on education at private schools. States that promise low-cost college education to every qualifying state resident can save some parents a bundle.

The sources below will help you determine which states provide good public education. You can obtain a variety of statistics from state educational agencies. Contact the state government operator in the state capital to find the state's education departments. Remember that school districts within a state may vary markedly and that the quality of school systems can vary greatly from neighborhood to neighborhood. Most education experts suggest that you visit several school districts to learn which neighborhoods are best for your future home. If you can't visit the schools, contact the local school boards. Also consult *Places Rated Almanac*, which ranks some cities on education criteria, to make quick comparisons between cities.

To evaluate elementary and secondary schools, ask questions such as the following:

What is the dropout rate?

Will my children be educated in the neighborhood?

What is the amount spent per pupil in the district?

What is the teacher/pupil ratio?

What are the average teacher salaries? (Remember to evaluate teacher salaries in the light of the cost of living in the area.)

If your child has a learning or physical disability, also ask about special education programs.

The following table, published by the National Education Association, shows the dollar amount each state spends per pupil in public education. It will give you some idea about the education level in the state, but remember that a dollar goes much further in terms of teachers' salaries and facilities in New Mexico than it does in New York. Likewise, the figures provided are state averages. Per-pupil expenditures can range widely within the state, so make appropriate allowances.

## TABLE 10: ESTIMATED EDUCATION AND EXPENDITURES, 1992–1993

| | Total (000) | Revenue State and local (000) | Receipts State contribution (%) | Local contribution (%) | Current Amount (000) | Expenditures Per pupil | Average Instructional staff* | Salaries Classroom teachers |
|---|---|---|---|---|---|---|---|---|
| 50 states & D.C. | $246,733,013 | $230,109,763 | 50.2 | 46.4 | $221,925,695 | $5,216 | $36,846 | $35,443 |
| Alabama | 2,605,225 | 2,254,251 | 74.8 | 21.8 | 2,580,281 | 3,550 | 28,737 | 27,490 |
| Alaska | 1,016,150† | 888,030† | 72.8† | 23.8† | 988,865† | 8,111† | 46,400† | 46,373† |
| Arizona | 3,362,851 | 3,020,080 | 45.9 | 48.6 | 3,248,271 | 4,830 | 38,221 | 32,403 |
| Arkansas | 1,791,466 | 1,617,466 | 68.9 | 28.1 | 1,599,532 | 3,630 | 28,645 | 27,598 |
| California | 27,559,848 | 25,246,466 | 65.4 | 31.7 | 23,769,619 | 4,585 | 42,800† | 41,400† |
| Colorado | 3,209,896 | 3,065,217 | 41.0 | 56.3 | 2,940,037 | 4,799 | 35,212 | 33,541 |
| Connecticut | 4,320,789† | 4,153,623† | 42.4† | 55.4† | 4,067,596† | 8,444† | 50,820† | 48,850† |
| Delaware | 648,883 | 593,883 | 73.3 | 24.4 | 601,217 | 5,763 | 37,691 | 36,217 |
| Dist. of Columbia | 581,552 | 513,552 | 0.0 | 88.3 | 570,000 | 7,043 | 39,382 | 38,168 |
| Florida | 11,218,438 | 10,325,079 | 50.8 | 45.3 | 9,594,795 | 4,846 | 32,453 | 31,153 |
| Georgia | 6,380,724 | 5,907,431 | 56.9 | 39.9 | 5,632,393 | 4,669 | 32,609 | 30,626 |
| Hawaii | 1,053,561 | 974,636 | 98.0 | 1.9 | 938,841 | 5,306 | 37,586 | 36,470 |
| Idaho | 905,889† | 838,273† | 67.2† | 30.3† | 818,384† | 3,537† | 28,334 | 27,156 |
| Illinois | 10,294,875 | 9,431,975† | 36.8† | 57.9† | 8,751,020† | 4,705† | 39,925 | 38,576 |
| Indiana | 5,977,360† | 5,698,345† | 55.2† | 42.8† | 5,124,534† | 5,350† | 37,264† | 37,446† |
| Iowa | 2,496,490 | 2,360,774 | 54.0 | 43.5 | 2,452,621 | 4,963 | 31,180 | 30,124 |
| Kansas | 2,355,792 | 2,232,686 | 54.6 | 43.0 | 2,234,588 | 4,949 | 34,269 | 33,133 |
| Kentucky | 3,171,609 | 2,846,521 | 75.8 | 21.7 | 2,969,048 | 4,636, | 32,733 | 31,487 |
| Louisiana | 3,663,956† | 3,314,360† | 61.3† | 35.0† | 3,366,496† | 4,231† | 29,783† | 26,074 |
| Maine | 1,261,393 | 1,173,055 | 55.7 | 41.2 | 1,205,643 | 5,692 | 31,293 | 30,258 |
| Maryland | 4,840,808 | 4,570,720 | 43.5 | 53.3 | 4,493,826 | 5,977 | 40,524 | 39,141 |
| Massachusetts | 5,730,703† | 5,399,371† | 32.7† | 63.4† | 5,216,939† | 6,162† | 47,510† | 39,245† |
| Michigan | 9,538,959 | 8,988,366 | 28.4 | 67.5 | 9,029,068 | 5,736 | 43,231† | 43,331† |
| Minnesota | 4,529,500 | 4,301,850 | 53.5 | 44.1 | 3,938,360 | 5,022 | 38,303 | 35,656 |
| Mississippi | 1,817,454 | 1,508,978 | 62.9 | 30.8 | 1,675,569 | 3,323 | 25,178 | 24,369 |

**TABLE 10:** continued

| | Total (000) | Revenue State and local (000) | Receipts State contribution (%) | Local contribution (%) | Current Amount (000) | Expenditures Per pupil | Average Instructional staff* | Salaries Classroom teachers |
|---|---|---|---|---|---|---|---|---|
| Missouri | 4,307,282 | 4,037,282 | 39.6 | 56.6 | 3,361,300 | 4,007 | 30,630 | 29,410 |
| Montana | 796,090 | 726,746 | 60.0 | 36.5 | 746,914† | 4,676† | 28,344† | 28,514† |
| Nebraska | 1,428,682† | 1,344,383† | 40.1† | 56.4† | 1,311,144† | 4,660† | 30,463 | 28,718 |
| Nevada | 1,167,223 | 1,117,765 | 39.2 | 58.2 | 1,022,973 | 4,590 | 35,764 | 34,119 |
| New Hampshire | 1,094,125 | 1,062,825 | 8.4 | 89.0 | 935,888 | 5,165 | 36,456† | 33,931 |
| New Jersey | 10,765,331 | 10,410,130 | 44.4 | 53.7 | 10,391,632 | 9,192 | 46,055 | 43,997 |
| New Mexico | 1,342,881 | 1,172,678 | 87.1 | 11.2 | 1,252,145 | 4,249 | 27,356 | 26,355 |
| New York | 22,234,500 | 21,034,500 | 41.4 | 55.5 | 20,744,400 | 7,767 | 46,300 | 44,600 |
| North Carolina | 5,978,417† | 5,593,260† | 69.8† | 28.3† | 5,314,621† | 4,801† | 30,678 | 29,367 |
| North Dakota | 574,684† | 516,784† | 46.2† | 48.4† | 504,224† | 4,270† | 26,058 | 25,211 |
| Ohio | 10,213,000 | 9,629,000 | 44.0 | 52.8 | 9,883,000 | 5,576 | 34,700 | 34,600 |
| Oklahoma | 2,546,270 | 2,344,925 | 70.3 | 27.4 | 2,273,900 | 3,808 | 26,977 | 26,051 |
| Oregon | 2,944,300 | 2,752,000 | 40.2 | 55.9 | 2,930,900 | 5,754 | 36,882† | 35,435† |
| Pennsylvania | 14,060,849† | 13,415,525† | 49.5† | 48.2† | 11,427,311† | 6,657† | 42,736 | 41,580 |
| Rhode Island | 928,725 | 877,515 | 42.1 | 54.7 | 905,165 | 6,328 | 38,282 | 37,510 |
| South Carolina | 3,133,290 | 2,848,800 | 50.9 | 44.6 | 2,733,652 | 4,319 | 30,477 | 29,151 |
| South Dakota | 604,364 | 529,549 | 29.8 | 61.5 | 548,814 | 4,100 | 24,470 | 24,125 |
| Tennessee | 3,179,479 | 2,854,829 | 49.8 | 45.1 | 3,148,494 | 3,724 | 30,451 | 29,313 |
| Texas | 17,826,663 | 16,471,236 | 47.2 | 48.8 | 15,665,353 | 4,395 | 20,452 | 29,935 |
| Utah | 1,608,525 | 1,503,333 | 60.9 | 36.5 | 1,361,827 | 2,952 | 27,859 | 26,997 |
| Vermont | 709,575† | 670,009† | 34.6† | 61.8† | 684,138† | 6,974† | 36,217† | 34,824 |
| Virginia | 5,673,547 | 5,405,806 | 35.5 | 61.4 | 5,060,147 | 4,903 | 35,093 | 32,356 |
| Washington | 5,372,273 | 5,076,391 | 77.4 | 21.4 | 4,681,489 | 5,213 | 37,495 | 35,070 |
| West Virginia | 1,867,096 | 1,721,410 | 72.7 | 25.1 | 1,680,041 | 5,288 | 31,428 | 30,301 |
| Wisconsin | 5,403,662 | 5,163,094 | 41.4 | 56.0 | 4,987,680 | 6,077† | 36,668† | 36,477 |

* Includes teachers of art, music, and so on.
† Estimates made by the National Education Association.

SOURCE: *1992 Estimates of School Statistics*, National Education Association, 1993.

## AIR QUALITY

We all want a cleaner, healthier environment. For some, however, the purity of the air and water are paramount. If you have a lung or heart condition, you may require a higher standard of environmental quality than other job hunters would. Likewise an allergy to pollens may drive you from the lush Southeast to the arid Southwest.

You can get free, detailed charts, published by the Environmental Protection Agency, to compare chemical air-pollutant and ozone levels in metropolitan statistical areas (MSAs) throughout the United States. To order the *National Air Quality and Emissions Trends Report*, call or write the Environmental Protection Agency, 401 M Street S.W., Washington, DC 20460; 202-260-4361.

To learn more about a particular area, contact the regional Environmental Protection Agency office that monitors the area. The addresses are listed on pages 179-180.

For information about pollen counts and other natural environmental pollutants, contact one of the area's local television stations and ask for the weather office. You can find the television stations by contacting the chamber of commerce or using the local yellow pages.

## HEALTH CARE

If you or someone in your family has a health problem requiring special treatment, you will want to research medical facilities and treatment programs carefully. Even if you have no special requirements, you may feel more secure living in an area with well-equipped medical facilities. There will be tradeoffs. A town that is too small to attract an obstetrician or have kidney-dialysis equipment may have excellent doctors who cheerfully make house calls and charge only a fraction of their city counterparts' fees.

To learn more about the availability of health care in a particular region, contact the county or state health department. You can reach the department by calling the state or county government operator. You can also get a good idea of the variety and number of hospitals and clinics by looking at the local yellow pages.

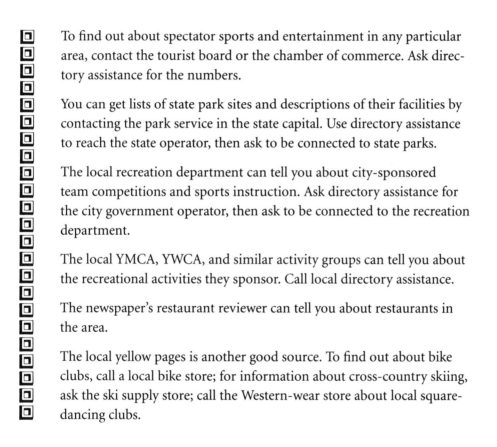

## RECREATION, SPORTS, AND LEISURE

If hiking or white-water rafting is your favorite pastime, you can learn about the facilities for that activity in your target area. If Little League baseball quenches your thirst for spectator sports, you have many more options than your job-hunting counterpart who demands season tickets to a professional team's home games. For the best information, you should focus on sources that specialize in your particular interests.

To find out about spectator sports and entertainment in any particular area, contact the tourist board or the chamber of commerce. Ask directory assistance for the numbers.

You can get lists of state park sites and descriptions of their facilities by contacting the park service in the state capital. Use directory assistance to reach the state operator, then ask to be connected to state parks.

The local recreation department can tell you about city-sponsored team competitions and sports instruction. Ask directory assistance for the city government operator, then ask to be connected to the recreation department.

The local YMCA, YWCA, and similar activity groups can tell you about the recreational activities they sponsor. Call local directory assistance.

The newspaper's restaurant reviewer can tell you about restaurants in the area.

The local yellow pages is another good source. To find out about bike clubs, call a local bike store; for information about cross-country skiing, ask the ski supply store; call the Western-wear store about local square-dancing clubs.

## TRANSPORTATION

You may spend an hour or more per day commuting to and from work. Living and working in an area with good, minimally congested roads and effective public transportation systems can mean more leisure time or at the very least, more comfortable commuting. Likewise, if the job you hope to have requires frequent travel, convenient air transportation is crucial.

As you consider the area in which you wish to live, find answers to these questions:

What is the average round-trip commute from specific residential neighborhoods to the city?

Is there reliable, convenient mass transit for commuters?

Where is the nearest airport, and what airlines service it? (Then call the airlines and ask how many flights there are per day.)

How many connections are required to reach major U.S. cities? (Or, if you already have a prospective job in mind, how many connections are required to travel to cities you will most often visit?

Does Amtrak make scheduled stops in the locality?

If you have special needs such as transportation for an elderly or disabled family member, be sure to ask about the availability and prices of such services.

To learn more about the transportation systems in local areas, contact the local transportation authority through local directory assistance. If you would like to compare several systems, *A Directory of Urban Public Transportation Service* (U.S. Department of Transportation) lists public transportation systems and contact information for metropolitan transit authorities in hundreds of cities.

▣▣▣▣▣▣▣▣▣▣▣▣▣▣▣▣▣▣▣▣▣▣▣▣▣▣▣▣▣

You may also get an accurate picture of local commuting from the chamber of commerce. Ed was considering several jobs in different cities. He asked the chamber of commerce in each community to provide average rush-hour commuting times from various neighborhoods. He learned that he could spend anywhere between ninety minutes and ten hours a week commuting—valuable input for his job decision.

▣▣▣▣▣▣▣▣▣▣▣▣▣▣▣▣▣▣▣▣▣▣▣▣▣▣▣▣▣

# REFERENCES FOR RESEARCH

The remainder of this chapter consists of listings of references for information about various aspects of the quality of life.

## A National Perspective

The Bureau of the Census in Washington, D.C. publishes several books that give an overview of demographics, (population), employment and unemployment, and general income levels in hundreds of cities across the United States. You can use these publications for a quick first look at various localities. Of the publications listed below you can find the *Statistical Abstract of the United States* in most public libraries. The others are available for purchase from the Government Printing Office or can be found in U.S. government depository libraries (see page 101) and large public libraries.

- *Statistical Abstract of the United States* (general)—Includes data on regions, states, metropolitan areas, and cities; subjects include population, employment, and income

- *County and City Data Book* (general)—Supplement to the *Statistical Abstract*; for counties, MSAs, and cities: published every five years

- *State and MSA Data Book* (general)—Statistical data at the state and MSA level

- *Current Population Reports* (general)—Population estimates and projections; income and special studies for localities across the United States

- *Current Government Reports* (general cost of living)—City, county, and public employment and finances; state tax revenues

## A State Level Perspective

The following publications are general directories for states and municipalities and can be found in most libraries. Use them to find state, county, and municipal agencies.

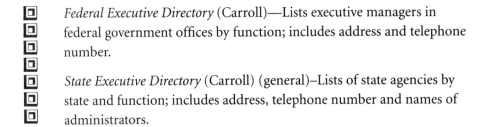 *Federal Executive Directory* (Carroll)—Lists executive managers in federal government offices by function; includes address and telephone number.

*State Executive Directory* (Carroll) (general)–Lists of state agencies by state and function; includes address, telephone number and names of administrators.

Most state chambers of commerce publish a variety of materials, including those described below, that can help you understand the state's economy and standard of living. (For a list of state chambers of commerce, refer to appendix IV.)

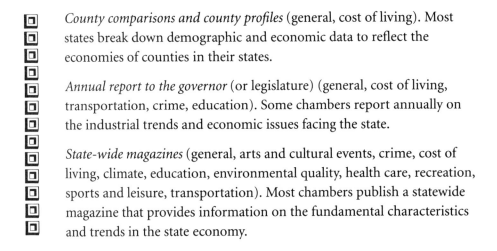 *County comparisons and county profiles* (general, cost of living). Most states break down demographic and economic data to reflect the economies of counties in their states.

*Annual report to the governor* (or legislature) (general, cost of living, transportation, crime, education). Some chambers report annually on the industrial trends and economic issues facing the state.

*State-wide magazines* (general, arts and cultural events, crime, cost of living, climate, education, environmental quality, health care, recreation, sports and leisure, transportation). Most chambers publish a statewide magazine that provides information on the fundamental characteristics and trends in the state economy.

### State Economic Analyses

Most states have an office devoted to analyzing employment trends, population, and other economic data. (There is a list of them on page 259.) The office is usually associated with the state's commerce or economic development department. The types of information published vary from state to state. Call the state government operator and ask to be connected to the office that oversees economic development in the state. When you reach the appropriate office, ask if the state provides:

*State economic profiles* (general, cost of living). Current and historical statistical, economic and demographic data for the entire state.

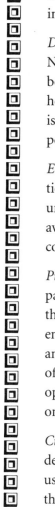

*State price-level indexes* (cost of living). Some states publish an annual index of price differences across the state at the county level.

*Data for site selection* (general, cost of living, education, transportation). Normally published with the potential businessperson in mind, these booklets provide excellent data on living conditions and the economic health of the state—information that is valuable to job seekers. The text is intended to describe the region's economy in the most favorable terms possible, so read the data and tables carefully.

*Economic statistics* (general, cost of living). Akin to data for site selection, publications of economic statistics normally present data such as union activity, cost of living, county and MSA economic indicators, average temperatures and precipitation, average wages and taxes, utility costs, and labor-market information.

*Publications on specific subjects.* Most states publish a wide variety of pamphlets describing various aspects of life within the state. Usually, the pamphlets include discussions about education, cost of living, energy, financing, population, transportation, training services, state and local services, and sports and leisure facilities. You can find a variety of such publications about the state in the state library. Ask the state operator for the telephone number, or use one of the directories listed on page 86.

*Current Employment Developments* (general)—A monthly newsletter describing employment on the state and county level. The publication usually includes statistics and news of industrial events, such as layoffs, that affect the labor market. It is available from the state's labor department. Contact the state operator to find the department, or use one of the directories listed on page 86.

State libraries can also point you towards specialized publications that are not listed elsewhere in this chapter.

## A Local Perspective

The best way to get a feel for a particular area is to visit it. Use the time not only to pursue job opportunities, but also to learn what it would be like to live in the area. If education is a priority, drop in on the local schools. If skiing is your passion, check out the slopes. Use the opportunity to make contacts—meet the local banker and visit the chamber of commerce; tell a reporter that you enjoyed reading his or her stories, and ask for further information. These contacts give you a good feeling for the area's personality and features, and may eventually lead you to a job offer.

If you cannot visit the area, conduct telephone interviews with people who have interests similar to your own. For example, you might want to contact the local Parent-Teacher Association (PTA), the ski club, an environmental organization, or the local church or synagogue. You can find such groups by contacting the local chamber of commerce or library, or you can order the local yellow pages from the telephone company.

The following information sources can give you an in-depth look at any specific community.

*Local newspaper.* This is probably the best way to get an in-depth look at any locality without actually visiting it, and you can subscribe to most newspapers from anywhere in the world. Read all the sections of the paper—you will learn about special events, weather, crime, and politics. You can learn a great deal about a community's priorities and politics when you see what news is covered regularly by the journalists. You can also get a good overview of local home prices and salary ranges from the classified advertising. In addition, check the clothing and food prices, the range of cultural events, and everything else that is important to you.

Newspaper research was the chief factor behind Francine's change of plans. She lived and worked in San Diego. Her fiancé worked in Seattle, and she had begun searching for employment there. Having visited the city only a few times, she subscribed to the Seattle Times to learn more about her prospective home. Day after day she read reports of cloudiness and rain. An avid tennis player and lover of sunshine, she began to have serious misgivings. Eventually she convinced her fiancé to join her in San Diego.

*Local chamber of commerce or mayor's office.* Both of these offices are interested in attracting business to the area, so do not be surprised if they paint an optimistic picture of all aspects of the area's quality of life. Ask questions that require quantitative answers: What is the local unemployment rate? rather than How healthy is your local economy? Also ask these organizations to send you any printed information they may have on the community. You can visit or call, depending upon your time and budget.

*Local economic development offices.* Most counties, and some cities, have their own economic development office, similar to the state agencies listed in appendix V. They can provide a range of data about a particular area, including unemployment, business development, inflation, population growth, and cost of living. Visit or call for information.

*Local library.* Most cities and towns have at least one public library (If your prospective area does not, check with the library in a nearby town.) The library will probably have information about local history as well as demographic and economic data for the area. Talk with the librarian by telephone to assess the value of visiting the library to review its collection.

In summary, decide what community attributes are important to you and your household. If you are free to live anywhere, balance your life-style priorities with your job priorities, and find out where you can make the best of both. If you are interested in specific areas, evaluate those attributes that are important to you in each prospective community. With a few hours of research, you can learn a tremendous amount about a community—enough to make well-informed job decisions.

# INTERVIEWING EMPLOYERS

The research that you do on industries, companies, and professions helps you not only to target employers and jobs, but also to land the job you want. First, research acquaints you with important background information and lingo, making you more comfortable in your contacts with employers. Second, because of what you have learned in your research on industries, companies, and professions, you will be more knowledgeable. This knowledge will impress your prospective employer and put you well ahead of less-informed job applicants. Few job candidates know much about the companies they interview with, so you will stand out above the crowd. Study the examples we have outlined below. They illustrate ways in which the research you have already conducted can give you the edge you need to land the job you want.

## THE COVER LETTER

Begin using your special insights in your cover letter. Showing knowledge of an employer will help you obtain an interview. The cover letter and a résumé provide the interviewer's first impression of you. Most experts agree that a cover letter should provide more than an overview of your experience. It should be written to show how you could fill the needs of an employer. Through your research, you can spot the employer's needs; show how your experience and skills will enable you to meet those needs.

Consider the case of Jason, a bright business graduate of a little-known midwestern college. He wanted to get a job as an assistant product manager at a large, profitable confectionery company, but he know that only Ivy League graduates were considered for positions in the company. Jason was determined to get noticed, so he set out to research the company to gather some ammunition. The company was privately held, so there were no filings at the Security and Exchange Commission. In addition, the company had a reputation of being extremely secretive—very little information about it was reported in the trade or popular press.

With so few published sources available to him, Jason got on the phone. He first called associations and Wall Street analysts, but their knowledge about the company was sketchy. He decided to call the company directly. Instead of starting at the headquarters where he would be applying for a job, he contacted several of the regional sales offices. He explained his plans to apply for a position with the company. Through the conversations he was able to piece together the strengths and weaknesses of a particular product line.

With this information, Jason targeted his cover letter directly to the product manager. He described what he understood about the marketing of the product, and cited acknowledged weaknesses in two of the company's sales regions. He further described how he thought they might be corrected. The sales manager was so impressed with Jason's insights and his research that he immediately called him in for an interview.

## YOUR APPEARANCE

You are not the only one that is looking for a good match during the interview. The employer is looking for someone who is not only qualified, but also possesses the personality and demeanor appropriate to the position. As part of your research about the target company you may well have learned something about its style. (The topic is covered in chapters 16 and 17.) Use that knowledge to help you prepare yourself for the interview. If employees wear Brooks Brothers suits, dust yours off and put it on. If a more casual atmosphere prevails, dress down a bit so that you will not appear stodgy. In any event, your appearance for the interview should reflect the company's style. Look as if you will fit in.

## ASKING GOOD QUESTIONS

What you ask during a job interview can be as important as the information you provide to the prospective employer. Most interviewers allot time for questions from the applicant. This is generally considered an open forum where you can address any topic that may concern you. This session gives you the opportunity to show the employer how much you have learned about the company before the interview. Your preparation, culminating with intelligent and well-conceived questions, will reveal your eagerness to make a good employment decision, reflect your skill as an information gatherer, emphasize your analytical research skills, and set you apart from less-informed candidates.

For example, a career services director in Washington, D.C. remembers a graduating student who was one of dozens interviewing with a large industrial company whose representatives had come to campus. The student, eager to get the position, had studied the company's annual reports and read several articles about recent developments in the company. The student was hired because, according to the employer, she was the only one who had asked questions about a recent merger between the company and another major employer. The employer felt that a student who came prepared for an interview would be prepared for the job.

In some cases, you may want to use the interview to supplement what you have already learned, while winning over the interviewer. Consider these examples.

• You may have learned that the industry in question is growing rapidly. You want to know how the prospective employer plans to take advantage of this growth. Instead of simply asking "What are the company's long-term goals?" you might phrase your question this way:

> I have spoken to analysts at the U.S. Department of Commerce
> who tell me that the semiconductor industry is growing by nearly
> 15 percent annually. The Semiconductor Association is even more
> optimistic, predicting growth at 20 percent. Do you agree with

these projections, and how does your company plan to capitalize on this growth?

In this question you have taken the opportunity to demonstrate the insights that you have acquired, your research methodology, and your knowledge of information sources. You have also made it clear that you take initiative and are interested enough in the industry and this company to become informed and to be prepared.

· If you have learned that your prospective employer is an industry leader in some segments of the medical products market, but are not sure how committed it is to the particular segment, medical instruments, that interests you, you might take this approach.

> Through your annual report, I learned that your research and development budget increased by 35 percent last year. What proportion of the R&D expenditures is earmarked for medical instruments? Do you have plans to expand this division?

In this discussion, you have let the employer know that you have done some research, and that budgets and corporate planning are areas familiar to you.

## GIVING GOOD ANSWERS

During the interview, your prospective employer will ask a series of questions designed to learn as much about you and your skills as quickly as possible. You can use what you have learned in the preceding chapters to impress your employers with well-thought-out answers.

Under each question set out below are two sample answers, the first, a reply that you may have made before you read this book, the second a reply that will illustrate the ways in which you can use what you have learned to make a good impression on the interviewer.

**Interviewer: Why do you want this job?**

BEFORE DOING RESEARCH
I learned about this job in the paper and it looked interesting.

AFTER DOING RESEARCH

Since beginning my employment research, I have learned a great deal about this industry, your company, and how my interests fit in. I believe this position gives me the opportunity to make a sizable contribution to the company as well as help me grow in my field. Your company has impressed me. You are considered a leader in the field by most analysts. Your growth record in recent years has been impressive and you have given your employees the opportunity to grow along with you and profit through your expansion. Experts believe that the industry will continue to expand, so I feel certain that your company has a bright future. I'd like to be a part of its future.

### Interviewer: How would you describe yourself?

BEFORE DOING RESEARCH

I feel I'm a conscientious, likable person, and easy to get along with.

AFTER DOING RESEARCH

I believe that, to get the most out of life, you need to explore possibilities and go after opportunities. I am the kind of person who is willing to work hard to get ahead. Some people will settle for just any job. I have done months of research to find the best job for myself. I believe this is the job.

### Interviewer: What are your qualifications for this job?

BEFORE DOING RESEARCH

I have a bachelor's degree in engineering.

AFTER DOING RESEARCH

I understand that your organization is not only looking for degrees, but also for proven innovativeness. I have a bachelor's degree in engineering, and I have experience in finding more efficient ways to accomplish tasks. For example, during college I created a system that could be used by our department secretary to collect, tally, and file all the student's grades with a minimum of effort. The device has since been adopted in four other departments.

**Interviewer: What do you see yourself doing five years from now?**

BEFORE DOING RESEARCH
I would like to be in some sort of managerial position.

AFTER DOING RESEARCH
In five years, I hope to be holding a responsible position in [company name]. Through my research, I've learned that [company name] traditionally promotes from within, and that the best of your trainees can expect to become managers within five years. I hope to perform well enough to earn a management position on, or ahead of schedule. I believe in [XYZ company's] long-range objectives, and I'm flexible enough to move where I'm needed.

The difference between these before and after answers can make or break an interview. Before you go to an interview, practice formulating your answers to the questions typically asked by employers. Use what you have learned from your research to identify the company's strengths and weaknesses, interests and needs, priorities and peculiarities, and think through how your talents fit in. Certain questions are commonly asked by employers.

What do you consider your strengths? Your weaknesses?

Do you like to work with people or alone?

What do you think about our company?

Do you work well under pressure?

What would you consider an ideal position?

What did you like most/least about your last job?

What do you do in your free time?

How long do you plan to live in this area?

Would you object to moving to a different city?

Why did you leave your last position?

Where else are you applying for a job?

How did you learn about this opening?

What are your salary requirements?

What interests you most about this job?

Many career-placement professionals agree that careful research into a company and an industry can be the difference between an unproductive job interview and a job offer. Do your research to find the best positions, then reuse what you have learned to capture the interest of your prospective employers.

# EMPLOYMENT ABROAD

The focus of this book is on finding the best jobs in the United States of America. If the travel bug bites and you want to explore opportunities overseas, here are some sources to get you started.

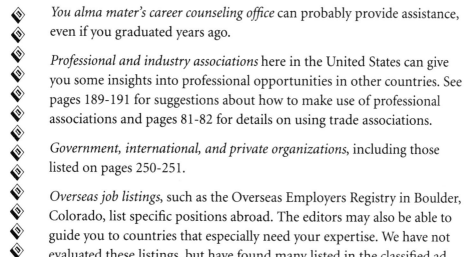

*You alma mater's career counseling office* can probably provide assistance, even if you graduated years ago.

*Professional and industry associations* here in the United States can give you some insights into professional opportunities in other countries. See pages 189-191 for suggestions about how to make use of professional associations and pages 81-82 for details on using trade associations.

*Government, international, and private organizations*, including those listed on pages 250-251.

*Overseas job listings*, such as the Overseas Employers Registry in Boulder, Colorado, list specific positions abroad. The editors may also be able to guide you to countries that especially need your expertise. We have not evaluated these listings, but have found many listed in the classified ad sections of international-interest magazines. Check for them in your library.

The target country's embassy or consulate. Check directory assistance in Washington, D.C. for the number.

You may obtain an overseas job with a U.S. company. In that case, the guidelines in parts I and IV of this book will serve you well. If you are targeting a job with a foreign firm, you can use the sources beginning on page 140. If you need additional resources, refer to *How to Find Information About Foreign Firms, How to Find Information About Companies, Volume 3, European Markets: A Guide to Company and Industry Information Sources,* and *Asian Markets: A guide to Company and Industry Information Sources,* all published by Washington Researchers. Look for them in your library or university career-services office.

# PUBLICATIONS

Aulick, Jane, *Looking for Employment in Foreign Countries* (World Trade Academy Press)—This book addresses current conditions. It explains opportunities and procedures for seeking and securing jobs overseas with the U.S. government, religious and nonprofit organizations, and private enterprises. Sample résumés and cover letters are included. Profiles of forty-six countries give historical and cultural backgrounds, the foreign employment situation, and the number of U.S. multinational corporations maintaining branches there.

*Employment Abroad: Facts and Fallacies* (Chamber of Commerce of the United States)—General discussion of the major points to be considered in looking for employment that may result in foreign travel or residence. The selected references at the end of the pamphlet provide a comprehensive of standard reference sources and inexpensive or free materials. Request with code #6867.

Cohen, Marjorie Adoff, *Work, Study, Travel Abroad: Whole World Handbook* (St. Martin's Press)—Guide to work, study, and travel abroad geared mainly to students.

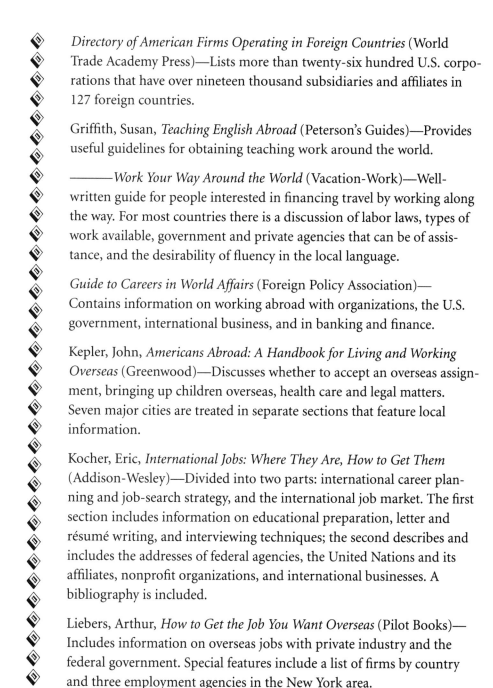

*Directory of American Firms Operating in Foreign Countries* (World Trade Academy Press)—Lists more than twenty-six hundred U.S. corporations that have over nineteen thousand subsidiaries and affiliates in 127 foreign countries.

Griffith, Susan, *Teaching English Abroad* (Peterson's Guides)—Provides useful guidelines for obtaining teaching work around the world.

————*Work Your Way Around the World* (Vacation-Work)—Well-written guide for people interested in financing travel by working along the way. For most countries there is a discussion of labor laws, types of work available, government and private agencies that can be of assistance, and the desirability of fluency in the local language.

*Guide to Careers in World Affairs* (Foreign Policy Association)—Contains information on working abroad with organizations, the U.S. government, international business, and in banking and finance.

Kepler, John, *Americans Abroad: A Handbook for Living and Working Overseas* (Greenwood)—Discusses whether to accept an overseas assignment, bringing up children overseas, health care and legal matters. Seven major cities are treated in separate sections that feature local information.

Kocher, Eric, *International Jobs: Where They Are, How to Get Them* (Addison-Wesley)—Divided into two parts: international career planning and job-search strategy, and the international job market. The first section includes information on educational preparation, letter and résumé writing, and interviewing techniques; the second describes and includes the addresses of federal agencies, the United Nations and its affiliates, nonprofit organizations, and international businesses. A bibliography is included.

Liebers, Arthur, *How to Get the Job You Want Overseas* (Pilot Books)—Includes information on overseas jobs with private industry and the federal government. Special features include a list of firms by country and three employment agencies in the New York area.

*Foreign Service Careers* (U.S. Department of State)—Provides information on application procedures, training, and benefits of Foreign Service employment, as well as an account of the work of the Service.

Williams, John, *Evaluating an Overseas Job Opportunity* (Pilot Books)—Written for the company employee who is offered an overseas position. Emphasized are comparisons to be made when considering such a position, including items such as possible changes in standard of living, taxation, and health care and other benefits.

Win, David, *International Careers* (Williamson)—Surveys the international career-building process; includes discussions on private- and public-sector employment, U.S. government and foreign government jobs, and international trade and business opportunities.

*International Living* (Agora) newsletter has a regular feature on employment. The December 1991 issue described how to find teaching jobs abroad and the January 1992 issue featured employment opportunities in Hong Kong. Write for information about subscription rates.

# ORGANIZATIONS

Listed below are some organizations that may be able to provide helpful information. Other sources not listed include trade associations and international corporations, which can be located through your local library.

### U.S. Government Organizations

*For teaching dependents of employees of the Defense Department:*
Department of Defense Dependent Schools
Teacher Recruitment Sections
2461 Eisenhower Avenue
Alexandria, VA 22331

*For positions as Foreign Service officers:*
Board of Examiners for the Foreign Service
Department of State
1800 N. Kent Street
Arlington, VA 22209

*For positions as Foreign Service support personnel:*
Recruitment Branch
Employment Division
Department of State
Washington, DC 20520

*For volunteer work:*
Peace Corps
Office of Personnel Management
Washington, DC 20526

## International Organizations

*For volunteer work:*
Coordinating Committee for International Voluntary Service
UNESCO
1 rue Miollis
Paris 75015, France

*For U.N. employment abroad:*
Office of Personnel
United Nations
1 United Nations Plaza
New York, NY 10017

## Private Organizations

Chamber of Commerce of the United States
1615 H Street NW
Washington, DC 20062

# APPENDIX III

# DATABASE VENDORS

BRS Information Technologies
A Division of Maxwell Online
8000 Westpark Drive
McLean, Virginia 22102
800-289-4277 or 703-442-0900

CompuServe Information Service
P.O. Box 20212
Columbus, OH 43220
800-848-8199 or 614-457-8600

Data-Star
Radio-Suisse Services
485 Devon Park Drive, Suite 110
Wayne, PA 19087
800-221-7754 or 215-687-6777

DIALOG
Information Services, Inc.
3460 Hillview Avenue
Palo Alto, CA 94304
800-334-2564 or 415-858-2700

Dow Jones & Company, Inc.
Dow Jones News/Retrieval
P.O. Box 300
Princeton, NJ 08543
609-520-4638

Dun & Bradstreet Information Services
3 Sylvan Way
Parsippany, NJ 07054
800-526-0651 or 201-605-6751

Mead Data Central—NEXIS
9443 Springboro Pike
Miamisburg, OH 45342
800-227-4908

NewsNet
945 Haverford Avenue
Bryn Mawr, Pennsylvania 19010
800-345-1301 or 215-527-8030

Wilsonline
H. W. Wilson Company
950 University Avenue
Bronx, NY 10452
800-367-6770 or 212-588-8400
NY State: 800-462-6060

# APPENDIX IV

# STATE CHAMBERS
# OF COMMERCE

**Alabama**
Business Council of Alabama
468 S. Perry Street
P.O. Box 76
Montgomery, AL 36101
205-834-6000
Fax: 205-262-7371

**Alaska**
Alaska State Chamber of Commerce
217 2d Street, No. 201
Juneau, AK 99801
907-586-2323
Fax: 907-463-5515

**Arizona**
Arizona Chamber of Commerce
1221 E. Osborn Road, Suite 100
Phoenix, AZ 85014
602-248-9172
Fax: 602-265-1262

**Arkansas**
Arkansas State Chamber of Commerce
410 Cross Street
P.O. Box 3645
Little Rock, AR 72203-3645
501-374-9225
Fax: 501-372-2722

**California**
California Chamber of Commerce
1201 K Street, 12th Floor
Sacramento, CA 95814
916-444-6670
Fax: 916-444-6685

**Colorado**
Colorado Association of
    Commerce & Industry
1776 Lincoln Street, Suite 1200
Denver, CO 80203-1029
303-831-7411
Fax: 303-860-1439

**Connecticut**
Connecticut Business & Industry
    Association, Inc.
370 Asylum Street
Hartford, CT 06103
203-244-1990
Fax: 203-278-8562

**Delaware**
Delaware State Chamber of
    Commerce, Inc.
1 Commerce Center, Suite 200
Wilmington, DE 19801
302-655-7221
Fax: 302-654-0691

**Florida**
Florida Chamber of Commerce
136 S. Bronought Street
P.O. Box 11309
Tallahassee, FL 32302
904-425-1200
Fax: 904-425-1260

**Georgia**
Georgia Chamber of Commerce
233 Peachtree Street NE, Suite 200
Atlanta, GA 30303
404-223-2264
Fax: 404-223-2290

**Hawaii**
The Chamber of Commerce of Hawaii
Dillingham Building
735 Bishop Street
Honolulu, HI 96813
808-522-8800
Fax: 808-522-8836

**Idaho**
Idaho Association of Commerce &
    Industry
802 W. Bannock Street, Suite 308
P.O. Box 389
Boise, ID 83701
208-343-1849
Fax: 208-342-6891

**Illinois**
Illinois State Chamber of Commerce
20 N. Wacker Drive
Chicago, IL 60606
312-372-7373
Fax: 312-372-7382

**Indiana**
Indiana State Chamber of Commerce, Inc.
Indiana Commerce Center
1 N. Capitol, Suite 200
Indianapolis, IN 46204-2248
317-264-3110
Fax: 317-264-6855

**Iowa**
Iowa Association of Business & Industry
431 E. Locust Street
Des Moines, IA 50309
800-383-4224 (Iowa only)
515-244-6149
Fax: 515-244-8907

**Kansas**
Kansas Chamber of Commerce & Industry
500 Bank IV Tower
1 Townsite Plaza
Topeka, KS 66603
913-357-6321
Fax: 913-357-4732

**Kentucky**
Kentucky Chamber of Commerce
Versailles Road
P.O. Box 817
Frankfort, KY 40602
502-695-4700
Fax: 502-695-6824

**Louisiana**
Louisiana Association of
  Business & Industry
P.O. Box 80258
Baton Rouge, LA 70898
504-928-5388
Fax: 504-929-6054

**Maine**
Maine Chamber of Commerce & Industry
126 Sewall Street
Augusta, ME 04330
207-623-4568
Fax: 207-622-7723

**Maryland**
Maryland Chamber of Commerce
275 West Street, Suite 400
Annapolis, MD 21401
410-269-0624
Fax: 410-269-5247

**Massachusetts**
Massachusetts Association of
  Chamber of Commerce Executives
c/o Chamber of Commerce and Industry
  of Northern Middlesex
45 Palmer Street
Lowell, MA 01852
508-937-9300

**Michigan**
Michigan State Chamber of Commerce
600 S. Walnut Street
Lansing, MI 48933
517-371-2100
Fax: 517-371-7224

**Minnesota**
Minnesota Chamber of Commerce
  & Industry
480 Cedar Street, Suite 500
Minnesota Chamber Building
St. Paul, MN 55101
612-292-4650
Fax: 612-292-4656

**Mississippi**
Mississippi Economic Council
620 North Street
P.O. Box 23276
Jackson, MS 39225-3276
601-969-0022
Fax: 601-353-0247

**Missouri**
Missouri Chamber of Commerce
P.O. Box 149
Jefferson City, MO 65102
314-634-3511
Fax: 314-634-8855

**Montana**
Montana Chamber of Commerce
2030 11th Avenue
P.O. Box 1730
Helena, MT 59624
406-442-2405

**Nebraska**
Nebraska Chamber of Commerce &
   Industry
1320 Lincoln Mall
P.O. Box 95128
Lincoln, NE 68509
402-474-4422
Fax: 402-474-2510

**Nevada**
Nevada Chamber of Commerce
   Association
P.O. Box 3499
Reno, NV 89505
702-786-3030
Fax: 702-323-3499

**New England Council**
New England Council, Inc.
581 Boylston Street, 7th Floor
Boston, MA 02116
617-437-0304
Fax: 617-437-6279

**New Hampshire**
Business & Industry Association
   of New Hampshire
122 N. Main Street
Concord, NH 03301
603-224-5388
Fax: 603-224-2872

**New Jersey**
New Jersey State Chamber of Commerce
1 State Street Square
50 W. State Street, Suite 1110
Trenton, NJ 08608
609-989-7888
Fax: 609-989-9696

**New Mexico**
Association of Commerce
   & Industry of New Mexico
2309 Renard Place SE, Suite 402
Albuquerque, NM 87106
505-842-0644
Fax: 505-842-0734

**New York**
Business Council of New York State, Inc.
152 Washington Avenue
Albany, NY 12210
518-465-7511
Fax: 518-465-4389

**North Carolina**
North Carolina Citizens for
   Business & Industry
225 Hillsborough Street
P.O. Box 2508
Raleigh, NC 27602
919-828-0758
Fax: 919-821-4992

**North Dakota**
Greater North Dakota Association/
State Chamber of Commerce
808 3d Avenue S.
P.O. Box 2467
Fargo, ND 58108
701-237-9461
Fax: 701-237-9463

**Ohio**
Ohio Chamber of Commerce
35 E. Gay Street, 2d Floor
Columbus, OH 43215-3181
614-228-4201
Fax: 614-228-6403

## Oklahoma

Oklahoma State Chamber of Commerce
 & Industry
4020 N. Lincoln Boulevard
Oklahoma City, OK 73105
405-424-4003
Fax: 405-424-3137

## Oregon

Associated Oregon Industries, Inc.
1149 Court Street NE
P.O. Box 12519
Salem, OR 97309
503-588-0050
Fax: 503-588-0052

## Pennsylvania

Pennsylvania Chamber of Business
 & Industry
222 N. 3d Street
Harrisburg, PA 17101
717-255-3252
Fax: 717-255-3298

## Puerto Rico

Chamber of Commerce of Puerto Rico
100 Tetuan Street
Old San Juan, PR 00904
809-721-6060
Fax: 809-723-1891

## Rhode Island

Rhode Island Chamber
 of Commerce Federation
300 Richmond Street
Providence, RI 02903
401-272-1400
Fax: 401-453-3799

## South Carolina

South Carolina Chamber of Commerce
NCNB Tower
1201 Main St., Suite 1810
AT&T Building
Columbia, SC 29201
803-799-4601
Fax: 803-779-6043

## South Dakota

Industry & Commerce Association
 of South Dakota
P.O. Box 190
Pierre, SD 57501
605-224-6161
Fax: 605-224-7198

## Tennessee

Tennessee Association of Business
611 Commerce Street, Suite 3030
Nashville, TN 37203
615-256-5141
Fax: 615-256-6726

## Texas

Texas Chamber of Commerce
900 Congress, Suite 501
Austin, TX 78701-2447
512-472-1594
Fax: 512-320-0280

## Utah

Utah State Chamber
 of Commerce Association
c/o Cache Chamber of Commerce
160 N. Main Street
Lugan, UT 84321
801-752-2161

**Vermont**
Vermont Chamber of Commerce
P.O. Box 37
Montpelier, VT  05601
802-223-3443
Fax: 802-229-4581

**Virginia**
The Virginia Chamber of Commerce
9 S. 5th Street
Richmond, VA 23219
804-644-1607
Fax: 804-783-6112

**Washington**
Association of Washington Business
P.O. Box 658
1414 S. Cherry Street
Olympia, WA  98507-0658
206-943-1600
Fax: 206-943-5811

**West Virginia**
West Virginia Chamber of Commerce
1000 Kanawha Valley Bldg.
P.O. Box 2789
Charleston, WV 25330
304-342-1115
Fax: 304-342-1130

**Wisconsin**
Wisconsin Manufacturers & Commerce
501 E. Washington Avenue
P.O. Box 352
Madison, WI  53701
608-258-3400
Fax: 608-258-3413

# APPENDIX V

# STATE ECONOMIC DEVELOPMENT OFFICES

**Alabama**
Department of Economic
   and Community Affairs
Office of the Governor
401 Adams Avenue
Montgomery, AL 36130
205-242-5100

**Alaska**
Division of Economic Enterprise
Department of Commerce
   and Economic Development
P.O. Box 110804
Juneau, AK 99811-0804
907-465-2018

**Arizona**
Office of Economic Development
Department of Commerce
3800 N. Central Avenue
Phoenix, AZ 85012
602-280-1331

**Arkansas**
Industrial Development Commission
1 Capitol Mall, Room 4C-300
Little Rock, AR 72201
501-682-1121

**California**
Department of Commerce
801 K Street, Suite 1700
Sacramento, CA 95814
916-322-1394

**Colorado**
Office of Business Development
1625 Broadway
Denver, CO 80202
303-892-3840

**Connecticut**
Department of Economic Development
865 Brook Street
Rocky Hill, CT 06067
203-258-4200

**Delaware**
Development Office
Department of Economic Development
P.O. Box 1401
Dover, DE 19903
302-739-4271

**District of Columbia**
Office of Business &
    Economic Development
Executive Office of the Mayor
717 14th Street NW
Washington, DC  20005
202-727-6600

**Florida**
Bureau of Industry Development
Division of Economic Development
Department of Commerce
310 Collins Building
107 W. Gaines Street
Tallahassee, FL 32399-2000
904-488-9360

**Georgia**
Department of Industry and Trade
P.O. Box 1776
285 Peachtree Center Avenue
Marquis Tower II, Suite 1100
Atlanta, GA  30301
404-656-3545

**Hawaii**
Research and Economic Analysis Division
Department of Business, Economic
    Development, and Tourism
220 S. King Street, 4th Floor
Honolulu, HI 96813
808-586-2466

**Idaho**
Division of Economic Development
Department of Commerce
700 W. State Street
Boise, ID 83720
208-334-2470

**Illinois**
Department of Commerce
    and Community Affairs
620 E. Adams Street
Springfield, IL 62701
217-782-7500

**Indiana**
Department of Commerce
Community Development Division
1 N. Capitol, Suite 700
Indianapolis, IN 46204-2288
317-232-8911

**Iowa**
Department of Economic Development
200 E. Grand Avenue
Des Moines, IA 50309
515-281-3251

**Kansas**
Department of Commerce
700 S.W. Harrison Street, Suite 1300
Topeka, KS 66603-3712
913-296-3481

**Kentucky**
Cabinet for Economic Development
2400 Capital Plaza Tower
Frankfort, KY 40601
502-564-7670

**Louisiana**
Department of Economic Development
P.O. Box 94185
Baton Rouge, LA 70804-9185
504-342-5359

**Maine**
Office of Business Development
State House, Station 59
Augusta, ME 04333
207-287-3153

**Maryland**
Department of Economic and
    Employment Development
100 Community Place
Crownsville, MD  21032
410-514-7005

**Massachusetts**
Office of Business Development
100 Cambridge Street, 13th Floor
Boston, MA  02202
617-727-3206

**Michigan**
Department of Commerce
P.O. Box 30004
Lansing, MI  48909
517-373-1820

**Minnesota**
Department of Trade
    and Economic Development
500 Metro Square
121 Seventh Place E
St. Paul, MN  55101-2146
612-297-1291

**Mississippi**
Department of Economic
    and Community Development
P.O. Box 849
Jackson, MS 39205
601-359-3449

**Missouri**
Department of Economic Development
P.O. Box 118, Room 680
Jefferson City, MO 65102
314-751-3964

**Montana**
Montana Department of Commerce
Business Development Division
1424 Ninth Avenue
Helena, MT  59620
406-444-3814

**Nebraska**
Department of Economic Development
P.O. Box 94666
Lincoln, NE 68509-4666
402-471-3111

**Nevada**
Commission on Economic Development
Capitol Complex
5151 S. Carson, 4th Floor
Carson City, NV 89710
702-687-4325

**New Hampshire**
Division of Economic Development
Department of Resources
    and Economic Development
P.O. Box 856
Concord, NH 03302-0856
603-271-2341

**New Jersey**
Division of Economic Development
Department of Commerce
  and Economic Development
20 W. State Street, CN 823
Trenton, NJ 08625
609-292-2462

**New Mexico**
Economic Development Division
Economic Development Department
Joseph Montoya Building
1100 St. Francis Drive
Santa Fe, NM 87503
505-827-0272

**New York**
State Department of
  Economic Development
Bureau of Research and Policy
1 Commerce Plaza
Albany, NY 12245
518-474-1161

**North Carolina**
Department of Economic
  and Community Development
Business Industry Development Division
430 N. Salisbury Street
Raleigh, NC 27611
919-733-4151

**North Dakota**
Department of Economic Development
  and Finance
1833 E. Bismarck Expressway
Bismarck, ND 58504
701-221-5300

**Ohio**
Department of Development
Ohio Data User Center
P.O. Box 1001
Columbus, OH 43266-0101
614-466-2115

**Oklahoma**
Department of Commerce
6601 Broadway Extension
P.O. Box 26980
Oklahoma City, OK 73126-0980
405-843-9770

**Oregon**
Department of Economic Development
775 Summer Street NE
Salem, OR 97310
503-373-1200

**Pennsylvania**
Office of Economic Development
  and Marketing
Department of Commerce
439 Forum Building, Room 454
Harrisburg, PA 17120
717-783-5698

**Rhode Island**
Department of Economic Development
7 Jackson Walkway
Providence, RI 02903
401-277-2601

**South Carolina**
State Development Board
P.O. Box 927
Columbia, SC 29202
803-737-0400

**South Dakota**
Governor's Office of
    Economic Development
Capitol Lake Plaza
711 E. Wells Avenue
Pierre, SD 57501-3335
605-773-5032

**Tennessee**
Division of Research
Department of Economic &
    Community Development
Rachel Jackson Building, 8th Floor
320 6th Avenue N
Nashville, TN 37243-0405
615-741-1995

**Texas**
Department of Commerce
P.O. Box 12728,
Capitol Station
Austin, TX 78711
512-472-5059

**Utah**
Department of Community
    and Economic Development
Division of Business and Economic
    Development
324 S. State Street, Suite 200
Salt Lake City, UT 84111
801-538-8700

**Vermont**
Economic Development Department
Development and Community
    Affairs Agency
109 State Street
Montpelier, VT 05609
802-828-3221

**Virginia**
Department of Economic Development
1021 E. Cary Street
Richmond, VA 23219
804-371-8100

**Washington**
Department of Trade
    & Economic Development
P.O. Box 42500
Mail Stop AX-13
Olympia, WA 98504-2500
206-753-7426

**West Virginia**
Governor's Office of Community
    and Industrial Development
Industrial Development Division
Capitol Complex, Building 6, Room 517
Charleston, WV 25305
304-348-2234

**Wisconsin**
Department of Development
P.O. Box 7970
Madison, WI 53707
608-266-1018

**Wyoming**
Division of Economic and
Community Development
Herschler Building, 2d Floor, West
122 W. 25th Street
Cheyenne, WY 82002
307-777-7287

# APPENDIX VI

# PUBLISHERS AND OTHER ORGANIZATIONS

T his section consists of the names, addresses, and telephone numbers of book publishers and of other organizations that have been cited in the text as sources of information.

Bob Adams Inc.
260 Center Street
Holbrook, MA 02343
800-872-5627

ACCRA. *See* American Chamber of
Commerce Research Association

Addison-Wesley Publishing Co., Inc.
1 Jacob Way
Reading, MA 01867
800-447-2226

AFL-CIO
815 16th Street NW
Washington DC 20006
202-637-5000

Agora, Inc.
824 E. Baltimore Street
Baltimore, MD 21202
410-234-0515

*The Almanac of the Unelected*
P.O. Box 3785
Washington, DC 20007
202-296-2297

American Business Information Inc.
5711 S. 86th Circle
Omaha, NE 68127
402-331-7169

American Chamber of Commerce
Research Association (ACCRA)
4232 King Street
Alexandria, VA 22302
703-998-0072

American Mathematical Society
P.O. Box 6248
Providence, RI 02940
401-272-9500

Arbor Consulting Group, Inc.
P.O. Box 5813
Bethseda, MD 20814

The Associated Press
50 Rockefeller Plaza
New York, NY 10020
212-621-1500

Avon Books
1350 Avenue of the Americas
New York, NY 10016
800-238-0658

Bureau of the Census. *See* U.S.
Department of Commerce

Bureau of Labor Statistics. *See* U. S.
Department of Labor

Business Publications, Inc.
9605 Scranton Road, Suite 503
San Diego, CA 92121
619-457-7577

BusinessWire
44 Montgomery Street, 39th Floor
San Francisco, CA 94104
800-227-0845 or,
in California, 415-986-4422
800-221-2462 or,
in New York, 212-575-8822

Cambridge Information Group
7200 Wisconsin Avenue, Suite 601
Bethesda, MD 20814
800-843-7751 or 301-961-6750

Cantrell Corp.
P.O. Box 3030
Oakton, VA 22124
703-620-1972

Carroll Publishing Company
1058 Thomas Jefferson Street NW
Washington, DC 20007
202-333-8620

Chamber of Commerce
of the United States
International Group
1615 H Street NW
Washington, DC 20062
202-463-5460

Columbia Books, Inc.
1212 New York Avenue NW, Suite 330
Washington, DC 20005
202-898-0662

Congressional Information Service, Inc.
4520 East West Highway, Suite 800
Bethesda, MD 20814-3389
800-638-8380 or 301-654-1550

Congressional Quarterly Books
300 Raritan Center Parkway
P.O. Box 7816
Edison, NJ 08818
800-638-1710

Contemporary Books, Inc.
180 N. Michigan Avenue
Chicago, IL 60601
800-691-1918 or 312-782-9182

Council on Economic Priorities
30 Irving Place
New York, NY 10003
212-420-1133

Disclosure, Inc.
5161 River Road
Bethesda, MD 20816
800-638-8241 or 301-951-1350

Dow Jones & Company, Inc.
P. O. Box 300
Princeton, NJ 08543
800-522-3567 or 609-520-4638

Dun & Bradstreet Information Services
3 Sylvan Way
Parsippany, NJ 07084
800-526-0651 or 201-605-6000

Environmental Opportunities
P.O. Box 4957
Arcata, CA 95521
707-839-4640

Equal Opportunity Publications
150 Motor Parkway
Hauppage, NY 11788
516-273-0066

Extel Financial Ltd.
Fitzroy House
13-17 Epworth Street
London EC2A 4DL
England
071-251-3333

Federal Information Center
Pueblo, CO 81009

Federal Research Service Inc.
243 Church Street NW
P.O. Box 1059
Vienna, VA 22183
703-281-0200

Forbes, Inc.
60 Fifth Avenue
New York, NY 10011
800-772-9200 or 212-620-2200

Foreign Policy Association
729 7th Avenue
New York, NY 10019
212-764-4050

The Foundation Center
79 5th Avenue
New York, NY 10003
212-620-4230

The Foundation for Public Affairs
1019 19th Street NW, Suite 200
Washington DC 20036
202-872-1750

Gale Research Company
835 Penobscot Building
Detroit, MI 48226
800-877-4253

Georgia State University Business Press
College of Business Administration
University Plaza
Atlanta, GA 30303-3093
404-651-4253

Glencoe Publishing Company
15319 Chatsworth Street
Mission Hills, CA 91345
800-257-5755 or 818-898-1391

Global Research
1605 S. Big Bend Boulevard
St. Louis, MO 63117
314-647-0081

GPO. *See* U.S. Government Printing
Office

Greenwood Publishing Group
88 Post Road W
P.O. Box 5007
Westport, CT 06881
203-226-3571

Harper/Perennial
10 E. 53d Street
New York, NY 10022
212-207-7000

Hoppenstedt Wirtschaftsdatenbank,
GmbH
Havelstrasse 9
6100 Darmstadt, Germany
001-49-6151-380272

ICC Information Group, Ltd.
Field House
72 Oldfield Road
Hampton, Middlesex TW1 22HQ
England
081-783-1122

Information Access Company
362 Lakeside Drive
Foster City, CA 94404
800-227-8431

Intermountain Referral Service
311 14th Street
Glenwood Springs, CO 81601
303-945-8991

International City and County
    Management Association
777 N. Capitol Street NE, Suite 500
Washington, DC 20002
202-289-4262

Island Press
1718 Connecticut Avenue NW
Washington, DC 20009
202-232-7933

ITA. *See* U.S. Department of Commerce

Kyodo News International, Inc.
50 Rockefeller Plaza, Room 803
New York, NY 10020
212-586-0152

McGraw-Hill, Inc.
Princeton-Hightstown Road
Hightstown, NJ 08520
609-426-5000

Market Service Corporation
49 Glen Head Road
Glen Head, NY 11545
516-759-1253

Mead Data Central
9443 Springboro Pike
Miamisburg, OH 45342
800-227-4908 or, in Ohio, 800-227-9547

Moody's Investors Service, Inc.
99 Church Street
New York, NY 10007
800-342-5647 or 212-553-0435

National Ad Search
2328 W. Daphne Road
Milwaukee, WI 53209
800-992-2832

National Association of Business
 Economists
28790 Chagrin Boulevard, Suite 300
Cleveland OH 44122
216-464-7986

National Safety Council
1121 Spring Lake Drive
Itasca, IL 60143
800-621-7619

Nelson Publications
1 Gateway Plaza
P.O. Box 591
Port Chester, NY 10573
800-333-6357 or 914-937-8400

NewsNet
945 Haverford Road
Bryn Mawr, PA 19010
800-345-1301

New York Times Co.
229 W. 43d Street
New York, NY 10036
212-556-1234

Oxbridge Communications, Inc.
 *See* Gale Research, Inc.

Pharos Books
1 International Boulevard
Mahwah, NJ 07495
201-529-6904

Penguin USA
375 Hudson Street
New York, NY 10014
212-366-2000

Peterson's Guides, Inc.
P.O. Box 2123
Princeton, NJ 08543
800-338-3282 or 609-243-9111

Pilot Books
103 Cooper Street
Babylon, NY 11702
516-422-2225

Predicasts
11001 Cedar Avenue
Cleveland, OH 44106
800-321-6388 or 216-795-3000

Prentice-Hall
15 Columbus Circle
New York, NY 10023

PR Newswire, Inc.
150 E. 58th Street
New York, NY 10155
800-832-5522 or 212-832-9400

Public Affairs Information Service, Inc.
521 W. 43d Street, 5th Floor
New York, NY 10036
212-736-6629

Reed Reference Publishing
121 Chanlon Road
New Providence, NJ 07974
800-521-8110

St. Martin's Press
175 5th Avenue
New York, NY 10010
212-674-5151

SDC Publishing
40 W. Fifty-seventh Street, Suite 802
New York, NY 10019
212-572-2600

Signet Books. *See* Penguin USA

Charles E. Simon & Company
1090 Vermont Avenue NW, Suite 430
Washington, DC 20005
202-408-3120

Staff Directories Ltd.
P.O. Box 62
Mt. Vernon, VA 22121
703-739-0900

Standard & Poor's Corporation
25 Broadway
New York, NY 10004
212-208-8000

Surrey Books, Inc.
230 E. Ohio Street, Suite 120
Chicago, IL 60611
312-751-7330

Theater Communications Group, Inc.
355 Lexington Avenue
New York, NY 10017
212-697-5230

Thomson Financial Networks, Inc.
11 Farnsworth Street
Boston, MA 02210
800-662-7878 or 617-345-2000

UMI/Data Courier
620 S. 3d Street
Louisville, KY 40202-2297
800-626-2823

University of California Press
2120 Berkeley Way
Berkeley, CA 94720
800-822-6657 or 510-642-4247

U.S. Department of Commerce
Data Users Services Division
Bureau of the Census
Washington, DC 20233
301-763-4100

U.S. Department of Commerce
Industry Publications Division
International Trade Administration
Washington, DC 20230
202-482-5487

U.S. Department of Labor
Bureau of Labor Statistics
Postal Square Building
2 Massachusetts Avenue NE
Washington, DC 20212
202-606-5886

U.S. Department of Labor
Room S-1032
200 Constitution Avenue NW
Washington, DC 20210
800-877-4253 or 202-219-7316

U. S. Department of State
Bureau of Personnel,
Recruitment Division
1800 N. Kent Street
Arlington, VA 22209

U.S. Department of Transportation
Federal Transit Administration
Office of Technical Assistance and Safety
400 7th Street SW
Washington, DC 20590

U. S. Government Printing Office
Superintendent of Documents
Washington, DC 20402
202-512-2051

Vacation-Work. *See* Peterson's Guides

Value Line Publishing, Inc.
711 3d Avenue
New York, NY 10017
212-687-3965

VGM Career Horizons
National Textbook Company
4255 W. Touhy Avenue
Lincolnwood, IL 60646
800-323-4900

Wall Street Transcript Corporation
99 Wall Street
New York, NY 10005
212-747-9500

Washington Monitor, Inc.
104 5th Avenue, 2d Floor
New York, NY 10011
212-627-4140

The Washington Post Company
1150 15th Street NW
Washington, DC 20071
202-334-7341

Washington Researchers Publishing
2612 P Street NW
Washington, DC 20007
202-333-3533

Williamson Publishing Co.
Churchill Road
P.O. Box 185
Charlotte, VT 05445
802-425-2102

H. W. Wilson Company
950 University Avenue
Bronx, NY 10452
800-367-6770 or 718-588-8400

World Trade Academy Press
50 E. 42d Street
New York, NY 10017
212-697-4999

# INDEX

*100 Best Companies to Work for in America, The,* 113, 161, 164-165
*100 Best Small Towns in America, The,* 187
ABI/Inform, 152-153
academic institutions, 9-10
    *See also* universities
*Acquisition Mart,* 151
air quality, 232
Alabama
    Chamber of Commerce, 253
    Economic Development, 259
    JTPA liaison officer, 213
    OCS, 207
    OICC, 201
    securities office, 130
    SESA, 195
Alaska
    Chamber of Commerce, 253
    Economic Development, 259
    JTPA liaison officer, 213
    OICC, 201
    securities office, 130-131
    SESA, 195
*Almanac of Jobs and Salaries,* 59
*Almanac of the Unelected,* 100
American Business Directory, 139
*Americans Abroad: A Handbook for Living and Working Overseas,* 249
*America's Corporate Families: Billion Dollar Directory,* 120
*America's Corporate Families and International Affiliates,* 120
*Annual Survey of Manufacturers,* 103
AP News, 153
Arizona
    Chamber of Commerce, 253
    Economic Development, 259
    JTPA liaison officer, 213
    OCS, 207
    OICC, 201
    securities office, 131
    SESA, 195
Arkansas
    Chamber of Commerce, 253
    Economic Development, 259
    JTPA liaison officer, 213
    OCS, 208
    OICC, 201
    securities office, 131
    SESA, 195
arts and cultural events, 225-226
*Artsearch,* 59
associations, 220
    finding, 7, 8, 80, 82, 116, 117, 182, 184, 191
    special-interest, 191-192

*See also* professional associations; trade associations

barriers, overcoming, 17-19
    advice, 18
    reluctance and, 17
    time limitations and, 19
benefits, employee, 168-171
    contribution plans, 170
    disability income, 171
    family, 170
    flexible, 171
    health care, 170-171
    paid leave, 171
    pension plans, 170
Bureau of Labor Statistics, 53
    offices, 56-57
Bureau of the Census Industry Specialists, 93
*Business Conditions Digest,* 102
Business Dateline, 153
*Business Index,* 152
Business Information Report, 121
*Business Information Sources,* 108
*Business Organizations, Agencies, and Publications Directory,* 89
business periodicals, 105-107
    indexes, 106-107
    list of, 105
*Business Periodicals Index,* 106, 152
*Business Rankings Annual,* 108, 115
*Business Statistics,* 102
*Business Week,* 115
BusinessWire, 150, 153

California
    Chamber of Commerce, 253
    Economic Development, 259
    JTPA liaison officer, 214
    OCS, 208
    OICC, 202
    securities office, 131
    SESA, 196
*Career Guide to Industries,* 102
*Career Information Center,* 58
careers. *See* occupations
*Careers for Dreamers and Doers: A Guide to Management Careers in the Voluntary Sector,* 191
caucuses, 94-95
CD-ROMs, 151
    using, 152-155
    *See also* databases
chambers of commerce, 85, 173, 219, 239
    quality of life materials, 236
    state listing of, 253-258

United States, 251
charitable contributions, 177-178
climate, 226
Colorado
    Chamber of Commerce, 253
    Economic Development, 259
    JTPA liaison officer, 214
    OCS, 208
    OICC, 202
    securities office, 131
    SESA, 196
community resources, 10
companies
    annual reports, 174
    best, 166
        corporate headquarters, 167
        job security, 166
        opportunities, 167
        pay and benefits, 166
    community action contributors, 178
    compatibility with, 62-167
    competitiveness of, 145
    congenial, 164-167
        criteria, 165-166
    culture, 173-175
    divisions. *See* subsidiaries
    environmental conscious, 178
    foreign, 112, 121
        financial information about, 140-143
    industry rankings of, 115-117
    information sources on, 149-155
    investing in future, 147-148
    library info on, 125
    management aptitude, 146-147
    mergers and acquisitions, 150-151
    on-site observation of, 175
    ownership of, 118-121
    private, 112, 119
        determining, 120
    financial information about, 136-139
    professional contribution within, 156-161
    most profitable, 114-117
    public, 112, 119
        financial information about, 123-135
    recruitment brochures, 174
    reputation, 144-149
    SEC info on, 124-125
    social conscience of, 176-184
    subsidiaries of, 112, 119, 120-121
        financial information about, 140
    successful, 113-117
        regionally, 117
    training programs, 169

*See also* employers; not-for-
  profit organizations
CBO. *See* Congressional Budget Office
competition, in industries, 79
computer field, 4
Congress
  caucuses, 94-95
  committees, 100
  Representatives and Senators of, 100
Congressional Budget Office
  (CBO), 95-96
  experts, 95-96
Congressional Clearinghouse on the
  Future, 88
*Congressional Directory*, 100
Congressional Research Service (CRS),
  96-98
  experts, 97-98
*Congressional Staff Directory*, 100
Connecticut
  Chamber of Commerce, 254
  Economic Development, 259
  JTPA liaison officer, 214
  OCS, 208
  OICC, 202
  securities office, 131
  SESA, 196
*Corporate 500: The Directory of
Corporate Philanthropy*, 177
cost of living, 227-228
*Cost of Living Index*, 228
*County Business Patterns*, 103, 212
cover letter, 240-241
crime rates, 228
CRS. *See* Congressional Research
  Service
*Current Industrial Reports*, 103

databases, 151
  directories of, 155
  on foreign companies, 142-143
  for private company finances, 139
  for public company finances, 128
  using, 152-155
  vendors, 252
  *See also specific databases*
Delaware
  Chamber of Commerce, 254
  Economic Development, 260
  JTPA liaison officer, 214
  OCS, 208
  Office of Occupational and
    Labor Market Information, 202
  securities office, 131
  SESA, 196
*Dictionary of Occupational Titles*, 53
directories, 85, 108-109
  association, 82
  business organizations and
    agencies, 89
  company, 86

company subsidiary, 120-121
congressional, 100
database, 155
DOC telephone, 93
executive, 86
FTC telephone, 94
on government experts, 91-93
government telephone contacts, 93
of information centers, 88
ITC telephone, 94
municipal, 86
occupational titles, 53
of periodicals, 213
in print, 89
publications and broadcast media,
  6, 213
SEC report filing companies, 120
of special libraries, 88
state industrial, 139
Who's Who, 147
*See also* publications; *specific
  directories*
*Directories in Print*, 89, 108
*Directory of American Firms Operating
  in Foreign Countries*, 249
*Directory of Corporate Affiliations*,
  120-121, 138
*Directory of Corporate Affiliations/
  International*, 121
*Directory of Publications and Broadcast
  Media*, 6, 213
*Directory of Special Libraries and
  Information Centers*, 88
*Disclosure SEC Database*, 128
District of Columbia
  Economic Development, 260
  JTPA liaison officer, 214
  OCS, 211
  OICC, 202
  securities office, 131
  SESA, 196
DOC. *See* U.S. Department of Commerce
DOL. *See* U.S. Department of Labor
*Dun's Business Rankings*, 84, 115-116
Dun's Electronic Business Directory, 139
*Dun's Employment Opportunities
  Directory/The Career Guide*, 161
Dun's Financial Records Plus, 139
Dun's Market Identities, 121

economic development offices, 85
*Editor and Publisher International
  Yearbook*, 6
*Editor and Publisher Yearbook*, 183
education, 228-231
  evaluation questions, 229
  state listing of money spent on,
    229-231
Educational Resources Information
  Center (ERIC), 58
  clearinghouses, 58

employees, 11
  benefits, 168-171
  interviewing, 160, 174-175
employers, 111
  buying stock in, 10
  compatibility with, 162-167
  employees and, 11
  industry leading, 115
  interviewing, 240-246
    appearance and, 241
    asking questions and, 242-243
    commonly asked questions
      and, 245-246
    giving answers and, 243-246
  newsletter, 10
  ownership of, 118-119
  public information office, 149
  research, viii, ix
  for research information, 10-11
  SEC filings, 124
  *See also* companies
employment
  agencies, 221
  environment, 172-173
    characteristics, 164
    information sources, 173
    questions, 172
  equal, 183-184
  foreign, 247-251
    organizations and, 250-251
    publications on, 248-250
  increase in, 69
  by industry, 70-76
  job listings and, 60
  newsletters, 59
  projections, 52
*Employment Abroad: Facts and Fallacies*,
  248
*Employment and Earnings*, 55, 189
Employment and Training
  Administration, 53
  offices, 57-58
*Employment Information in the
  Mathematical Sciences*, 59
*Employment Opportunities*, 59
*Employment Opportunities for Business
  Economists*, 59
*Encyclopedia of Associations*, 7, 8, 80, 82,
  116, 117, 182, 184, 191
*Encyclopedia of Business Information
  Services*, 108
*Encyclopedia of Government Advisory
  Organizations*, 92
environmental awareness, 178-180
  references, 178
  watchdog groups, 180
Environmental Protection Agency
  (EPA), 179-180
EPA. *See above*
Equal Employment Opportunity
  Commission, 184

*Equal Opportunity Publications*, 58
ERIC. *See* Educational Resources
    Information Center
*Evaluating an Overseas Job Opportunity*,
    250
evaluation, industry, 77-80
experts
    CBO, 95-96
    CRS, 97-98
    in government, 90-100
    in industry, 84-86
        regional, 85-86
    OTA, 98-99
    in private sector, 81-89
    professional association, 189-190
Extel International Financial Cards, 143

*Federal Career Opportunities*, 161
*Federal Executive Directory*, 86, 92
*Federal Information Centers*, 92
Federal Trade Commission (FTC), 94
*Federal Yellow Book*, 92
financial information
    divisions and subsidiaries, 140
    foreign companies, 140-143
    not-for-profit organizations, 143
    private companies, 136-139
    public companies, 123-135
FINDEX: The Worldwide Directory of
    Market Research Reports, Studies,
    and Surveys, 108
Florida
    Bureau of Labor Market
        Information, 202
    Chamber of Commerce, 254
    Economic Development, 260
    JTPA liaison officer, 214
    OCS, 208
    securities office, 131
    SESA, 196
FOIA. *See* Freedom of Information Act
*Forbes* , 115
foreign companies, 112, 121
    annual reports, 141
    employment in, 247-251
    financial information, 140-143
        databases, 142-143
        publications, 142
    U.S. offices, 140
    *See also* companies
*Foreign Service Careers*, 250
*Fortune*, 115
    America's Most Admired
        Corporations, 145
*Foundation Directory, The*, 177
*Foundation for Public Affairs*, 8
Freedom of Information Act (FOIA), 112
    Reading Room, 143
FTC. *See* Federal Trade Commission
*Futurist, The*, 87

*Gale Directory of Databases*, 155
Geographic locations, 185-187
    life-style and, 186
    for occupations, 188-193
    references, 187
    targeting, 194-223
    *See also* quality of life
Georgia
    Chamber of Commerce, 254
    Economic Development, 260
    JTPA liaison officer, 214
    OCS, 208
    OICC, 202
    securities office, 131
    SESA, 196
government experts, 90-100
    advantages to, 90
    caucuses and, 94-95
    CBO, 95-96
    congressional committees, 100
    congressional Representatives
        and Senators, 100
    CRS, 96-98
    departments and agencies, 93-94
    library research on, 91-93
    OTA, 98-99
    publications on, 91
    using, 91
    *See also* experts
government publications, 52-58
    clearinghouses for, 56-58
    earnings projection, 55-56
    occupational guides, 54-55
    *See also* publications
government reports, 101-104
    best and quickest, 102
    individual industries, 102-103
    industry statistics, 102
    on industries by region, 103
    publications, 104
GPO. *See* U.S. Government Printing Office
growth rate, industry, 77
*Guide to Careers in World Affairs*, 249

Harvard University case study catalog, 10
Hawaii
    Chamber of Commerce, 254
    Economic Development, 260
    JTPA liaison officer, 214
    OICC, 202
    securities office, 131
    SESA, 196
health care, 232
high-technology fields, 4
    industry growth rate, 63
Hoppenstedt Directory of German
    Companies, 143
*How to Be Happily Employed in
    Washington D.C.*, 222
*How to Find Business Intelligence in
    Washington*, 92

*How to Find Information about
    Companies*, 86, 155
*How to Find Information About Foreign
    Firms*, 248
*How to Get a Job in the San Francisco
    Bay Area*, 222
*How to Get the Job You Want Overseas*, 249

ICC British Company Directory, 143
ICC British Company Financial
    Datasheets, 142
Idaho
    Chamber of Commerce, 254
    Economic Development, 260
    JTPA liaison officer, 214
    OCS, 208
    OICC, 202
    securities office, 131
    SESA, 196
Illinois
    Chamber of Commerce, 254
    Economic Development, 260
    JTPA liaison officer, 215
    OCS, 208-209
    OICC, 202
    securities office, 132
    SESA, 196
indexes, 106-107
    using, 151-152
Indiana
    Chamber of Commerce, 254
    Economic Development, 260
    JTPA liaison officer, 215
    OCS, 209
    OICC, 203
    securities office, 132
    SESA, 197
industries, 61-109
    competition in, 79
    consumer base for, 79
    defined, 61
    emerging, 86-88
    employment by, 70-76
    established, 81-84
    evaluation of, 77-80
        example, 80
        questions for, 77-79
    experts in, 84-86
    growth potential of, 77-78
    growth rates of, 63, 77
    high-growth, 62-76
    high-tech, 62-63
    manufacturing, 62
        declining, 64
        forecast growth rates for, 65-
            68
    product technology and, 78
    production technology and, 78
    projected growth of, 70-76
    prospects for, 79
    reading up on, 101-109

reports, 104
    individual, 102-103
    by region, 103
    researching, 79-80
    service, trends in, 63
    size of, 77
    supplies for, 79
    *See also* companies
industry
    regulators, 85-86
    reports, 107-108
    statistics, 102
    surveys, 104-105
*Industry Wage Surveys*, 103
information source, interviewing
    cooperation and, 19
    evaluating, 13-14
    getting through to, 14-15
*Insider's Guide*, The, 223
*International Careers*, 250
International Dun's Market
    Identifiers, 142
*International Employment Hotline*, 59
*International Jobs: Where They Are,
    How to Get Them*, 249
*International Living*, 250
International Trade
    Administration (ITA), 93
    for foreign company
        information, 141
    Periodic Reports, 103
    publications, 102-103
International Trade Commission
    (ITC), 94
interviewing, 12-20
    advice in, 18
    closing and, 20
    employers, 240-246
        appearance and, 241
        asking questions and, 242-243
        commonly asked questions
            and, 245-246
        giving answers and, 243-246
    follow through and, 18
    getting answers through, 16-17
    getting through to source and,
        14-15
    guidelines for, 15-16
    industry experts, 81
    introducing yourself and, 14,
        15-17
    maintaining cooperation and, 19
    mental preparation and, 14
    nervousness and, 14
    overcoming barriers and, 17-19
    preparation for, 13-14
    questions, 13-14
    response evaluation, 17
    uneasiness and, 12
Investest, 129
Iowa
    Chamber of Commerce, 254

Economic Development, 260
JTPA liaison officer, 215
OCS, 209
OICC, 203
securities office, 132
SESA, 197
ITA. *See* International Trade
    Administration
ITC. *See* International Trade
    Commission

Japan Economic Newswire Plus, 142
"Job Bank" publications, 222
job clearinghouses, 221-222
    electronic, 222
    government publications and,
        56-58
job-counseling services, 221
job hunting, viii
    *See also* local-level job search
job listings, 60
    *See also* employment
Job Outlook Handbook, The, 54
job research, viii, ix
    interviewing and, 12-20
    local-level, 206-223
    process of, 51-60
    state-level, 195-206
    *See also* research
job security, 166
*Job Seeker's Guide to Private and
    Public Companies*, 161
*Jobs Rated Almanac, The*, 59
Job Training Partnership Act
    (JTPA), 213
    offices, 213-218
JTPA. *See above*

Kansas
    Chamber of Commerce, 254
    Economic Development, 260
    JTPA liaison officer, 215
    OCS, 209
    OICC, 203
    securities office, 132
    SESA, 197
Kentucky
    Chamber of Commerce, 255
    Economic Development, 260
    JTPA liaison officer, 215
    OCS, 209
    OICC, 203
    securities office, 132
    SESA, 197

labor unions, 7-8, 159, 173, 192
    AFL-CIO and, 8
    finding, 8
    list of, 182
    local, offices, 182-183

management styles and, 147
*Liberal Arts Jobs: Where They Are
    and How to Get Them*, 161
libraries
    indexes, 106-107
    local, 212, 239
    state, 86
    U.S. government depository,
        101
library research, 2-3
    advantages, 3
    FINDEX and, 107-108
    on company financial
        information, 125-135
    databases, 128
    microfiche, 126-128
    publications, 126-128
    on government experts, 91-93
    on industries, 79
    resources for, 2
*Livable Cities Almanac, The*, 187
local-level job search, 206-223
    boards of trade, 219
    chambers of commerce and, 219
    county business patterns and,
        212
    employment agencies and, 221
    job clearinghouses and, 221-222
    job counseling services and, 221
    JTPA and, 213-219
    local associations and, 220
    local libraries and, 212
    local press and, 212-213
    publications for, 222-223
    regional wages and, 206-211
    universities/colleges and, 220-
        221
*Looking for Employment in Foreign
    Countries*, 248
Louisiana
    Chamber of Commerce, 255
    Economic Development, 261
    JTPA liaison officer, 215
    OCS, 209
    OICC, 203
    securities office, 132
    SESA, 197

M & A Filings, 151
McGraw-Hill Publications Online,
    153
Magazine Index/Magazine ASAP,
    153
*Magazines for Libraries*, 151
Maine
    Chamber of Commerce, 255
    Economic Development, 261
    JTPA liaison officer, 215
    OCS, 209
    OICC, 203
    securities office, 132
    SESA, 197

management
    aptitude, 146-147
    strengths, 146
    styles, 146
manufacturing industries, 62
    declining, 64
    forecast growth rates for, 65-68
    SIC code, 64
    *See also* industries
*Market Guide*, 126-127
Maryland
    Chamber of Commerce, 255
    Economic Development, 261
    JTPA liaison officer, 215
    OCSs, 209
    OICC, 203
    securities office, 132
    SESA, 197
Massachusetts
    Chamber of Commerce, 255
    Economic Development, 261
    JTPA liaison officer, 215
    OCS, 209
    OICC, 203
    securities office, 132
    SESA, 197
*Mergers Yearbook, The*, 151
Michigan
    Chamber of Commerce, 255
    Economic Development, 261
    JTPA liaison officer, 216
    OCS, 209
    OICC, 203
    securities office, 132
    SESA, 197
*Million Dollar Directory*, 138
Minnesota
    Chamber of Commerce, 255
    Economic Development, 261
    JTPA liaison officer, 216
    OCS, 210
    OICC, 203
    securities office, 132
    SESA, 197
Mississippi
    Chamber of Commerce, 255
    Economic Development, 261
    JTPA liaison officer, 216
    OCS, 210
    OICC, 203
    securities office, 133
    SESA, 198
Missouri
    Chamber of Commerce, 255
    Economic Development, 261
    JTPA liaison officer, 216
    OCS, 210
    OICC, 204
    securities office, 133
    SESA, 198
*Money*, 187
Montana
    Chamber of Commerce, 255

    Economic Development, 261
    JTPA liaison officer, 216
    OCSs, 210
    OICC, 204
    securities office, 133
    SESA, 198
*Monthly Catalog of U.S.
Government Publications*, 80, 104
*Monthly Labor Review*, 54
Moody's
    Corporate News, 129, 142-143
    Corporate Profiles, 129
    *Industrial Manual*, 126, 142
    *Industry Review*, 104, 116
    specialized titles, 126
*Municipal Yearbook*, 86

*National Air Quality and Emissions
    Trends Report*, 232
*National Business Employment
    Weekly*, 223
National Newspaper Index, 153-154
*National Trade and Professional
Associations of the United States*, 7,
    82, 191
Nebraska
    Chamber of Commerce, 256
    Economic Development, 261
    JTPA liaison officer, 216
    OCS, 210
    OICC, 204
    securities office, 133
    SESA, 198
*Nelson's Directory of Investment
    Research*, 9, 117, 173
Nevada
    Chamber of Commerce, 256
    Economic Development, 261
    JTPA liaison officer, 216
    OICC, 204
    securities office, 133
    SESA, 198
New Hampshire
    Chamber of Commerce, 256
    Economic Development, 261
    JTPA liaison officer, 216
    OCS, 210
    OICC, 204
    securities office, 133
    SESA, 198
New Jersey
    Chamber of Commerce, 256
    Economic Development, 262
    JTPA liaison officer, 216
    OCS, 210
    OICC, 204
    securities office, 133
    SESA, 198
New Mexico
    Chamber of Commerce, 256
    Economic Development, 262
    JTPA liaison officer, 216
    OICC, 204

    securities office, 133
    SESA, 198
Newsearch, 154
newsletters, employment, 59
NewsNet Business and Industry
    Newsletters, 154, 252
Newspaper Abstracts, 154
newspapers, 159
    for company financial
        information, 137
    equal opportunity and, 184
    local, 212-213, 238
    locating, 183
    for occupational news, 52
    *See also* periodicals
Newswire ASAP, 154
New York
    Chamber of Commerce, 256
    Economic Development, 262
    JTPA liaison officer, 217
    OCS, 210
    OICC, 204
    securities office, 133
    SESA, 198
*New York Times Index*, 107
NEXIS, 154
North Carolina
    Chamber of Commerce, 256
    Economic Development, 262
    JTPA liaison officer, 217
    OCS, 210
    OICC, 204
    securities office, 133
    SESA, 198
North Dakota
    Chamber of Commerce, 256
    Economic Development, 262
    JTPA liaison officer, 217
    OICC, 204
    securities office, 133
    SESA, 199
not-for profit organizations, 112
    financial information, 143
    *See also* companies

Occupational Compensation
    Surveys (OCS), 206
    ordering, 207
    *Selected Metropolitan Areas*, 207
    by state, 207-211
Occupational Health and Safety
    Administration. *See* OSHA
*Occupational Outlook Handbook*,
    54, 188
*Occupational Outlook Quarterly*, 54
*Occupational Projections and
    Training Data*, 54
*Occupational Projects and Training
    Data*, 55
occupational safety, 180-183
    health departments and, 182
    National Safety Council, 180-
        181

OSHA, 181-182
  union offices and, 182-183
occupations, 21-60
  administrative, 27
  administrative support, 33
  agriculture, forestry, fishing,
    38-39
  architectural, 29
  changing, 22
  cleaning and building service, 36
  clerical/administrative support
    workers, 35-36
  communications equipment
    operators, 33
  computer, mathematical
    research analysts, 29
  engineering, 28-29, 32
  events that effect, 52
  executive, 27
  extractive, 39-40
  fastest growing, 25
  fields of, decreasing size, 51
  financial records processing,
    33-34
  firefighting, 38
  food preparation and service,
    36-37
  food workers, precision, 42
  geographic focus for, 188-193
    placement organizations
      and, 192-193
    professional associations
      and, 189-191
    special interest associations
      and, 191-192
  guides on, 54-55
  hand workers, 48-49
  health and diagnosing, 30-31
  health service, 37
  helpers, laborers, 50
  information on, 52-60
  inspectors, testers, graders, 42-
    43
  with large job numbers, 51
  with largest projected job
    growth, 26
  law enforcement, 38
  lawyers and judicial workers,
    29-30
  life scientists, 29
  listing of, 27-50
  management support, 27-28
  managerial, 27
  marketing and sales, 32-33
  material moving equipment,
    49-50
  material recording, dispatching,
    distributing, 34-35
  mechanics, installers,
    repairers, 40-42
  operators, fabricators, laborers,
    44-46

operators/tenders, 47-48
  personal service, 37
  physical scientists, 29
  plant and system, 43-44
  printing workers, 43
  private household workers, 37
  production, craft and repair, 39
  production, precision, 42
  prospects for, 79
  rail transportation workers, 49
  records processing, 35
  religious workers, 29
  researching, 21-22, 51-60
    example, 22
  science technicians, 32
  service, 36-38
  social scientists, 29
  social workers, 29
  teachers, librarians, counselors,
    30
  technicians, related support,
    31-32
  textile and related setters, 46-47
  textile, apparel, furnishings, 43
  transportation/material
    moving, 49
  water transportation workers, 49
  woodworkers, 43
  woodworking machine setters,
    operators, 47
  writers, artists, entertainers, 31
OCS. *See specific state Occupa-*
  *tional Compensation Survey*
Office of Technology Assessment
  (OTA), 87, 88, 98-99
  experts, 98-99
Ohio
  Chamber of Commerce, 256
  Economic Development, 262
  JTPA liaison officer, 217
  OCS, 210
  OICC, 204
  securities office, 134
  SESA, 199
OICC. *See* specific state
  Occupational Information
  Coordinating Committees
Oklahoma
  Chamber of Commerce, 257
  Economic Development, 262
  JTPA liaison officer, 217
  OICC, 205
  securities office, 134
  SESA, 199
*Omni*, 87
  *Opportunities in...*, 58
Oregon
  Chamber of Commerce, 257
  Economic Development, 262
  JTPA liaison officer, 217
  OCS, 210
  OICC, 205

securities office, 134
  SESA, 199
organizations
  future-oriented, 88
  listing of, 264-270
  *See also* not-for-profit
    organizations
OSHA, 181
  regional offices, 181-182
OTA. *See* Office of Technology
  Assessment
Overseas Employers Registry, 247


Pennsylvania
  Chamber of Commerce, 257
  Economic Development, 262
  JTPA liaison officer, 217
  OCS, 211
  OICC, 205
  securities office, 134
  SESA, 199
periodicals, 105-107
  *Business Week*, 115
  *Forbes*, 115
  *Fortune*, 115
  indexes, 106-107
  lists of, 105
  local, 213
  *Omni*, 87
  *See also* newspapers
*Peterson's Engineering, Science &*
  *Computer Jobs 1993*, 161
placement organizations, 192-193
*Places Rated Almanac*, 187, 228
*Predicasts Basebook*, 104
*Predicasts F&S Index United States*,
  107, 152
*Predicasts Forecasts*, 105
press reporters, 6
  special interest groups and, 8
*Principle International Business*, 142
private companies, 112, 119
  determining, 120
  financial information, 136-139
    databases, 139
    publications, 138-139
  *See also* companies
private sector experts, 81-89
  association executives, 81
  in emerging industries, 86-88
  in established industries, 81
  in industry, 84
    regional, 85-86
  securities analysts, 83
  specialized information on,
    88-89
  trade journalists, 83-84
  *See also* experts
PR Newswire, 150
*Productivity Measures for Selected*
  *Industries*, 102

professional associations, 158-159,
189-191
  experts, 189-190
  finding, 191
  interviewing members of, 190
  local, 220
  publications, 190
  *See also* associations; trade
    associations
professions. *See* occupations
PTS
  Annual Reports Abstracts, 129
  New Product
    Announcements-Plus, 150
  P&S Indexes, 154
  PROMT, 154-155
*Public Affairs Information Service
  Bulletin*, 107
publications
  charitable contributions and, 177
  company future and, 150
  on employment within
    companies, 160-161
  on foreign companies, 142
  foreign employment, 248-250
  future-oriented, 87
  government, 52-56
    catalog of, 104
  on government experts, 91
  non-government, 58-59
  on private company finances,
    138-139
  professional association, 190
  on public companies, 126-128
  on quality of life
    local, 238-239
    national, 235
    state, 236-237
  regional career opportunity,
    222-223
  state economic analysis, 236-237
  *See also* directories; *specific
    publications*
public companies, 112, 119
  financial information, 123-135
    databases, 128
    publications and microfiche,
      126-128
  interstate, 123-130
  intrastate, 130-135
  *See also* companies
*Public Interest Profiles*, 9
  publishers, 264-270
Puerto Rico
  Chamber of Commerce, 257
  JTPA liaison officer, 217
  OICC, 205
  SESA, 199
quality of life, 224-239
  air quality and, 232

arts and cultural events and,
  225-226
climate and, 226
cost of living and, 227-228
crime rates and, 228
education and, 228-231
health care and, 232
recreation and, 233
references, 235-239
  local, 238-239
  national, 235
  state, 235-237
transportation and, 233-234
*See also* geographic locations
questions, employer, 157-159
questions, interviewing, 13-14
  asking, 13
  backing off from, 17
  follow-up, 16
  getting answers to, 16-17
  keeping track of, 13
  leading, 16

recreation, sports, leisure, 233
*Reference Book of Corporate
  Managements*, 146
Rehabilitation Act, 52
*Report to the Nation on Crime and
  Justice*, 228
reputation, company, 144-149
  competitiveness, 145
  current events and, 148-149
  future investment, 147-148
  management aptitude, 146-147
research
  industry, 79-80
  job, x-xi
  library, 2-3, 79, 91-93, 107-
    108, 125-128
  occupation, 21
  professions, 51-60
  telephone, 3-11, 93-100
Rhode Island
  Chamber of Commerce, 257
  Economic Development, 262
  JTPA liaison officer, 217
  OCS, 211
  OICC, 205
  securities office, 134
  SESA, 199
*Rocky Mountain Employment
  Newsletter*, 59

safety, 228
SEC. *See* Securities and Exchange
  Commission
securities analysts, 9
  as experts, 83
  finding, 9, 173
  for foreign companies, 141
  for leading companies, 117
  Securities and Exchange

Commission (SEC), 119
  directory of companies, 120
  employer's filings, 124
  main office, 124
  management styles and, 146
  regional offices, 124-125
service industries
  growth in, 69
  trends in, 63
  *See also* industries
*Shopping for a Better World*, 177, 178
SESA. *See specific state* State
  Employment Security Agency
SIC codes, 64, 91
  by industry, 70-76
  industry experts and, 84
  for manufacturing industries,
    65-68
  using, 9!
social conscience, company, 176-184
  charitable contributions, 177-178
  environmental awareness, 178-
    180
  equal employment
opportunities, 183-184
  occupational safety, 180-183
  reference, 177
SOICC. *See specific state
  Occupational Information
  Coordinating Committees*
South Carolina
  Chamber of Commerce, 257
  Economic Development, 262
  JTPA liaison officer, 217
  OCS, 211
  OICC, 205
  securities office, 134
  SESA, 199
South Dakota
  Chamber of Commerce, 257
  Economic Development, 263
  JTPA liaison officer, 218
  OICC, 205
  securities office, 134
  SESA, 199
special-interest groups, 8-9
  finding, 8-9
Standard & Poor's
  Corporate Descriptions, 129-130
  *Industry Surveys*, 105
  News, 130
  Register, 139, 147
  *Register of Corporations,
    Directors, and Executives*, 138
  *Stock Reports*, 127
*Standard Corporation Descriptions*,
  127
Standard Industrial Classification
  Codes. *See* SIC codes
*Standard Industrial Classification
  Manual*, 91
*Standard Periodical Directory*, 6, 213

State Employment Security Agency (SESA). *See* by state
*State Executive Directory*, 86, 92
state offices
  for company financial information, 137-138
  economic development, 259-263
  employment security agencies, 195-200
  JTPA, 213-219
  securities, 130-135
  SOICC, 201-206
  *See also* chambers of commerce
*Statistical Abstract of the United States*, 103, 235
*Statistical Reference Index*, 109
*Statistics Sources*, 109
subsidiaries, 112, 119, 120-121
  financial information, 140
*Survey of Current Business*, 102
surveys, industry, 104-105

*Teaching English Abroad*, 249
technology
  product, 78
  production, 78
*Telephone Contacts for Data Users*, 93
telephone research, 3-11
  academic institutions and, 9-10
  advantages, 3-4
  with company employees, 160
  disadvantages, 4
  example, 5
  for government experts, 93-100
  labor unions and, 7-8
  local communities and, 10
  on industries, 79
  press reporters and, 6
  prospective employers and, 10-11
  security analysts and, 9
  special interest groups and, 8-9
  trade associations and, 6-7
Tennessee
  Chamber of Commerce, 257
  Economic Development, 263
  JTPA liaison officer, 218
  OCS, 211
  OICC, 205
  securities office, 134
  SESA, 199
Texas
  Chamber of Commerce, 257
  Economic Development, 263
  JTPA liaison officer, 218
  OCS, 211
  OICC, 205
  securities office, 134
  SESA, 200
Trade and Industry Index/Trade and Industry ASAP, 155

trade associations, 6-7
  director of, 82
  executives, 81-82
  for leading companies, 116-117
  listings for, 7
  local, 220
  special interest groups and, 8
  ways of using, 7
  *See also* associations; professional associations
trade journalists, 83-84, 150
  for leading companies, 117
transportation, 233-234

*Ulrich's International Periodicals Directory*, 6
unions. *See* labor unions
U.S. Department of Commerce (DOC), 62, 269
  internal directory, 92
U.S. Department of Labor (DOL), 52-53, 270
  Bureau of Labor Statistics, 53
    offices, 56-57
  Employment and Training Administration, 53
    offices, 57-58
  publications, 53-56
    earnings projections, 55-56
    occupational guides, 55-56
*United States Government Manual*, 92
U.S. government depository libraries. *See* libraries
U.S. Government Printing Office, 207, 270
*U.S. Industrial Outlook*, 102
universities, 9-10, 220
  career guidance offices, 220
  faculty, 220-221
  Harvard University case study catalog, 10
  researchers at, 87
Utah
  Chamber of Commerce, 257
  Economic Development, 263
  JTPA liaison officer, 218
  OCSs, 211
  OICC, 205
  securities office, 134
  SESA, 200

Value Line Investment Survey, 105, 125, 127-128
Vermont
  Chamber of Commerce, 258
  Economic Development, 263
  JTPA liaison officer, 218
  OICC, 205
  securities office, 134
  SESA, 200

Virginia
  Chamber of Commerce, 258
  Economic Development, 263
  JTPA liaison officer, 218
  OCSs, 211
  OICC, 206
  securities office, 135
  SESA, 200
Virgin Islands
  OICC, 206
  SESA, 200

*Wage Surveys*, 55
*Wall Street Journal Index*, 107, 152
*Wall Street Journal National Ad Search*, 223
*Wall Street Transcript*, 105, 128, 155
*Ward's Business Directory of U.S. Private and Public Companies*, 84, 116
Washington
  Chamber of Commerce, 258
  Economic Development, 263
  JTPA liaison officer, 218
  OCSs, 211
  OICC, 206
  securities office, 135
  SESA, 200
*Washington Information Directory*, 92
Washington Post Electronic Edition, 155
West Virginia
  Chamber of Commerce, 258
  Economic Development, 263
  JTPA liaison officer, 218
  OICC, 206
  securities office, 135
  SESA, 200
*Who Knows: A Guide to Washington Experts*, 91, 92-93
Wisconsin
  Chamber of Commerce, 258
  Economic Development, 263
  JTPA liaison officer, 218
  OCSs, 211
  OICC, 206
  securities office, 135
*Work, Study, Travel Abroad: Whole World Handbook*, 248
*Work Your Way Around the World*, 249
  World Future Society, 88
Wyoming
  Economic Development, 263
  JTPA liaison officer, 218
  OICC, 206
  securities office, 135
  SESA, 200